From School Improvement to Sustained Capacity

From **School Improvement** to **Sustained Capacity**

THE PARALLEL LEADERSHIP PATHWAY

Foreword by **ANDY HARGREAVES**

FRANK CROWTHER

CORWIN
A SAGE Company

FOR INFORMATION:

Corwin
A SAGE Company
2455 Teller Road
Thousand Oaks, California 91320
(800) 233-9936
Fax: (800) 417-2466
www.corwin.com

SAGE Ltd.
1 Oliver's Yard
55 City Road
London EC1Y 1SP
United Kingdom

SAGE India Pvt. Ltd.
B 1/I 1 Mohan Cooperative Industrial Area
Mathura Road, New Delhi 110 044
India

SAGE Asia-Pacific Pte. Ltd.
33 Pekin Street #02-01
Far East Square
Singapore 048763

Acquisitions Editor: Debra Stollenwerk
Associate Editor: Desirée Bartlett
Editorial Assistant: Kimberly Greenberg
Production Editor: Amy Schroller
Copy Editor: Brenda Weight
Typesetter: C&M Digitals (P) Ltd.
Proofreader: Wendy Jo Dymond
Indexer: Jean Casalegno
Cover Designer: Scott Van Atta
Permissions Editor: Adele Hutchinson

Printed in the United States of America

Library of Congress Cataloging-in-Publication Data

Crowther, Frank, 1942-
From school improvement to sustained capacity : the parallel leadership pathway / Frank Crowther ; foreword by Andy Hargreaves.

p. cm.
Summary: "Bestselling author Frank Crowther makes a compelling case for capacity building and parallel leadership as the keys to ensuring sustainable improvement. Research-based with tools and examples"— Provided by publisher.

Includes bibliographical references and index.

ISBN 978-1-4129-8694-6 (pbk.)

1. School improvement programs—United States.
2. School management teams—United States.
3. Educational leadership—United States. I. Title.

LB2822.82.C795 2011
371.2′07—dc22
2011001808

This book is printed on acid-free paper.

11 12 13 14 15 10 9 8 7 6 5 4 3 2 1

❖ Contents ❖

❖ List of Tables ❖

List of Figures and Diagrams

❖ Foreword ❖

I have been traveling to Australia and working with its educators in one capacity or another for more than 20 years. In all that time, one of the most iconic and influential as well as indefatigable characters in Australian education has undoubtedly been and continues to be Professor Frank Crowther.

Frank Crowther has seen it all—as a teacher, principal, researcher, university dean, president of the Australian Council for Educational Leaders, and now also of the world's most expansive educational administration organization, the Commonwealth Council for Educational Administration. He has been a relentless champion, and not always a politically popular one, of all that is just and right for dedicated professionals and disadvantaged pupils. In some of the bleakest years of educational reform, when budgets were cut back and standardized solutions were imposed with insensitivity and inflexibility, Frank was foremost among state governments' caustic critics—to the point where, as the years came upon him, he seemed at risk of turning into a borderline curmudgeon. Courageously critical, he might well have pursued the path that is all too tempting for many of us in this work—to be clearer and more articulate about what we are against than what we are for.

Defending the rearguard was more comforting and familiar than advancing the vanguard. You can gain a lot of professional popularity this way, and the approach does validate those who feel they have been victimized by politically driven reforms. But in the end, it doesn't get much done.

Then a little over a decade ago, it became clear to me that something in Frank—an educator whose courage and candor I had always admired—had changed, developed, or transformed. Over ten years or more, I had returned time and again to Australia not only to enjoy its cosmopolitan culture and spectacular natural scenery, but also to engage with teachers and leaders across every state about how to build more professionally collaborative cultures in schools and direct these toward making school-driven changes that would benefit all students. Frank—always the avid learner and never one to turn a soapbox into a high horse—participated with his colleagues in many of these extended learning sessions: asking challenging questions while also embracing promising and proven ideas.

And so, when I visited Brisbane in Queensland, Frank invited me to meet several of his colleagues in a restaurant by the river. The occasion was memorable for two reasons. First was the food. This was my first experience of Moreton Bay bugs—a trilobite-like crayfish that must be one of the ugliest items ever to be presented on a high-class menu. Moreton Bay bugs are like crusty old teachers who seem resistant to change. Beneath their brittle carapaces are mellifluous contents that can melt any soul, if you can only figure out how to break through the surface. Second, was the company—school leaders, teacher leaders, and now action researchers who, with Frank, had established and were now developing an innovative network of schools called IDEAS. IDEAS wanted to do for schools and their children what Moreton Bay bugs had done for their diners—take schools and teachers that had become ossified and ostracized and turn them into deliciously dynamic centers of change.

Frank Crowther and his colleagues spoke in excited and animated cadences about the IDEAS schools network that they had created and were developing. They were passionate about what teachers could do with other teachers and how schools could help lift other schools. For all their commitment and enthusiasm, though, they were not naive about networks, nor were they innocents abroad when it came to educational change. In Australia and elsewhere, they had seen networks come and go. Some, like Australia's own National Schools Network, flourished well under government sponsorship, but collapsed just as quickly when political caprice shifted the focus somewhere else. Others that encouraged schools to share practices, commit to common principles, or even become critical friends tended to preach to the converted and attract schools that already possessed an innovative edge. As architects of the IDEAS network, Crowther and colleagues knew that they needed to avoid overdependence on political patronage or excessive reliance on like-minded volunteers and develop something more robust that would embolden leaders and both challenge and support professionals to bring about changes that would benefit all their students.

At the same time, committing to a clear architecture of change meant avoiding becoming a restrictive and even oppressive structure of the kind that has become all too common in the past decade of imposed systemwide reform among controlling governments and the change consultants whose ideas and expertise have legitimized them. Targets, testing, and the standardized curriculum requirements that pander to the narcissism of political control have fabricated appearances of improvement, created false recoveries that manifest themselves in sudden spikes of improvement, turned the self-help of authentic capacity building into the cultlike compliance of imposed training, and narrowed the learning to a diet of basics that is the opposite of what creative and advanced knowledge societies require.

IDEAS sought to avoid the two extremes that Dennis Shirley and I have called the First and Second Ways of educational change (Hargreaves & Shirley, 2009). The First Way of voluntary innovation created interesting islands and even archipelagoes of change, but these did not spread or last. The Second Way of market competition and standardization established a little more urgency and coherence but at the expense of professional commitment and authentic improvement. Instead, IDEAS was a Third and even a Fourth Way change strategy that established a firm framework to enable educators to support and challenge themselves and each other in achieving a higher purpose for the good of all students, especially the most disadvantaged—involving those very students and their communities in the change process itself. IDEAS and its champions understood that students and their lives were the purpose, teachers were the key, and that whatever the reasons for previous failure, the past was the past, and no blame would be assigned as schools forged a better path ahead.

In time, the IDEAS network spread across Australia and then to other parts of the world and I had the privilege, if only briefly, to work with scores of teams from its schools. Frank and his colleagues began to document what they had learned and achieved and wrote two inspiring and informative books that turned into the best and most strongly supported accounts that have been written of teacher leadership in the educational literature. Believing at first that teacher leadership could sometimes supersede or even be developed in the absence of principal leadership, they continued to learn from their schools over longer periods and eventually revised their view, grasping that strong teacher leadership and effective principal leadership go together, enhancing both dissemination and sustainability. Their concept of parallel leadership, the basis of this book, emerged from that understanding.

This is the third book arising from the IDEAS Project and the body of knowledge that has accumulated from its experience and achievements. It is a book based on compelling examples of schools that have made remarkable and sustainable breakthroughs in Australia, Asia, and Europe. It is a book that embeds what IDEAS has contributed within a wider and supporting literature of school improvement, leadership development, and educational change. And it is a book that shows how the principles of effective school change are also those of effective organizational change in social justice–driven organizations like Doctors Without Borders, Al Gore's environmental movement, the emergence of micro-credit as an alternative source of financing and development, or Mother Theresa's community in India.

In the six dynamics of change that underpin the successes of IDEAS schools, Frank Crowther turns abstract ideas into common sense and makes common sense an inspiring and innovative force in turn. IDEAS schools must commit to the idea of revitalizing themselves; to the belief that things must dramatically change. They must do this in an organized and coherent way through moral commitments and common beliefs, not just through technical plans; they must almost literally "pull themselves together." They must set a vision for the future that moves on but does not cast them adrift from their past. They must deepen the approach to teaching and learning, building on, challenging, and drawing together people's diverse talents as they do so. IDEAS schools must go public, share their practice, and advocate for what they believe in. And on top of all this, they must seek ways to sustain their success through widely distributed leadership, pervasive embedding of new beliefs, and orderly management of leadership succession.

There is so much in this book to be learned and so many opportunities to apply it. In engaging and original exercises, you will have the chance as you work with these ideas to rehearse resistance, eat all your greens, go diving for treasures, and cross the Rubicon. This book is an invitation to change, an opportunity to learn, and an affirmation of the power of self-initiated improvement in a Kafkaesque world of systemic top-down models promoted by politically sycophantic consultants who have given up too easily on their belief in the power of teacher-driven change and the professionals who make it possible. It is a book that is the life work of someone who has helped change very many others by first changing himself. Admirable. Enviable. Unavoidable. Pick it up and you will not be able to put it down. I certainly couldn't!

—Andy Hargreaves
Thomas More Brennan Chair in Education
Boston College
November 2010

❖ Preface ❖

Islands of hope existed in each decade yet even these remarkable islands drop below sea level when founders, principals or key teachers, leave. As long as any one individual is indispensible, sustainability is a distant dream.

—Linda Lambert
(2007, p. 311)

WHY THIS BOOK AND WHY NOW?

School leaders in today's world often seem to be caught between the proverbial rock and hard place. School improvement is a case in point. If, on the one hand, principals and their co-leaders are *not* leading a comprehensive process of school improvement, they may be accused of "near enough is good enough" complacency by their system supervisors and also by their school boards and councils. But if they *are* leading such a process, they may harbor deep-seated doubts as to whether the immense effort that the process requires of them and their colleagues will have commensurate payoff.

According to leading international authorities, their doubts are justified. For even if their process of improvement is sound in theory, it may not be responsive to key systemic priorities or contextual values. Moreover, important infrastructural considerations that are required to see the improvement process through to a point of long-term embeddedness—such as retention of key staff, continuity in systemic priorities, provision of external supports, and leadership succession strategies—may not be in place, resulting in the jeopardizing, or even undoing, of their efforts.

It is for reasons such as these, says Linda Lambert in our opening quote, that the sustainability of hard-earned success remains for many schools a distant dream. While islands of educational hope may occasionally be built, they are of limited value if they drop below sea level whenever a new educational wave sweeps through.

It is in the context of this debilitating void in educational understanding and practice that this book has been written.

I became convinced in early 2008 that major developments in educational thinking during the preceding decade had resulted in the evolution of a very powerful new concept—"capacity building." This concept appeared to me to be essential to the work of 21st-century school leaders because it goes beyond processes of improvement to emphasize the sustainability of what has been achieved through an improvement process. In so doing, it appeared to provide an overdue response to the expressed needs of school leaders for guidance about how to get past the "boom and bust" cycle of school improvement that has plagued them since the school improvement movement began about 30 years ago.

My confidence in the concept of capacity building as a critically important tool for 21st-century educational leaders derived in large part from my analysis of five highly credible school capacity-building models that had been developed internationally over the previous decade. This examination led me to believe that capacity building may very well represent the missing link between school improvement and sustained school success. If principles of capacity building are not acknowledged in a school's improvement process, I deduced from my analysis, school improvement is conceptually, strategically, and practically incomplete.

But this book derives also from serious research with which I have had personal involvement. In mid-2008 I turned my attention to a major school improvement initiative—the IDEAS Project—with which I had close association (co-director) and which had enjoyed apparent success in 300-plus schools in a range of international contexts. The IDEAS Project was about to be evaluated in one large education district where it had been comprehensively implemented. Based on perceptual data, the 22 schools in question had shown important improvements in teacher morale and student engagement over a four-year period and were in the process of attempting to consolidate those improvements. What insights, I wondered, could the impending research reveal about sustainability as a feature of hard-earned school success? And what implications might ensue about the promising new concept of school capacity building?

The research project that was undertaken over the next six months resulted in the COSMIC C-B capacity-building model that provides the basis for this book. It was with a sense of deep satisfaction that I decided in early 2009 that answers to three core questions were within grasp:

- What is needed for school improvement to become sustainable school success?
- What are the constituent parts of capacity building as a process of building and sustaining school success?
- What forms of leadership are needed in order to ensure capacity building for sustainable school success?

And so my colleagues and I began to think about the possibility of this book.

So, Why This Book and Why Now?

In a nutshell, the answers to three questions of critical importance to school leaders are now available. But they have only just become available. This book represents a state-of-the-art description of what capacity building means and how to use a particular form of distributed leadership—"parallel leadership"—to achieve and sustain it. The book not only presumes to provide insights, processes, and skills that are essential to 21st-century school leadership and management, but it may well be the first major publication to illustrate how the roles of school leaders—principals and teacher leaders—vary and strengthen in relation to each other as a successful school improvement process evolves into a sustainable capacity-building process. It is a cutting-edge book that will help ensure that hard-earned improvements in school outcomes can be sustained, that professional effort toward school improvement can be justified—and that school leaders' sanity can be preserved (or restored).

WHAT MAKES THIS BOOK UNIQUE?

This book has four features that make it unique.

First, it describes in detail not just what capacity building means, but the constituent elements (we call them "dynamics") that schools should engage in to achieve enhanced school success and to sustain that success. COSMIC C-B details the six process dynamics that school leaders can employ to ascertain the quality of their school improvement processes and, if necessary, adjust in the interests of achieving sustained school success. There exists no other educational resource, to my knowledge, that interprets and explains capacity building in this way. In essence, if the COSMIC C-B model is applied in a school's improvement process, then enhancing school quality need not be the hit-and-miss business that it has been far too often in recent decades.

Second, this book develops the emerging concept of parallel leadership to a new level of understanding by demonstrating its distinct meanings at different stages of the capacity-building process. Almost without exception, school-based leadership has been regarded over the past 30 years as one-dimensional, with little or no allowance for the developmental phase of a school's improvement process. This book not only elevates parallel leadership to a new level of understanding; it also outlines the various functions of principalship and teacher leadership that are pertinent to each of the six capacity-building dynamics. In this regard, this book can be said to break very important new ground.

Third, Chapters 2 through 7, which are devoted to the COSMIC C-B dynamics, contain an unconventional feature. That is, each chapter contains two case studies—one being a snapshot that illustrates the meaning of the respective dynamic in a school setting and the other being a description of the dynamic in the workings of another human service institution. Readers will find that the six noneducational case studies relate clearly to the education snapshots and to the theme of the chapter. School capacity building, it becomes apparent, is not dissimilar from capacity building in other sectors of community life.

Fourth, each chapter concludes with a simulation that has been developed specifically to enable school leaders to develop advanced understanding of, and expertise in working with, the six COSMIC C-B dynamics. By completing the full sequence of six simulations, school leaders can have confidence in their ability to apply comprehensive capacity-building criteria in school improvement processes that they may have in train and in leading school workshops relating to the various dynamics.

Each of these four features makes this book distinctive. Taken together, the four features make it unique, a "book with a real difference." In summary, my associates and I undertake in this book to provide school leaders with three specific means of professional assistance:

- A research-based, capacity-building model—COSMIC C-B—that shows what must be done in a school if school outcomes are to be improved and those improved outcomes sustained
- New insights into a particular form of distributed leadership—parallel leadership—that has been demonstrated as fundamental to sustained school capacity building
- Professional learning experiences, in the way of original simulations, that can be experienced as a means of internalizing the essence of the six COSMIC C-B dynamics

HOW TO MAKE THE MOST PRODUCTIVE USE OF THIS BOOK

There are three ways that you might use this book productively. But where to start?

Before addressing this question, examine the COSMIC C-B diagram (Figure 1.1) with the following questions in mind:

1. Which of the six dynamics do you think you probably understand reasonably well already? Which do you probably understand least well?
2. Why do you think the dynamics expand and deepen as the C-B process unfolds?
3. Why do you think the arrows that link the dynamics, and that represent parallel leadership processes, expand as the six-dynamic C-B process unfolds?

As an experienced—or, equally important, aspirational—educational leader, you have no doubt drawn on a wealth of background understanding in answering the three questions. What you have undoubtedly seen for yourself is that you already have at least a cursory understanding of what this book is about. That being the case, you can proceed with confidence to determine how to use the book in any of three important ways.

The first use you might make of the book is needs based. For example, your need may be for increased understanding of how to create energy and excitement for what your school's improvement process might achieve. If that is the case, then Chapters 2 and 4—the first and third COSMIC C-B dynamics—would be your immediate reference point. You will find that the combination of case studies, relevant literature, leadership analyses, and simulation exercises relating to *committing to revitalization* and *seeking new heights* go a long way toward showing how you can enthuse your school and community for your personal goals and convictions.

But you may want more from this book. You may feel the need for understanding capacity-building as a holistic process and also for the leadership underpinnings of the six constituent C-B dynamics. If that is the case, then the Introduction and Chapter 1 provide a brief overview of school improvement and school capacity-building models, Chapters 2 through 7 provide detailed analyses of the six individual dynamics, and Chapter 8 provides a reflective summation of the COSMIC C-B model and of new insights into parallel leadership. The eight chapters, taken together, contain what we regard as the essential insights for 21st-century school leaders regarding holistic capacity building.

But you may want more than understanding. You may feel the need to become an expert practitioner in capacity building as a schoolwide developmental process. If that is the case, the simulations that are outlined in the final section of each chapter are intended to serve your purposes. Having read the chapters, find several colleagues with needs similar to your own and work your way through the simulations. That task completed, not only will you have acquired important practice-based insights into the six dynamics, but you will also be ready to lead capacity building with school or cluster colleagues. Given the fundamental importance of capacity building as a 21st-century educational process, that is an exciting and important day to look forward to.

How to use this book? Decide which of these purposes, or combination of purposes, suits your needs and proceed from there.

ORGANIZATION OF THE BOOK

This book follows a straightforward organizational format.

The Introduction sets the scene by providing an up-to-date analysis of international developments in both school capacity building and distributed leadership. In Chapter 1, the COSMIC C-B model is introduced along with a description of the research design that was used to assess the IDEAS School Improvement Project, and that led to the creation of the COSMIC C-B model.

A uniform format is used to organize each of Chapters 2 through 7. That is, following a brief introduction, a real-life snapshot description of the workings of the dynamic is presented. The meaning of the dynamic is then explored, drawing on material from the snapshot as well as authoritative literature. This analysis is followed by examination of school leadership principles in relation to the dynamic, once again using a combination of material from the snapshot and recent authoritative literature. That done, a noneducation case study of the dynamic is presented, along with a series of reflective questions. To conclude the chapter, an original simulation activity is outlined, incorporating comprehensive guidelines for use by school leadership teams, school staffs, or cluster members.

Two resources are contained in the final section of the book. The first outlines the IDEAS Project core concepts. The second outlines the research design and methodology for the evaluation of the IDEAS Project. It was this examination that provided the stimulus for development of the COSMIC C-B model.

CONCLUSION

The past decade has posed immense challenges for educators. One challenge in particular may be regarded as standing above all others—the school improvement movement, where so many doubts have been raised about sustainability that many committed principals and teacher leaders have been left wondering whether their energy-consuming efforts are justified.

The next decade should be much better. For while current challenges will no doubt continue—and new challenges will no doubt emerge—we finally have within our grasp a detailed understanding of school capacity building—what it means, its constituent parts, and its underpinning leadership principles. In the chapters that follow, we endeavor to bring the capacity-building process alive and to illuminate how you, as a "parallel" school leader, can use it to enhance the success of your school and sustain that success into the long-term future.

—Frank Crowther
November 2010

❖ Acknowledgments ❖

This book results from a decade or more of concerted thinking about one question: How can educational leaders ensure that the successes of their schools become valued and permanent fixtures rather than fleeting and peripheral ornaments? In my inquiring, researching, and building of tentative explanations over this time, I have been aided by a distinguished network of professional colleagues.

Of most importance have been the nine co-contributors of the book: Lindy Abawi, Dorothy Andrews, Joan Conway, Rosalia Cutaia, Senthu Jeyaraj, Marian Lewis, Giuseppe Micciche, Allan Morgan, and Shauna Petersen. Their chapter contributions have given the book "spice" as well as academic rigor and practical relevance. And then there are my "critical friends," people whose job it was to tell me I had more to learn—particularly Trish Bevan, Emma Brennan, Steve Brown, Trish Browne, Susan Callaghan, Bryan Connors, Natalie Crowther, Mark Dawson, Ross Dean, Sybil Dickens, Steve Dinham, Jim Dowie, Judy Dunne, Greg Duthie, David Eddy, Mike Gaffney, Marie Geoghegan, Tom Hart, Norm Hunter, Doug Jeanes, Bev Johnson, Colin Leech, Jenny Lewis, Mary L'Estrange, Angus Lucas, Warren Marks, Elena Masters, Chris McRae, Simon McGlade, Lee Mittens, Elizabeth O'Carrigan, Shirley O'Neill, Graeme Smith, Helen Starr, and Allan Walker.

A book of this type is dependent on the willing involvement of principals and teachers in those schools from which the case study data and descriptions are drawn. The staff of La Trobe Secondary College, Meadow Fair North Primary School, Mazzarino High School, All Hallows Catholic Elementary School, Woodlands Secondary School, and Eltham High School in that sense made this book possible. Also of great assistance to the chapter authors were the principals and teachers at a number of other schools, including Fairview Heights Primary School, Kealba Secondary College, and Duncraig Senior High School.

Corwin editors Desirée Bartlett and Debra Stollenwerk have been a professional pleasure to work with over the past year, considerate at all times but nevertheless totally straightforward and dependable in their judgment. Marlene Barron, who copyedited the manuscript, formatted it, and made numerous suggestions for literary enhancement, also deserves my deep gratitude. The Corwin reviewers who assessed the first draft—and seemed to almost gleefully destroy it—enjoy my ongoing gratitude and admiration.

Finally, it is now 30 years since I completed my doctoral studies under the tutelage of Professor Fred Newmann at the University of Wisconsin–Madison. This book reveals Fred's continuing extraordinary influence on my professional life.

Publisher's Acknowledgments

Corwin would like to thank the following individuals for providing their editorial insight and guidance:

David Freitas, Professor
Indiana University South Bend
South Bend, IN

David G. Hodgdon
Superintendent of Schools
SAU #38
Swanzey, NH

Ron MacDonald, Educational Consultant/Co-director
Model Secondary Schools Project
Bellevue, WA

Natalie Marston, Vice Principal
Mt. Hope/Nanjemoy Elementary
Nanjemoy, Maryland

Belinda J. Raines, Principal
Northwestern High School
Detroit, MI

About the Author and Collaborators

Frank Crowther, PhD, is Emeritus Professor of the University of Southern Queensland, where he was Pro Vice-Chancellor and Dean of Education before retiring in 2006 to research and write about teachers as leaders in school capacity building. His lifelong passion is for the status of the teaching profession. His book *Developing Teacher Leaders* is a bestseller.

Lindy Abawi lectures in curriculum and pedagogies at the University of Southern Queensland. She is a member of the Leadership Research Institute at the University of Southern Queensland and the IDEAS Project team. Her research interests relate to the intersection of school culture building and pedagogical enhancement.

Dorothy Andrews, PhD, is Associate Professor of Education and Director of the Leadership Research Institute at the University of Southern Queensland and National Director of the IDEAS Project. Her principal research interest is school improvement, with an emphasis on professional learning communities, particularly the IDEAS Project.

Joan Conway, PhD, lectures in pedagogies at the University of Southern Queensland. She is a member of the Univeristy of Southern Queensland Leadership Research Institute and the IDEAS Project team. Her research interests relate to collective intelligence and teachers' professional learning.

Senthu Jeyaraj lectures in psychology at James Cook University Singapore. Her doctoral thesis (almost completed) explores a cognitive dimension to the concept of schoolwide coherence. She is an associate member of the University of Southern Queensland Leadership Research Institute.

Marian Lewis, PhD, is a senior lecturer in education at the University of Southern Queensland. A member of the University of Southern Queensland Leadership Research Institute and the IDEAS Project team, her research interests focus on knowledge creation in schools, professional learning communities, and teacher leadership.

Allan Morgan, PhD, is an educational researcher and consultant, with a particular interest in school leadership processes and approaches. He is a member of the University of Southern Queensland Leadership Research Institute and the IDEAS Project team.

Shauna Petersen lectures in literacy education at the University of Southern Queensland. She is a member of the University of Southern Queensland Leadership Research Institute and the IDEAS Project team. Her research interests relate to teachers as leaders.

❖ Introduction ❖

Sustained School Success— What We Know, What We Don't Know, What We Need To Know

> *Without a clear focus on "capacity," a school will be unable to sustain continuous improvement efforts or to manage change effectively. That we know.*
>
> —David Hopkins and David Jackson (2003, p. 87)

Concern for capacity building has been a somewhat controversial topic of inquiry in educational research for more than a decade. The reason for this concern is well captured in our opening quotation by eminent British researchers Hopkins and Jackson.

But what, exactly, is "capacity"? Why is it important? How is it created? How is it sustained? And what forms of leadership underpin it? These questions have, until very recently, been unresolved. Now, fortunately, concrete, encouraging answers are becoming apparent. Taken together, the answers suggest that the education community now possesses the insights to ensure that school leaders can have a greater sense of strategic purpose during the next decade than was possible for the most part during the past decade.

In this introductory chapter, we outline briefly what is known about school capacity building. We also provide an up-to-date summary statement regarding distributed leadership, which is widely accepted as necessary if enhanced capacity is to be achieved and sustained. These tasks completed, the stage is set for the presentation in Chapter 1 of our response to the capacity-building challenge: the COSMIC C-B model.

SUSTAINABLE SCHOOL CAPACITY—WHAT WE KNOW

For the past two decades, educational researchers across the globe have expended massive effort attempting to uncover the school improvement equation. Literally hundreds of innovative approaches to school improvement, development, and revitalization have been created and implemented, encompassing the following range of widely used and well-known improvement approaches:

- Action learning, involving collaborative learning techniques, action research, and various forms of collegial learning circles
- School reculturing, involving values clarification and the development of school vision statements
- Coaching and mentoring, involving external experts and train-the-trainer strategies, usually in relation to school implementation of systemic priorities
- Cluster-based networking, involving district teams of school representatives sharing successes and needs
- Infrastructural design and reconstruction, involving the implementation of new facilities, technologies, and learning spaces

Some notable revitalization initiatives have in fact incorporated aspects of several of these approaches. Consider, for example, the ROUNDS Project (City, Elmore, Fiarman, & Teitel, 2009) in the United States; Manitoba School Improvement Project in Canada (Earl, Torrance, Sutherland, Fullan, & Ali, 2003); Improving the Quality of Education for All Project (Hopkins, West, & Ainscow, 1996) in the United Kingdom; and the IDEAS Project in Australia (Crowther, Andrews, Dawson, & Lewis, 2001). All are laudatory for their originality, comprehensiveness, and clarity. All have been methodically developed, comprehensively implemented, and systematically evaluated. And yet, as Levin (2010) has stated recently, their influence on school achievement has been disappointingly limited, with the focus of many schools and systems still on maintenance, not improvement. And why, one might ask, would this not be the case? After all, school improvement as currently construed provides no guarantee of a return that is commensurate with the effort expended and no assurance of sustainability, even if short-term success is achieved. The resultant frustration for school leaders is understandably and predictably debilitating.

Which leads us directly to the concept of capacity building . . .

It was probably Peter Senge who first introduced capacity building into the organizational and management literature. In attempting in 1990 to demonstrate a logical link between the concepts of knowledge society and organizational development, Senge asserted that two conditions must be met in the work of 21st-century organizations: first, the notion that the professional learning community must become accepted as integral to organizational development and, second, professional learning communities, once in operation, must accept that their core purpose involves the creation and sustainability of significant "new knowledge."

It was out of these dual premises that the concept of educational capacity building was born. For, according to Senge, when the professional community of an organization such as a school creates significant "new knowledge," and sets in place processes to ensure the ongoing refinement and dissemination of that knowledge, the organization's "capacity" to achieve and sustain success is greatly enhanced.

In the two decades since Senge's pioneering thinking, capacity building and its two key subordinate concepts—knowledge creation and professional learning community—have become fundamental organizational constructs. In education, the sequence of development as we see it can be linked to six key milestones.

Milestone one—1995—The idea that a school's "capacity" influences the nature and quality of student learning was introduced into the educational literature in 1995 by University of Wisconsin-Madison researchers Fred Newmann and Gary Wehlage. Subsequently, Bruce King and Newmann (1999, pp. 1-4) undertook nationwide research that enabled them to assert that a school's capacity to affect the quality of instruction in classrooms comprises four "dimensions":

- Teachers' knowledge, skills, and dispositions
- Professional learning, focused on (a) a concentration on student learning, (b) collaborative planning and decision making, (c) sustained effort, and (d) teachers learning as a community
- Program coherence
- Technical resources

Newmann and Wehlage's model is unique in the emphasis it places on teachers' use of the four dimensions to enhance their core work—their pedagogy.

Milestone two—2001—The notion of "spheres of capacity" was developed by Canadian researchers Coral Mitchell and Larry Sackney. Their model is based on three "spheres," which they assert must be developed concurrently if a school's overall capacity is to be enhanced. The spheres are

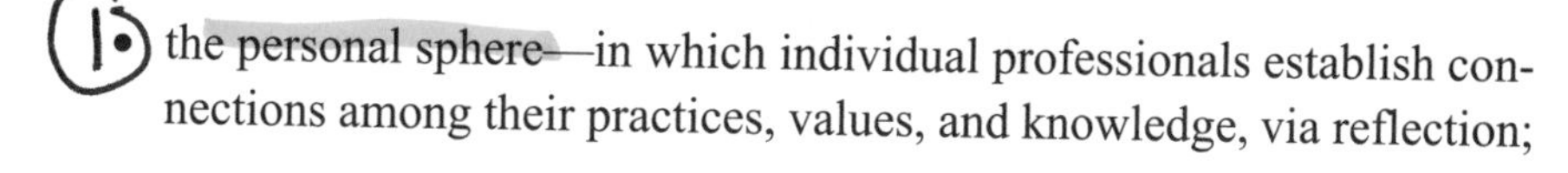

- the personal sphere—in which individual professionals establish connections among their practices, values, and knowledge, via reflection;

- the interpersonal sphere—in which groups and teams share knowledge about both good practice and how to build effective teams; and
- the organizational sphere—in which shared leadership, schoolwide collaborative practices, and associated supportive mechanisms are conceptualized, trialed, and refined.

Mitchell and Sackney's (2001) model is regarded by some authorities as the most comprehensive model of capacity building yet devised (Hadfield, Chapman, Curryer, & Barrett, 2002).

Milestone three—2001—The concept of "capital" was probably first introduced into the school improvement and capacity-building literature in a landmark publication by British researcher David Hargreaves in 2001. Hargreaves's model for building school success has four interrelated concepts:

- Social capital—the school's sociocultural (trust) and structural (networks) components
- Intellectual capital—the sum of the knowledge and experience of the school's stakeholders
- Leverage—the strategies that use teachers' invested energy to enhance the school's educational output
- Outcomes—the achievement of overt and unanticipated goals

Fundamental to Hargreaves's thinking is that an *improving* school increases its social and intellectual capital by using leverage strategies based on "what works." An *effective* school, on the other hand, uses leverage strategies that are grounded in evidence-informed practice. In either case, the enhancement of social capital, intellectual capital, and leverage strategies is asserted to facilitate the creation of better outcomes.

Milestone four—2003—The capacity-building model developed by British researchers David Hopkins and David Jackson is grounded in the rationale that capacity building is a plausible response to the fact of discontinuous societal change. Their capacity-building model contains five dimensions:

- Foundational conditions—creating both a sense of purpose and environmental orderliness
- The personal—constructing new knowledge and skills through reflective professional practice
- The interpersonal—working collaboratively and taking collective responsibility for learning and well-being

- The organizational—building, developing, and redesigning workplaces to create and sustain organizational improvement processes
- External opportunities—becoming entrepreneurial, creative, and resourceful in conjunction with external agencies and initiatives

The Hopkins and Jackson model is based on a conception of schools as organizations that are internally complex and externally interdependent. Hopkins and Jackson also assert the essential importance in capacity building of "dispersed leadership."

Milestone five—2005—The central role of the education system (as opposed to the individual school) in capacity building has been forcefully asserted by Canadian researcher Michael Fullan (2005b).

Fullan's concept of sustained capacity building incorporates eight system-level elements:

- Public service with a moral purpose
- A commitment to change as a multilevel process
- Lateral capacity building through networks
- Vertical relationships and intelligent accountability
- Deep learning
- A dual commitment to short-term and long-term results
- Cyclical energizing of staff
- The "long lever" of leadership (p. 14)

In placing the locus of capacity building outside the school, Fullan in a sense proposes radically new meanings for both "school" and "school leadership."

Milestone six—2006—Canadians Andy Hargreaves and Dean Fink (2006) have made the somewhat provocative point that educational development should be regarded as inseparable from global trends toward sustainable lifestyles and ecological conservation:

> The prominence and urgency of having to think about and commit to preserving sustainability in our environment highlights the necessity of promoting sustainability in many other areas of our lives. Foremost among these are leadership and education. (p. 2)

One might ask how school-level improvement initiatives might contribute to global sustainability. Hargreaves and Fink provide a very pointed answer by discussing not "education" but "non-education":

> Our consuming obsession with reaching higher and higher standards in literacy and numeracy within shorter and shorter time lines is exhausting our teachers and leaders, depleting and making it hard to renew the resources pool from which outstanding educators are drawn and turning vast tracts of the surrounding learning environment in humanities, health education, and the arts into barren wastelands as almost all people's achievement and improvement energies are channeled elsewhere. (pp. 2–3)

Hargreaves and Fink then proceed to propose seven principles of sustainable leadership that they (and we) regard as an educational antidote to the sustainability challenge:

- Depth—Sustainable leadership matters.
- Length—Sustainable leadership lasts.
- Breadth—Sustainable leadership spreads.
- Justice—Sustainable leadership actively improves the surrounding environment.
- Diversity—Sustainable leadership promotes cohesive diversity.
- Resourcefulness—Sustainable leadership develops, and does not deplete, material and human resources.
- Conservation—Sustainable leadership learns from the best of the past to create an even better future.

Each of these six highly credible research teams has made a vital contribution over the past decade to our understanding of school-based capacity building. But there is little of commonality in the six models, as is indicated in Table 1, where we indicate what we have borrowed from each model in creating our own capacity-building framework.

Table I.1 Key Contributions of Six Internationally Acclaimed Capacity-Building Models to COSMIC C-B

Model	*Context*	*Key contributions*
Newmann and Wehlage (1995) and King and Newmann (1999)	U.S.	• The concept of professional learning community is the central agency in school capacity building • Successful 21st-century teachers are both highly proficient individuals and collaborative professionals

Model	*Context*	*Key contributions*
Mitchell and Sackney (2001)	Canada	• Capacity building happens when personal, interpersonal, and organizational development intersect
D. Hargreaves (2001)	U.K.	• The generation of significant outcomes depends largely on the existence of high levels of social capital and intellectual capital, as well as leverage strategies
Hopkins and Jackson (2003)	U.K.	• Discontinuous change can be managed if capacity building processes are in place • Dispersed leadership is fundamental to successful capacity building
Fullan (2005b)	U.S.	• The basis of successful capacity building is systemwide supports, leadership networks, and incentives
A. Hargreaves and Fink (2006)	U.S./ Canada	• Sustainable capacity building in schools is inseparable from values associated with global sustainability and quality of life

LEADERSHIP AS A DISTRIBUTED QUALITY—WHAT WE KNOW

We indicated earlier that it was probably Peter Senge who introduced the concept of capacity building into our thinking and also into our vocabulary. But while immense progress has been made by educational researchers and thinkers since Senge's pioneering endeavors two decades ago, many questions remain unanswered. One question of particular importance is that of leadership: *What forms of leadership are needed to ensure success in school improvement and school capacity building?*

In our efforts over the past year or more to chart a leadership pathway for successful school improvement and school capacity building, we have been guided by our own inestimable confidence in the notion of teacher leadership, by our belief in the integrity of a particular form of distributed leadership that we call parallel leadership, and by compelling research from around the globe. Four insights appear to us to be irrefutable.

First is the establishment of a direct relationship between leadership as a distributed quality and successful school improvement. Traditional constructions of educational leadership, focused on the principalship, are now almost universally regarded as totally inadequate for processes of organizational learning, knowledge creation, and sustainability. In contrast, researchers such as Raelin (2005, p. 18) and Solansky (2008, p. 334), have asserted that constructs such as "team leadership," "leaderful organizations," and "we the leaders" are not only suited to sociocultural values associated with modern liberal democratic life but are justified for school applications on grounds of research into school effectiveness. There is also compelling evidence that distributed leadership can contribute to enhanced school outcomes by nurturing the development of pedagogical quality through highly the activities of professional learning communities. Mulford (2007), Harris (2004), and Timperley (2005) are leading international scholars who support this important conclusion.

Second is the lack of established clarity regarding what "distributed" leadership actually means in school affairs. Hopkins and Jackson (2003, p. 97) have noted that

> Despite more than two decades of writing about organizational learning . . . we are still in a position of needing to develop understandings about what leadership really involves when it is distributed, how schools might function and act differently, and what operational images of distributed leadership in action might look like.

In similar vein, Leithwood and Riehl (2003) have cautioned that distributed leadership has a variety of meanings and seems to have a variety of vague descriptors, including "devolved," "dispersed," "shared," "teamed," and "democratic." Consistent with this theme, Leithwood and Jantzi (2006, p. 202) have asserted that

> One slice of the educational literature seems mostly to be about "leadership by adjective"; a new qualifier is added to the term leadership at least annually, creating the misguided impression that something new has been discovered.

It can only be concluded that the international research agenda in relation to distributed leadership in school contexts is far from complete. Nevertheless, we have previously taken the position that what we call "parallel leadership" is identifiable, definable, and defensible on the basis of authoritative school-based research. Our research-based definition is

> Parallel leadership is a process whereby teacher leaders and their principals engage in collaborative action to build school capacity. It embodies three distinct qualities—mutual trust, shared purpose, and allowance for individual expression. (Crowther, Ferguson, & Hann 2009, p. 53)

Our construction of parallel leadership was described in our publication *Developing Teacher Leaders: How Teacher Leadership Enhances School Success* (Crowther et al., 2009, pp. 57–58) as follows:

> In advancing parallelism as a professionally appropriate approach to school-based leadership, we acknowledge, first of all, its dictionary definition: "agreement in direction, tendency or character" (Macquarie Library, 1998, p. 1560). Essential to our developmental work, however, have been the rich and complex meanings of this concept in a number of fields of cultural and intellectual endeavor.

Consider, for example, the field of *music,* where parallelism connotes the harmony derived when two independent parts or voices within a musical texture move up or down by the same distance in tandem (e.g., parallel fifths). In *language,* parallelism is well known. For example, analogies allow new meaning to be constructed through correspondence between two different concepts. In the world of *mathematics,* parallelism refers to forces that mirror each other. Parallel lines, for example, sustain their individual identities while maintaining a common direction and an unwavering distance from each other. In *computer science,* parallel processing refers to the management of complex data through systems that operate in a complementary fashion. Finally, consider the discipline of *philosophy,* in particular metaphysics, where parallelism connotes a doctrine of mind and body interacting synchronistically while remaining independent.

Parallelism in these human endeavors suggests values of respect, harmony, purposeful direction, alignment, individual presence, and complementarity. The three specific qualities that we have attributed to parallel leadership—mutual trust, shared purpose, and allowance for individualism—are readily discernible in these broader constructs and have been generated from our research with them in mind.

As would be expected, the three specific qualities that define parallel leadership are also to be found in other manifestations of contemporary culture.

In sports, for example, the notion that "A champion team will always beat a team of champions" implies at least two of the three qualities that we attribute to parallelism in school leadership. In musical performance, the complex relationship between a conductor, orchestral heads, and specialist performers can be viewed as reflecting aspects of all three underpinning qualities of parallelism—mutualism, shared purpose, and allowance for individual expression. The same is true in other performing arts, perhaps particularly dance, where ballet, rock 'n' roll, line dancing, and a preindustrial war dance may each be regarded as demonstrating particular forms of parallelism and manifesting varying degrees of each of the qualities of mutualism, shared purpose, and individuality.

But the three qualities are, we think, more deeply meaningful in leadership for successful school-based reform than in other culture forms that we have explored. We therefore assert that parallel leadership is a distinctive educational construct that has the potential to decisively advance the cause of schools and the teaching profession in the 21st century.

Diagram 4 (Resource A) shows the product of our research in conceptual terms.

In essence, to enhance a school's effectiveness necessitates a three-pronged strategy by a committed professional community over an extensive period (two years or more, in our case studies). That is, the school's professionals must engage in shared learning, focused reflection, and in-depth problem solving (outer circle of Diagram 4) while refining and deepening the school's culture and identity (middle circle) and simultaneously designing and implementing school-specific pedagogical principles and associated strategies (inner circle).

The daunting nature of this multifaceted challenge should not be underestimated. But it is within the capability of the modern teaching profession to achieve, as long as parallel leadership is used to guide school development and revitalization processes.

Our six school case studies in the chapters that follow substantiate this very important point. But, in this book, in charting a leadership pathway for schools pursuing enhanced success, we take our earlier definition of parallel leadership to a new level of understanding and justification.

Third is the rapidly evolving international policy context for distributed leadership in school practice. Pont, Nusche, and Moorman (2008) have noted that, as a result of the ever-growing phenomenon of the school as a learning organization, global interest in middle management is spreading and teachers are taking on an increasingly wide range of roles and responsibilities for leading and managing in schools. They note (pp. 78–80) that in Spain, teachers with specialist skills are now provided reduced workloads to assume the role of leadership assistants; in New Zealand, teachers have access to senior practitioner roles with schoolwide functions; in Finland, teachers assume districtwide educational coordination responsibilities; in the United States, many jurisdictions have introduced "lead teacher" classifications as a way of facilitating schoolwide curriculum and pedagogical development and mentoring junior staff; and in Korea, "chief teachers" take responsibility for staff and program supervision. In Australia, meanwhile, a 2010 Commonwealth proposal for the future teaching profession includes official designation of a "lead teacher" classification, with both classroom and schoolwide professional and pedagogical functions.

In this rapidly evolving policy context, featuring ongoing developments in the status, roles, and core functions of teacher leaders, it is important to recognize that as much remains unknown as is known about the machinations of school-based leadership as a distributed quality.

Fourth, Linda Lambert (2007) has postulated a major consideration for school leadership, given the capacity-building focus of this book. Lambert endorses the concept of distributed leadership but notes that leadership in different phases of capacity development requires different functions (p. 316). For example, she asserts, if schools are at "instructive," "transitional," and "high capacity" stages of development, the form of leadership that is required—of both principals and teachers—is necessarily different.

Lambert is one of the very few international thinkers to construe school-based leadership for capacity building as linked to phases of development. In so doing, she has made a singularly important contribution to the practice of modern school-based leadership and also to the research that underpins this book. Critical in Lambert's contribution is that there is no one "style" of educational leadership that fits all needs, situations, or contexts, a position that is supported by Maden (2001). We have previously made the point (Crowther et al., 2009, pp. 28–36) that contemporary school-based leadership approaches tend to fall into four broad categories:

- *Transformational,* emphasizing charisma, vision, inspiration, and intense energy
- *Strategic,* emphasizing planning, accountability, objectivity, and efficiency
- *Advocacy* (educative), emphasizing social justice, consciousness raising, culture struggle, and confronting barriers to fairness
- *Organizationwide,* emphasizing democracy, shared responsibility, synergies, and everyone a potential leader

The question of which, if any, leadership approach is most important at each of Lambert's three stages of school development is seriously under-researched. But Hallinger and Heck have recently captured the importance of this point:

> Leaders must be able to adapt their strategies to changing conditions at different stages in the journey of school improvement. (2010, p. 106)

Also of relevance to our concern about leadership and phases of school development is the very helpful postulation of Hallinger and Heck (2010) that school-based leadership and school-based capacity building may be characterized by a range of interactive relationships:

- A *direct effects* relationship, in which a school's leadership is the primary driver for student learning
- A *mediated effects* relationship, in which a school's leadership shapes the school's capacity for improvement
- A *reversed mediated effects* relationship, in which school outcomes shape a school's leadership
- A *reciprocal effects* model, in which a school's leadership and capacity building are mutually influential

Hallinger and Heck's (2010) research conclusions are very interesting: that the *reciprocal effects* model has greatest validity, and that leadership for successful school improvement should be viewed "as a highly responsive and contextualized relational process" (p. 106). But the question of what form of distributed leadership, if any, best suits the reciprocal effects model has not yet been explored in detail.

In summary, we conclude that leadership for capacity building is best thought of as a distributed quality. That much is agreed on by authoritative contemporary observers. But distributed among whom? How? And for what purposes? These questions continue to be explored by educational researchers. In our building of the leadership underpinnings of COSMIC C-B, we drew heavily on the four developments referred to in the previous paragraphs and summarized in Table 1.2.

Table 1.2 Key Contributions of Four Recent Educational Leadership Developments to COSMIC C-B

Model	*Key research-based contributions*
Mulford (2007) Harris (2004) Timperley (2005) Crowther et al. (2009)	• Distributed leadership is essential to school success
Pont, Nusche, and Moorman (2008)	• The teaching profession is maturing rapidly, with teachers in a wide range of countries assuming significant leadership roles and functions in school improvement
Lambert (2007)	• Principal and teacher leader functions should take into account the distinctive requirements of particular phases of their school improvement processes
Hallinger and Heck (2010)	• Successful school improvement and school leadership are reciprocally related

CONCLUSION

It might well be surmised from the analyses that we have completed in the preceding sections that more is *not* known about achieving school success than is known.

On one hand, we have ready access to a range of highly credible conceptual models that tell us what successful capacity building looks like. But, on the other hand, we don't know much about the actual school-based processes of capacity building. Perhaps most important, we don't possess clear understandings of how to sustain successes that have been achieved in the face of changing influences such as a new principalship, and we don't know how to avoid overload and burnout as the process unfolds. As Louise Stoll has stated, we learned ten years ago that multiple parts of the school as an organization have to be developed if capacity is to be built, but only now are we beginning to understand capacity as a holistic and generic process of continuous improvement (Stoll, 2009, p. 116).

We know also that distributed forms of leadership—involving the principal and teacher leaders—are fundamental to school success, but we know very little about the ways that the roles and functions of principals and teacher leaders should be defined in the different phases of a developmental process.

Thus, is more known or not known about how to achieve sustained school success? That question is too complex to be easily answered. What is comparatively easy to agree on is that we desperately need to know the criteria that define a successful school improvement process and just as desperately need to know the leadership forms that are part and parcel of those criteria.

These are the core challenges that guide this book.

1

The COSMIC C-B Approach

A Prelude

There is no chance that large-scale reform will happen, let alone stick, unless capacity building is a central component of the strategy.

—Michael Fullan (2005b, pp. 10–11)

INTRODUCTION

In our introductory chapter, we reviewed global developments in school improvement and also explored significant pioneering initiatives in school capacity building. We learned from our review that capacity building is much more than school improvement; it is school improvement that matters, that works, and, as Michael Fullan put it in our opening quote, that "sticks."

Our conclusions from our analysis of global capacity-building developments were largely, but not totally, encouraging. On one hand, we concluded, the range of explanatory conceptual models that is now available to educational leaders is very impressive. On the other hand, it is all too apparent that we know relatively little about the leadership and management strategies that are needed to proceed through a school improvement process to the point where success is achieved. We know even less about strategies that are needed to sustain that success. The net effect is that we can only agree with Fullan—immense professional effort is currently expended by school leaders in the name of school improvement but, because that effort does not incorporate capacity-building strategies, it is largely wasted.

In this chapter, we outline the features of a capacity-building model—COSMIC C-B—that we believe provides an antidote to this very serious educational concern. We say this because the six dynamics that make up the COSMIC C-B model contain criteria that can be employed by school leaders at either of two critically important stages of a school improvement process: first, during the project design stage; second, in conjunction with ongoing progress reviews.

If COSMIC C-B is used in conjunction with preimplementation, activities to design and plan a school's improvement project, then the improvement project will in all probability become hybridized with COSMIC C-B. That particular use of COSMIC C-B, we believe, is fully justified. If, on the other hand, the COSMIC C-B dynamics are used as yardsticks in conjunction with periodic progress reviews, then the essence of the school's own improvement process will probably be retained, enriched by the COSMIC C-B dynamics. This use of COSMIC C-B is also legitimate. In both instances, the application of COSMIC C-B to a school improvement initiative will, we believe, heighten the chances of achieving meaningful school-based success.

COSMIC C-B IN BRIEF

Figure 1.1 The COSMIC C-B Model

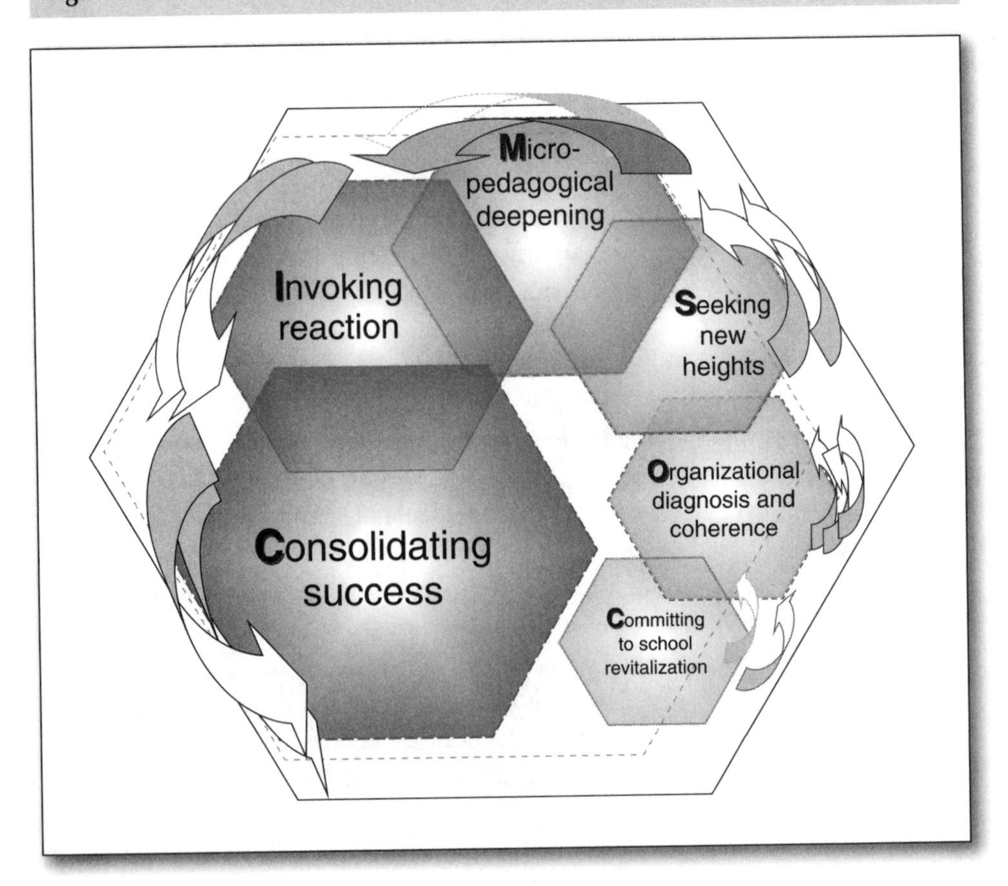

Our capacity-building framework is labeled COSMIC C-B for three reasons: first, C-B is our stylized representation of the concept of school capacity building, and second, COSMIC is an acronym drawn from the six dynamics that make up the model:

- ***C***ommitting to school revitalization
- ***O***rganizational diagnosis and coherence
- ***S***eeking new heights
- ***M***icro-pedagogical deepening
- ***I***nvoking reaction
- ***C***onsolidating success

Third, COSMIC derives from *cosmos*,which is not only ever-evolving but also dynamic, harmonious, and orderly—every school leader's dream.

The COSMIC C-B model represents what we regard as the clearest picture yet developed of how a school can achieve enhanced outcomes and sustain those outcomes in the face of changing times, changing circumstances, changing external priorities, and changing people. The C-B model has five features.

First, it contains six "dynamics," and associated criteria, that need to be clearly in evidence at particular junctures of a school improvement process if that process is to achieve sustained success.

Second, each dynamic provides a foundation for the other five dynamics. This particular feature of the model is reflected in Figure 1.1 in the overlaps of the dynamics and the increasing size of the hexagons as COSMIC C-B develops. The counterclockwise direction of the dynamics in Figure 1.1 indicates an important reality that we associate with successful school improvement—it frequently gets started "against the grain."

Third, while each dynamic is critically important in its own right, we regard the fourth dynamic, *micro-pedagogical deepening,* as the centerpiece of COSMIC C-B. It is this dynamic where teaching, learning, and assessment are the focus of concern. Our research showed that it is this dynamic that was most challenging for schools and where a new paradigm of leadership—one that emphasizes teachers as leaders—is most needed.

Fourth, the model is underpinned by a form of distributed leadership that we call "parallel leadership." The increased size of the arrows linking the six dynamics in the diagram in Figure 1.1 connotes the growth and maturation in parallel leadership as a school improvement process generates success.

Fifth, the model asserts that each school is primarily responsible for its own improvement. Thus, while we recognize the importance of systems, networks, clusters, and alliances, COSMIC C-B asserts that schools exist in individual contexts and must respond to particular circumstances. School leaders must, in the final analysis, assume responsibility for their individual school's developmental processes and outcomes.

The six dynamics that constitute COSMIC C-B are generic in the sense that they are fundamental in any process of school improvement that is designed to create and sustain enhanced success. But each of the dynamics must also be understood and valued in its own right.

The six dynamics that compose the model have precise meanings:

C-B dynamic 1—Committing to school revitalization—making a firm decision to undertake school improvement (or revitalization) as an immediate leadership priority.

C-B dynamic 2—Organizational diagnosis and coherence—facilitating shared understanding within the school community of the degree of alignment (or misalignment) of the school's key organizational elements.

C-B dynamic 3—Seeking new heights—developing an image of the future that is both inspirational and optimistic. This image manifests primarily in two interrelated forms—a motivational vision statement and a transformative schoolwide pedagogical framework (SWP).

C-B dynamic 4—Micropedagogical deepening—engaging teachers in forms of professional inquiry that will enhance schoolwide pedagogical practice. Professional inquiry for micro-pedagogical deepening incorporates three strategies: reflection on personal gifts and talents, conceptual exploration of the school's pedagogical principles, and development of classroom strategies relating to the SWP principles.

C-B dynamic 5—Invoking reaction—disseminating and refining significant new school-based knowledge (organizational and pedagogical) through networking, "double loop" learning, and professional advocacy.

C-B dynamic 6—Consolidating successes—identifying core processes that have contributed to enhanced school outcomes, and embedding these processes in the ongoing work of the school. The processes incorporate organizational, cultural, and professional learning strategies.

Thus, it can be seen that the origins of COSMIC C-B reside in three factors: a concern for contemporary school leaders' lack of ability to ensure that the effort they devote to school improvement has commensurate payoff, the emergence over the past decade of a number of authoritative explanations of the meaning of school capacity building, and research into a large-scale school improvement initiative that achieved documented success in a range of student outcomes areas. COSMIC C-B is undoubtedly not the final word in school capacity building, but it extends previous educational thinking to a new level of understanding. It does so primarily because its six dynamics provide practical and authoritative criteria that school leaders can use to ensure that their school improvement processes demonstrate the potential for sustained success.

THE SCHOOL RESEARCH ORIGINS OF COSMIC C-B

COSMIC C-B derives in part from research into a particular school improvement process, the IDEAS Project, which has been implemented in over 300 schools internationally. The major features of the IDEAS Project are described in Resource A. In summary, the features are

- a five-phase, three- to four-year revitalization process, supported by descriptive professional learning materials and ongoing assistance from the IDEAS Project consultancy team;
- a construction of parallel leadership roles and functions that recognizes metastrategic principalship and teacher leadership;
- an established framework for organizational alignment (the Research-Based Framework for Organizational Alignment) and survey instruments to ascertain a school's *index of coherence*; and
- a three-dimensional framework for expert pedagogical practice.

The IDEAS Project schools that participated in the research ($N = 22$) commenced their involvement as an "IDEAS cluster" in 2004. Nineteen of the schools completed the requirements of the project in the period 2004 to 2008 and were found to demonstrate important improvements in teacher esteem and morale, as well as student attitudes and engagement. A comprehensive three-phase research design was agreed on with state education officials in order to explore and explain these improvements.

THE PHASE A RESEARCH

The research problem that guided the Phase A research was as follows:

> What changes, if any, in school outcomes can be attributed to the research schools' implementation of the IDEAS Project, 2004 to 2008?

As a result of the Phase A research, significant improvements were identified in 17 of the 19 schools in teacher morale, teachers' perceptions of the effectiveness of their pedagogy, student engagement, and students' perceptions of the efficacy of their teachers' pedagogical strategies (see Resource B for details).

The following definition of "success" was then developed:

School success means the achievement of enhanced school outcomes in one or more agreed priority areas, based on documented evidence of those outcomes and teachers' confidence in their school's capacity to sustain its achievements into the future.

THE PHASE B RESEARCH

Analysis of five Phase A schools that had achieved documented success in an area of priority importance to the school (e.g., student literacy, student engagement) was then undertaken by the research team. The Phase B research problem was as follows:

> What lessons for school improvement can be learned from the experiences of schools that have achieved enhanced outcomes in conjunction with implementation of the IDEAS Project, 2004 to 2008?

As a result of the case study research, the research team developed the COSMIC C-B model (Figure 1.1) and also the following definition of "capacity building":

Capacity building is the intentional process of mobilizing a school's resources in order to enhance priority outcomes–and sustain those improved outcomes. It comprises six dynamics as outlined in Figure 1.1.

THE PHASE C RESEARCH

A follow-up research initiative was undertaken by the research team to explore the leadership constructs that underpinned the six capacity-building dynamics. The research problem that guided the Phase C research was the following:

> What forms of principal and teacher leadership are associated with successful implementation of the six COSMIC C-B dynamics?

The Phase C research resulted in four key outcomes:

1. Parallel leadership grows in maturity and importance as school improvement unfolds successfully.
2. Middle managers (deputy principals, heads of department) are critical to the success of parallel leadership.
3. Existing professional conceptualizations of teacher leadership and principal leadership should be expanded to incorporate capacity-building functions.
4. The leadership functions of principals and teacher leaders vary in accordance with the demands of individual capacity-building dynamics.

To conclude, the Phase C research revealed that parallel leadership is more definitive in nature than has often been presumed. It connotes variations in roles and functions for teacher leaders, middle managers, and principals, as well as linkages to systemic agencies, that have not been taken into full account in leadership research and theory building in the past. But that deficiency can now be addressed. It can be addressed because the dynamics of successful school capacity building have been identified and their underpinning leadership dimensions are beginning to take clear shape.

CONCLUDING COMMENT

We began this chapter with a statement in which Michael Fullan indicated that school improvement without a capacity-building component is a virtual waste of time, effort, and resources. But what is capacity building, and how can it be integrated with a school improvement initiative in the interests of heightened school success?

In this chapter, we have provided an overview of our response to this question—the COSMIC C-B model.

COSMIC C-B is a unique educational model. It captures features of six particularly significant and reputable approaches to school capacity building that we have reviewed but differs from them in two key respects: its process orientation and its grounding in a "parallel" leadership approach.

With this brief overview of COSMIC C-B completed, we now proceed to explore each of the six capacity-building dynamics in detail.

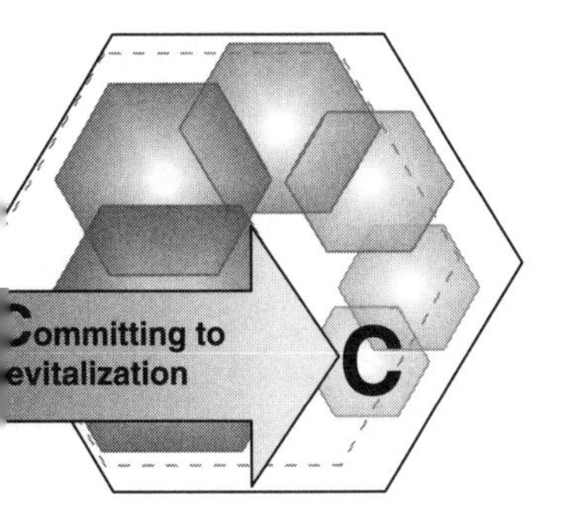

2

The First C-B Dynamic

Committing to Revitalization

(Prepared in collaboration with Dr. Marian Lewis)

> *Until one is committed, there is hesitancy, the chance to draw back, always ineffectiveness . . . the moment one definitely commits oneself, then providence moves too. A whole stream of events issues from the decision.*
>
> —W. H. Murray
> (*The Scottish Himalayan Expedition,* 1951,
> as cited in Gore, 1992, p. 16)

INTRODUCTION

What does it take to climb a Mt. Everest? First and foremost, according to renowned Scottish mountaineer W. H. Murray in our opening quote, it takes commitment. For, he says, "the moment one definitely commits oneself, then providence moves too."

In our Introduction, we established that many schools are currently operating in extremely challenging conditions, caught in the complexities of change and political demands for heightened effectiveness. Within that highly pressurized context, however, there is a lot of variation in the circumstances of individual schools. Some may be perceived by system supervisors as highly successful on the basis of their student data, while others are viewed in a less positive light, possibly as failing. Some may be seen by parents or students as having no particular direction, while others have a clear sense of purpose and self-belief. Some may be regarded by their teachers as frenzied, while others lack dynamism and energy. Leaders and teachers in some may recently have enjoyed a positive involvement with a school improvement process while others may have predominantly bad recollections. So, one might ask, can there be a generic starting point in building, and then sustaining, school success?

We believe there is indeed a common starting point in successful school capacity building. We say this because, regardless of circumstances, the processes of enhancing and sustaining school success meet six common criteria, the first of which is the same "elementary truth" that mountaineer W. H. Murray described as essential to embarking successfully on any serious "act of initiative"—that is, a firm decision to commit.

But knowledge of *how* to start a process of school revitalization is vague in the minds of many school leaders. We begin our exploration of the *committing to revitalization* dynamic with a snapshot description of a school that captured the essence of this C-B dynamic and proceeded to achieve and sustain enhanced school capacity. We place particular emphasis on the actions, motivations, and purposes of school leaders in getting the process of school improvement underway. We then develop a definition of the first C-B dynamic. That done, we explore the implications for school-based leadership before proceeding to apply and test our new understandings about committing to revitalization in a well-known international exemplar. We conclude the chapter with a professional learning exercise that is designed to enhance your personal proficiency in working with the first C-B dynamic in your school, and hopefully other schools.

It is now timely to turn to the story of one of our research schools where committing to revitalization was the first crucial step in a highly successful process of school improvement.

A SNAPSHOT OF COMMITTING TO REVITALIZATION

CARMICHAEL SECONDARY COLLEGE

A Struggling and Dispirited School . . .

Steven Walker came to Carmichael as the new principal early in 2004. A successful elementary school principal with a strong sense of social justice, Steve was looking for a way to expand his understanding of education and relished the prospect of a challenge in a high school. But he was surprised by what he found. Located in one of the more disadvantaged areas of a large city, Carmichael Secondary College was a school with major problems. Once large and successful, the school had gradually slipped into decline, a situation worsened by falling enrollments and diminished subject choices for senior students. Those students who remained were mostly struggling, and in comparison with other schools across the state, Carmichael ranked in the lowest percentiles on a number of important measures. The future looked dismal. At the same time, as part of a broader education restructuring process in the district, discussions were being held about school amalgamations. It was determined that Carmichael would amalgamate in three years with a nearby secondary college, a move that would, in effect, bring this low period in its history to an end.

The decline at Carmichael had been gradual and many of the longer term teachers were struggling, seemingly unable to provide for their students. There were few, if any, staff room conversations about educational topics. Morale was revealed in district surveys as rock bottom. Teachers had limited confidence in students and seemingly little trust in each other. They blamed each other, and they blamed students for not responding to their programs. Ben, a young teacher, recalled that the climate of blame was so bad he considered resigning after his first two weeks.

The hostility in the corridors and the conflict in the classrooms shocked Steve. He began to wonder whether it was possible to turn the school around, reconnecting teachers and students. After a range of discussions, he summed up his appraisal of the situation: there was no shared philosophy in place to support those who wanted to bring about positive change; Carmichael was not a school where the teachers genuinely provided for their students, understood their individuality, or expected them to work to the best of their abilities; and students were not focused on learning in respectful classroom environments.

At this critical point, Steve considered, and talked to trusted colleagues about, the three most obvious options that were available to him:

- *The planned merger is only three years away so let's just wait this mess out.*
- *I didn't create this situation and can therefore be justified in prescribing my own remedies to those who did create it.*
- *We owe it to the students to improve the situation as much as we possibly can in the time remaining available to us.*

Which way to go?

A Principal With the Courage of His Convictions

Steve knew that he needed to be true to himself. He wanted in a personal sense to be in an environment where students were respectful and enjoyed learning. Moreover, he knew that some teachers in the school were committed to building a positive environment but could not do so because their commitment was not linked to any coherent sense of purpose.

With this picture in mind, Steve went looking for a process of school revitalization that had an established history of success and that was grounded in a belief in teachers' professionalism. What he found was the IDEAS Project, a process that appeared to align with his educational and social justice values and that used the sort of language that he needed in order to persuade staff to embark on a schoolwide process of change—*no blame, teachers are the key, collective responsibility,* and *parallel leadership.*

A Process That Fits the Situation

After listening to a briefing about IDEAS, Steve returned to Carmichael and discussed the possibility of taking it on with his leadership team at a full staff meeting. He was forthright about not being the sole individual to bring about change—collective responsibility was needed. In his work with staff, he began to focus on ways of fundamentally changing the culture of the school, because, as he stated regularly, "Unless you fundamentally change the culture of how people operate together, I don't believe you can bring about educational change."

The Carmichael staff gave approval to the IDEAS Project at a staff meeting, with several noting that their vote was an act of faith, given the absence of full understanding. An IDEAS Project School Management Team (ISMT), comprising three teachers and a deputy principal, was then created. With the agreement of the staff, the ISMT began its work, taking stock of the school through use of the IDEAS Project Diagnostic Inventories. While the outcomes of this analysis presented a depressing picture of the school, the teachers made a critical discovery—that their students were just as concerned about high-quality teaching and learning as they were. Another discovery was that the data weren't totally about negatives—there were also successes to be celebrated. Buoyed by the positives, the staff chose to engage in frank and open conversations, formally endorsing the IDEAS "no blame" principle and making extensive use of the IDEAS "professional conversation" protocols (Table B.6). They began to openly, if somewhat tentatively, acknowledge the need, and the real possibility, for change.

A Teacher Leader With Optimism

The action of the principal in taking a stand about what was right, and in actively challenging the status quo, opened new leadership opportunities for others. Of importance was the emergence of Jenny, a particularly well-regarded and committed teacher who spoke openly of her optimism for the school and its students and who became the official IDEAS facilitator. She and two other teachers worked with Steve to co-lead the IDEAS process, particularly the processes of visioning and schoolwide pedagogical development (Table 2.1). It was a process that quickly gathered momentum and retained that momentum over a three-year period until the school was amalgamated. It is significant that Jenny shared the same fundamental values and educational goals as Steve. It is significant also that the ISMT group was a diverse array of individuals with very different leadership and management skills. If the group had one quality in common, it was that it was very strategic in its intent, developing time frames, analyzing data, organizing workshops, synthesizing staff ideas, and preparing community communications.

The Transformation at Carmichael College

Picking up the impetus for action, the staff began to move forward, reorganizing the teaching day, working together in year-level teams, and using student assessment data to inform their teaching. The teachers became much more involved in their school's big-picture challenges, creating the vision and schoolwide pedagogical framework statements that are contained in Table 2.1.

By year three of the IDEAS Project, Carmichael College was on the way to becoming a transformed educational institution. Teacher morale and student engagement data showed dramatic improvement (Resource B). Steve and Jenny were selected to lead other revitalization approaches throughout the district, based on the Carmichael success story.

Table 2.1 Carmichael College Vision and SWP

VISION: *Be Brave, Lead, Succeed*

VALUES: Perseverance, Respect, Attitude

SCHOOLWIDE PEDAGOGICAL FRAMEWORK:

- Knowing each student personally
- Clear expectations for learning engagement
- A culture of respect
- Building confidence to engage with the outside world
- Thinking deeply
- Reflection and self-assessment

Steve's courage, confidence in others, educational insight, and personal convictions, allied with the depth of concern felt by Jenny, had paid huge dividends for the students of Carmichael College.

COMMITTING TO REVITALIZATION

DEEPENING OUR UNDERSTANDING

The critical importance of one or more school leaders making a firm commitment if a process of successful school improvement is to get off the ground is readily apparent in the Carmichael College case study. But the concept of human commitment is as complex as it is powerful. It is multileveled and linked to both a sense of hopefulness and a concern for "good work," as the following explanations reveal.

The Multiple Levels of Commitment

The story of Carmichael Secondary College is illuminating in the way that it demonstrates that, at any time in the life of a school, there are likely to be different degrees and levels of commitment. The Carmichael story also illustrates that levels of commitment can change over time.

It seems fair to say that, initially, a number of teachers at Carmichael engaged with the prospect of school revitalization at a level of commitment that is sometimes called "political." According to Richards (2004), this is the most common, and also the shallowest, form of commitment, with the focus being on what might be gained (or lost) at a personal level. Political commitment "is frequently half-hearted and short-lived. It lacks the oomph, verve, and sheer stubbornness needed to achieve a challenging common purpose" (Richards, 2004, p. 14). This form of commitment—"I will go along with your proposal provided that it takes little of my time and can give me tangible rewards"—undoubtedly represents the entry point for many teachers who have been burned by bad experiences with school improvement processes. It was certainly the entry point for some of the disengaged teachers at Carmichael College.

But by the time the Carmichael improvement process got underway, deeper levels of commitment were already forming. Most notably, the principal—and increasingly, the teacher leaders, particularly Jenny—were demonstrating "intellectual" commitment in the form of a deep-rooted belief that they could create a sense of purpose and pedagogical practice that was tangibly better at Carmichael than currently existed. As the advocates of revitalization, they were able to draw in some of their colleagues through their ability to communicate the possibility of a better future. They painted a picture of "a new Carmichael world" and offered their time and resources to achieve it. Gradually they began to deepen the commitment of others until a majority of colleagues were on board. In so doing, they demonstrated that a political mind-set can be transposed into intellectual commitment by astute leaders who are armed with effective revitalization strategies and communicate with conviction.

The meaning of commitment as either political or intellectual has been extended to an even deeper level in the powerful notion of emotional intelligence. According to Goleman, Boyatzis, and McKee (2002), the most successful leaders tune in to people's emotions, inspiring them and "guid[ing] them in the right direction" (p. 26). This point is of importance because, while political commitment is about obtaining people's attention, and intellectual commitment is about convincing people of the worth of particular ideas, emotional commitment is about values and moving people and systems to concrete action.

Thus, in the story of Carmichael College, serious educational change came about when political agendas were set aside and both intellectual and emotional commitment were pursued—that is, when hearts and minds became engaged. This is not to say that all Carmichael College teachers were politically, intellectually, and emotionally engaged in changing their school. It is likely that at no time in the revitalization process were more than two-thirds of the staff actively involved. Goleman and his associates (2002, p. 8) point out that "people take their emotional cues from the top"—but note that many of the "emotional leaders" in an organization do not hold positions of formal authority. To the contrary, loyalty, trust, and cooperation can be molded by respected top colleagues. This was most certainly the case in the success of Carmichael College.

Hope and Commitment

I have a dream today.

I have a dream that my four little children will one day live in a nation where they will not be judged by the color of their skin but by the content of their character. I have a dream today.

—Martin Luther King, Jr.
(Washington, D.C., August 28, 1963,
as cited in Montefiore, 2005, p. 152)

Martin Luther King inspired a generation of Americans with the depth of his convictions and the power and inspiration of his oratory. In the process, he shaped modern America and much of the contemporary world. Indeed, his influence lives on, almost 50 years after his "I have a dream" speech. Such is the power of hope as an emotion in the enhancement of societies and their institutions.

As we have seen, the story of Carmichael College illustrates that committing to revitalization has a strong emotional-affective dimension. Of particular significance in bringing about change at the college was the use of fervor, passion, and affect to create a pervasive ethos of hopefulness in the school community. Sergiovanni (2005) captured the intent of this notion when he said that it is a sense of hope, linked to action, that enables leaders to change reality. Larson and Luthans (2006, p. 50) extend this point into the realm of strategic action when they state that "high hope leaders are stronger leaders because of their ability to set goals, create pathways, and think of alternatives."

Thus, Steve Walker communicated his positive emotions clearly and convincingly, with significant effects on staff and, at a later stage, on students and parents. He conveyed his goal to revitalize his school with what Snyder (as cited in Helland & Winston, 2005, p. 44) calls "affective zest" as opposed to "affective lethargy." In so doing, Steve created an expectation, based on both cognition and emotion, that his goal for Carmichael was reasonable, defensible, desirable, and achievable. Once a degree of schoolwide commitment to the idea of revitalization had been gained, he proceeded to facilitate the development of a school vision (Table 2.4) that captured his values, his emotional attachment to the school, and his sense of hope.

Emotions in organizations are contagious, as is evident in the case of Carmichael. Moreover, the spread of positive mood can have the effect of reducing interpersonal conflict, widening flexibility of thinking, fostering creativity and innovation, increasing openness to the ideas of others, and improving decision making (Isen, 1999). This would also seem to have been the case at Carmichael. Finally, Carmichael's staff-created schoolwide pedagogical framework mirrored the sense of optimism and hopefulness of the "brave" school vision. This would not have been possible without a sense of hope, trust, and self-belief in place by the end of the first year of the revitalization process.

Commitment and "Good Work"

The core human value of "goodness" is inseparable from commitment in educational leadership. While history is replete with descriptions of "leaders" who have wrought havoc while demonstrating their commitment to causes that were grounded in various forms of destruction, educational leadership resides in a very different world, one where "goodness" is a core value.

In exploring the meaning of the first C-B dynamic, therefore, it is important that we consider what is meant by "good work."

Gardner, Csikszentmihalyi, and Damon (2001) provide a very helpful starting point with their assertion that work that is "both excellent in quality and socially responsible" meets the criterion of "goodness." It does so because it implies acceptance of values that are grounded in concern for the well-being of people—human dignity, individual growth, and inclusivity, for example.

"Good work" was a significant aspect of the challenge facing Steve Walker as a newly appointed principal at Carmichael Secondary College. For him, committing to revitalization meant creating a new understanding of what high-quality work meant at Carmichael—and how that work might contribute to enhanced student well-being.

Educational philosopher Parker Palmer says that "good work is done with heart as well as knowledge and skill, done with a depth of commitment that brings integrity and courage to the workplace" (Center for Courage & Renewal, n.d.). Steve Walker appears to have embodied the intent of this assertion in the values he courageously embraced and the integrity with which he led the Carmichael revitalization process. The importance of this point cannot be overstated when a revitalization initiative is being considered. We say this because there is no reason to believe that an individual whose conception of good work is well developed for one context will necessarily find it applicable in another context. To the contrary, some educators feel a deeply rooted commitment to lead school development in schools in low socioeconomic communities, others in schools in culturally distinctive communities, and others again in schools with a high proportion of advantaged and talented students. The implication is significant—school leaders should attempt to establish a clear relationship between their personal values and the values that are implicit in the particular school that they are considering revitalizing. Steve Walker, whose personal values focused on justice and equity across the community, student-oriented pedagogy, and the well-being of disadvantaged students, was ideally situated to lead at Carmichael College. He connected who he was with what he did in a highly authentic way.

There are three conclusions that we can now draw about committing to revitalization:

- It implies acceptance at a personal level of values that are grounded in good work—values such as individual human dignity and inclusivity.
- It can be understood as encompassing four levels of meaning, with intellectual commitment being deeper than political commitment and emotional commitment being deeper than intellectual commitment. Integrated intellectual-emotional commitment is yet higher.

- Commitment that is tied to a sense of hope in the future is particularly likely to attract followership in the short term and to lead to shared ownership and responsibility in the long term.

Based on our research, the views of a range of experts, and the Carmichael College case study, we offer the following definition:

> **Committing to school revitalization** requires that school leaders make a firm decision to undertake school revitalization and communicate that decision as a leadership priority for their school.

LEADERSHIP FOR COMMITTING TO REVITALIZATION

With these insights in mind, we can begin to develop a conceptual understanding of leadership for committing to revitalization.

First, it can be deduced from the Carmichael case study that, in order to get a schoolwide process of revitalization underway, someone in a position of authority—most likely the principal or a senior officer acting on the principal's behalf—must identify the need for change and be prepared to advocate firmly for that change. Stated a little differently, the principal not only must have a genuine desire to take concerted action to make the school a better place but must also seek to work with and through others—understanding that hearts and minds need to be engaged.

Second, the principal and key other leaders must recognize that in a complex organization such as a school, different levels of commitment and engagement will be in place at any time. The importance of teacher leaders at this stage—volunteering to work with the principal, critiquing the process of revitalization, and proposing adjustments to it that reflect the interests of staff—cannot be overstated. Thus, Jenny, the teacher leader at Carmichael, made a personal commitment that captured collegial support and had dramatic schoolwide effects. This involved a high level of trust on Jenny's part (particularly of Steve, the principal, but also of the IDEAS Project process) as well as the courage to undertake leadership responsibilities that were new to her. Steve recognized that, initially, some staff would quite naturally resist the change process. He championed the notion of teacher leadership as a key ingredient of the revitalization process and explicitly supported Jenny and fellow teacher leaders in their efforts to take schoolwide responsibility, particularly for pedagogical development.

Third, the articulation of an "I have a dream" big picture of where the school might head, and how it might get there, is essential to the creation of a sense of hope for a better future and of confidence in the revitalization process being undertaken. Steve made apparent that he cared about doing "the right thing" in relation to student learning but, equally important, his commitment to bringing about positive change opened the opportunity for similarly concerned teacher leaders to step forward.

Fourth, a credible process of school improvement must be available. Moreover, the process that is chosen must fit the type of school need being addressed and must be seen by the staff as respectful of teachers' professionalism. In the case of Carmichael College, the principal made the decision to investigate the possibility of the IDEAS Project, but he went to considerable lengths to engage the staff in getting the process underway.

Thus, committing to revitalization requires principal-directed, values-based advocacy and inspired communication; it requires potential teacher leaders to put their hand up in the interests of meeting a whole-school challenge; and it requires access to a highly credible process of school revitalization.

The leadership that we have observed with the committing to revitalization exemplar has qualities that are associated with both advocacy and strategic leadership approaches. Richard Bates is one authority who has affirmed the importance of the advocacy approach, noting that it "involves the making and articulating of choices, the location of oneself within the cultural struggles of the times as much in the cultural battles of the school as in the wider society" (1983, p. 19). This description would seem to accurately capture Steve Walker's "I can't live with this mess" mind-set. The same might be said of Jenny at the point at which she decided to devote herself to the well-being of marginalized students and commit to Steve's espoused cause. John MacBeath has also asserted the critical importance of the advocacy leadership approach in 21st-century schools, provocatively labeling it "subversive." He has described this approach pointedly and eloquently:

> Subversive leadership is intellectual, moral and political. . . . It cannot accept children being shortchanged whether by government policies, by teachers unaccountable for their actions, or by young people who settle for the mediocre. . . . Subversive leadership is intolerant, not in a bullish or confrontative sense, neither personalized nor necessarily even direct, but implicit in the fostering of a climate in which critical inquiry is simply the way we do things around here. (2006b, p. 7)

While the principal of Carmichael College probably would not regard himself as "subversive," there is no doubting the "intolerant" nature of his leadership approach in opting to initiate and co-lead comprehensive school revitalization in the interests of an underachieving school community.

Equally important in getting the revitalization process underway at Carmichael College was Steve Walker's strategic leadership. Bennis and Nanus (1985, p. 89), pioneers of the strategic leadership movement, have described this approach to leadership in a way that appears to capture Steve Walker very precisely:

> To choose a direction, a leader must first have developed a mental image of a possible and desirable future state of the organisation . . . it must articulate a view of a realistic, credible, attractive future for the organisation, a condition that is better in some important ways than what now exists.

Steve Walker's commitment to revitalization was reinforced by his clear picture of what Carmichael College might become and a comprehensive strategy (the IDEAS Project) for getting there. His leadership orientation had a powerful strategic component.

While the principal was the dominant leadership figure in the research schools at the *committing* C-B stage, teacher leaders began to emerge in response to perceived need—in particular the perceived injustice of being ascribed "failing" status. It might be said that in most, perhaps all, of the schools, some teachers began to think of themselves as what Susan Baker (2007, p. 50) calls "active followers," laying the foundations for teacher leadership to emerge as the revitalization process took firm hold. According to Baker, active followership is in fact a form of leadership—it grants legitimacy to supervisors' directions and in so doing makes a powerful facilitative contribution to the organization's leadership (p. 56).

Thus, it can be concluded that leadership for committing to revitalization is distinguished by three qualities:

- An advocacy quality, particularly a grounding in both intolerance of disadvantage and hopefulness in the face of adversity
- A strategic quality, particularly the detailed articulation of carefully thought-out ideas for going forward
- A deliberate broadening out from the principalship to nurture the beginnings of teacher leadership and parallel leadership

THINKING OUTSIDE THE SQUARE: AL GORE AND COMMITTING TO REVITALIZATION

The following account is offered as a classic example of the committing to revitalization C-B dynamic. It has not been selected because of Al Gore's political beliefs or because we necessarily agree with all aspects of his controversial stance on global warming. After all, Gore himself has acknowledged he has made mistakes—while adding that "unfortunately the reality of the danger we are courting has not been changed by the discovery of . . . mistakes" (Norington, 2010, p. 7). No, we have selected Al Gore for analysis in relation to the first C-B dynamic because he is a figure whose deep convictions, combined with his extraordinary capacity for communication, has engendered a movement that has influenced hundreds of millions of people worldwide. He epitomizes what our review of literature revealed committing to revitalization to mean, namely, a sense of hopefulness, doing "good" work, and allowing for varying degrees of commitment in followers. Much is to be learned from his example.

Clarify and enhance your understanding of committing to revitalization by reading and reflecting on the description that follows. Ask yourself three questions:

1. In Al Gore's life work, what is the equivalent to the educational concept of committing to school revitalization?
2. How did Al Gore reach his convictions? What special qualities drive him to transpose those convictions into focused and concerted action?
3. Which of the four leadership approaches that we identified in our opening chapter as dominant in educational practice (transformational, advocacy, strategic, organizationwide) do you associate most with Al Gore's work as a global environmental leader?

The name Al Gore may well conjure up either or both of two images. On one hand, there is the well known U.S. politician—the congressman, senator, and two-term vice president whose political career was interrupted when he was narrowly, and somewhat controversially, defeated in the 2000 presidential election. On the other hand, there is the presenter in the Oscar-winning documentary *An Inconvenient Truth,* talking passionately about a "planet in crisis." This Al Gore is the environmental activist who uses his "slide show," and shares stories from his own life, to raise awareness on a global scale about the impact of carbon emissions on the delicate ecosystem of the planet. Although Al Gore the politician and Al Gore the environmental activist may seem separate, there is considerable interconnection between the two spheres of Gore's life. Climate change was not a cause adopted in the wake of political defeat. Rather, Al Gore's interest in the environment developed during his childhood, and the negative effects of high carbon emissions, in fact, constituted the focus of much of his work in his political career.

In 1992, while still a senator, Al Gore published *Earth in the Balance,* warning of the dangers of the degradation of the global ecological system. But his book was not about despair, it was a "call to action and hope." Gore acknowledged in that book that it is easy to feel overwhelmed, even helpless, in the face of such an enormous challenge as the survival of the planet, but he also insists that the crisis can be resolved—provided that people can be persuaded to take individual responsibility for it. Thus, personal values combined with a sense of hope constitute a critically important aspect of responsibility as Gore sees it. As he says, people need to assess their relationship to the natural world, and renew, at the deepest level of personal integrity, a connection to it (1992, p. 366). This moral stance is reiterated in his subsequent publications *An Inconvenient Truth* (2006) and *Our Choice* (2009b). The awarding of the Nobel Peace Prize to Al Gore in 2007 reinforced the world's acceptance of the depth of his commitment, his belief in the importance of individual integrity in human work, and his inspirational influence on millions of citizens worldwide. So, while lack of commitment can lead to ineffective action, deciding to commit can set off a continuous chain of events and mobilize individuals and communities:

> As more and more people understand what's at stake, they become a part of the solution, and share both in the challenges and opportunities presented by the climate crisis. (Gore, 2009a)

As a practical demonstration of his personal commitment, Al Gore presented his "slide show" more than 1,000 times throughout the world before the making of *An Inconvenient Truth.* In 2006, he established a climate change leadership program, The Climate Project, in order to educate people worldwide about the effects of climate change and stimulate grassroots solutions. Trained volunteer presenters have presented the updated "slide show" approximately 70,000 times, reaching an audience of more than 7 million worldwide.

Al Gore says that his most recent book, *Our Choice,* is solutions orientated. He optimistically states that

> We can solve the climate crisis. It will be hard, to be sure, but if we can make the choice to solve it, I have no doubt whatsoever that we can and will succeed. (Gore, 2009b)

These words—"We will succeed in addressing our problem if we can make the choice to solve it"—deriving from Al Gore's lifetime of commitment to environmental causes, provide us with a critically important starting insight in our understanding of the committing to revitalization dynamic in the work of school leaders.

CONCLUSION

In this chapter, we have introduced the first C-B dynamic, committing to revitalization. In considering it from a number of perspectives, we have concluded that committing to revitalization is grounded in both deep human conviction and a sense of hopefulness. Leadership for committing to revitalization is extremely challenging, making demands of school leaders that call on their personal resources much more than on their organizational resources. It is leadership that has strong elements of both strategic and advocacy leadership forms. It begins with the principal but cannot proceed far without teacher leaders beginning to come on board.

In the simulation that follows, you will have the opportunity to test and enhance your personal preparedness to engage in committing to revitalization. That done, we proceed to the second dynamic—organizational coherence—where quite different values come into play, quite different developmental processes are involved, and quite different leadership is required.

COSMIC C-B SIMULATION 1— CROSSING THE SCHOOL IMPROVEMENT RUBICON

COMMITTING TO REVITALIZATION: BUILDING PERSONAL CAPACITY

Purpose:

The purpose of this simulation is to provide an opportunity for school leaders to explore the nature and extent of their personal commitment in relation to crossing the school improvement Rubicon.

An explanation of "the Rubicon":

At the risk of simplifying history, in the first century BC the Rubicon River marked the boundary between Roman Italy and Gaul. Julius Caesar decided to cross the river with his army in full knowledge that he was breaking a significant law of the Roman Senate. Once across the river, there was no turning back. Upon reaching the shore, Caesar is alleged to have uttered the phrase, *alea iacta est*—"The die is cast!"

But what, you may ask, does "crossing the Rubicon" have to do with committing to school improvement? A great deal, actually, for in committing to school improvement, school leaders need to

- explore the underlying values to ascertain whether an improvement process is needed and/or worth the effort required;
- articulate personal goals in public forums, some of which may have adversarial elements;
- seek a degree of commitment from potential teacher leaders; and
- be prepared to share leadership of the project from initiation to completion.

Thus, if and when school leaders make a personal commitment to school improvement, it is indeed a matter of *alea iacta est*, of crossing the Rubicon.

Rationale:

Every school operates within its own particular context, and as a result, school leaders often have different reasons for wanting, or not wanting, to commit to improvement. Moreover, other professionals within the school can be expected to have different levels of commitment to the strong possibility of upheaval in their work and increased complexity in their professional lives.

So what do you need to know and do in order to meet your own expectations, and those of others, as a leader who is thinking about school improvement? What level of commitment should you expect of yourself in particular, once the decision to commit is made? Al Gore clearly had questions such as these on his mind when he wrote,

> As more and more people understand what's at stake, they become a part of the solution, and share both in the challenges and opportunities presented by the climate crisis. (Al Gore, 2009b)

This exercise enables you to explore the first C-B dynamic and to gain a better understanding of the depth of your personal convictions regarding the need for improvement in your school. The exercise is premised on the assumption that your commitment as a leader can be deepened and enriched, and, if that happens, your leadership will be significantly more effective.

Approximate time required:

Allow a minimum of 45 minutes for the values clarification activity and one hour for the major activity.

Organization:

This activity is aimed at school leaders, both individually (Exercise A) and as a school group (Exercise B).

Materials for each group:

- Exhibit 2.A–Ten Committing Statements
- Exhibit 2.B–A Range of Reactions to a Proposal for Change
- Worksheet 2.A–My Two Committing Statements

Process:

The process comprises a preparatory values clarification exercise (Exercise A, for individuals, in two parts) and a simulation (Exercise B) for groups of four to six members.

EXERCISE A

THE RUBICON VALUES CLARIFICATION ACTIVITY

Step 1–Exhibit 2.A contains a wide range of political, corporate, and educational quotations about "commitment." Select the one quotation that resonates most clearly with your current leadership work and that you think you aspire to live by in your work as a school leader.

Step 2–Why did you select that particular statement? What insights does it reveal about your values in both your *actual* leadership practice and in your *aspirational* leadership practice?

Step 3–How might "living" this statement help you initiate a process of school improvement in your school?

Step 4–Select a second statement that you think would enable you to progress your school improvement project even further and more successfully.

Complete Worksheet A.

EXHIBIT 2.A: TEN COMMITTING STATEMENTS

- *We can solve the . . . crisis. It will be hard, to be sure, but if we can make the choice to solve it, I have no doubt whatsoever that we can and will succeed.* (Gore, 2009a)
- *Unless commitment is made, there are only promises and hopes; but no plans.* (Peter Drucker, http://en.thinkexist.com)
- *Commitment unlocks the doors of imagination, allows vision, and gives us the "right stuff" to turn our dreams into reality.* (James Womack, http://en.thinkexist.com)
- *. . . the moment one definitely commits oneself, then providence moves too. A whole stream of events issues from the decision . . .* (W. H. Murray)
- *Change will not come if we wait for some other person or some other time. We are the ones we have been waiting for. We are the change that we seek.* (Barrack Obama, http://www.barackobama.com)
- *. . . leadership is intellectual, moral and political . . . it cannot accept children being shortchanged whether by government policies, by teachers unaccountable for their actions, or by young people who settle for the mediocre.* (John MacBeath, 2006a, p. 7)
- *A ruler should learn self-discipline, should govern his subjects by his own example and should treat them with love and concern.* (Confucius, http://plato.stanford.edu/entries/confucius/)
- *The buck stops here.* (Harry Truman)
- *In your hands, my fellow citizens, more than mine, will rest the final success or failure of our course.* (John F. Kennedy, http://www.quotedb.com/speeches/john-f-kennedy-inaugural-address, Para 19)
- *It is an ideal which I hope to live for and to achieve. But if needs be, it is an ideal for which I am prepared to die.* (Nelson Mandela, http://thinkexist.com)

WORKSHEET A

MY TWO PREFERRED COMMITTING STATEMENTS

My most preferred *committing to revitalization* quotation:

The special appeal of this particular quotation to me:

What this quotation affirms about my values as an educational leader:

How the story behind this quotation could help me "cross the Rubicon" and initiate a school improvement project:

My second preferred quotation and its special relevance:

My definition of committing to school revitalization:

What crossing the Rubicon means to me in my world as a school leader:

EXERCISE B

THE RUBICON SIMULATION ACTIVITY

This simulation builds on the Rubicon values clarification activity. It is intended as a problem-solving exercise for a school leadership team but can also be used purposefully and effectively with a school staff that is considering a whole-school revitalization project.

You are the principal and leadership team of a school where school revitalization is very much needed (in your view). You know from experience that you may receive a wide range of responses to your proposal to engage the services of a consulting company to work with the school through a formal improvement process. You need to prepare for this likelihood.

Step 1–As a group, discuss the range of reactions to change that is contained on the continuum in Exhibit 2.B. These are the sort of responses that school leaders frequently confront when a major change proposal is presented. Each member of the group assumes a position on the continuum and, in a simulated staff room chat, outlines his or her argument in relation to the change proposal. Typical starting point statements for the five points on the continuum include the following:

- Who cares? It's a mirage, won't happen.
- Fantastic. Way overdue. Let's get going.
- We're going as well as can be expected. No one wants this . . .
- Maybe we can make this work for our school.
- Speaking personally, it will bring on a nervous breakdown for sure.

Step 2–Guiding questions for group discussion following the brief role-play include the following:

- What instances of each reaction have members of the group seen in their schools?
- Which point(s) on the continuum is/are most difficult to deal with, as a school leader?

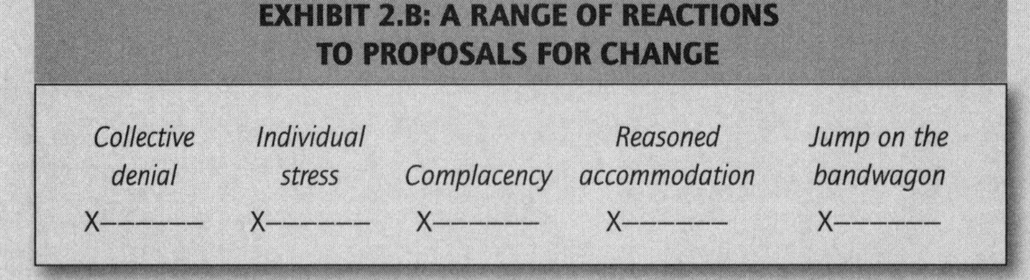

Step 3—As a group, select a quote from Exhibit 2.A that appears most suited to addressing the challenge at each point on the continuum. Justify your selection to the proponents of that position. Invite his or her or their reactions.

Step 4—Questions for reflection and deep discussion:

- What do you personally want to achieve from a process of revitalization in your school?
- What must you personally do to cross the Rubicon in relation to the proposal for change?
- How will you gain formal school endorsement for the proposed school improvement process?
- What lessons might be learned about leadership for commitment from the Carmichael College snapshot, the Al Gore case study, and the Rubicon simulation? How do these lessons reflect the scholarly constructs of multiple levels of commitment, hopefulness, and good work?
- How might you use advocacy leadership and strategic leadership to achieve the sort of success in your school that the Carmichael College principal achieved in getting an effective process of school revitalization underway?

We believe that you have now achieved a significant professional milestone. You are well placed to begin preparations to undertake a whole-school revitalization process.

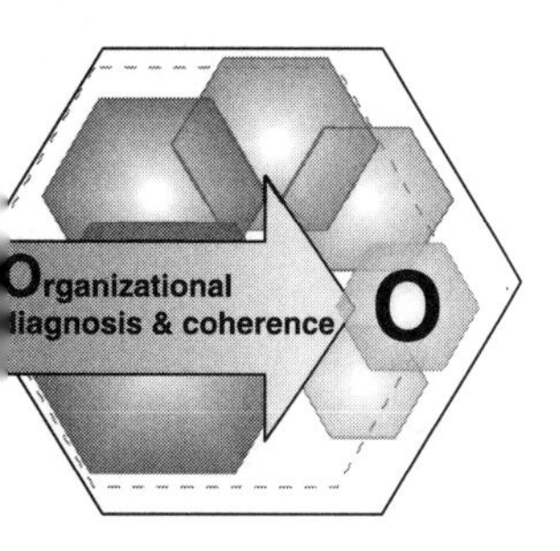

3

The Second C-B Dynamic

Organizational Diagnosis and Coherence

(Prepared in collaboration with Ms. Senthu Jeyaraj)

An institution is like a tune; it is not constituted by individual sounds but by the relations between them.

—Peter Drucker (1946, p. 26)

INTRODUCTION

The concept of organizational "coherence" is certainly not new, as the 1946 date for our opening quote from renowned theorist Peter Drucker indicates. Nor is it new to think of a school as a piece of music—images of in-tune schools and out-of-tune schools are easy enough to conjure up.

What *is* new is the understanding that, without a process in place to ensure a high level of "coherence" between key organizational factors, school leaders cannot easily proceed to create the fundamental conditions for sustainable school success. What are the key factors? And what are the implications for school leaders? These questions provide the impetus for this chapter on the second C-B dynamic.

The essential elements of organizational coherence are explicit in the case study of Bellwood Secondary School that follows. They are also apparent in recent organizational thinking, as we indicate in the review of international research that follows the Bellwood case study. The research analysis completed, we examine the distinctive features of leadership for organizational diagnosis and coherence and then explore coherence in a non-educational setting. We conclude the chapter with a simulation that is inspired by Peter Drucker's musical metaphor—*What tune is your school playing?* Having completed the simulation, you will be well qualified to lead initiatives to enhance coherence in your own school setting.

A SNAPSHOT OF ORGANIZATIONAL COHERENCE

BELLWOOD SECONDARY SCHOOL

The Decision to Commit

Bellwood Secondary School is a government school, founded in 1982, and located on the west side of the island of Singapore. Given its location within housing development areas, Bellwood is generally considered by the wider community to be a Malaysian/Indian/Chinese "neighborhood" school (in contrast to those schools in Singapore that are regarded as "privileged"). From 2003 to 2009, the school was led by a female principal. In 2009, the student enrollment was 1328 with 100 staff.

The principal spearheaded the decision in 2004 to embark on a process of school improvement, using the IDEAS Project. She did so because she had observed that Bellwood was characterized by a mind-set of "We are doing as well as we need to" complacency. She thought that IDEAS offered the opportunity to cultivate structural, pedagogical, and cultural enhancements. She therefore introduced IDEAS to the staff, informed them that she personally endorsed it, and organized the establishment of a representative IDEAS School Management Team (ISMT). She explained,

> In order to support structural and cultural changes driven by the ISMT team, I felt the composition required a delicate balance of strategic [HODs] and pedagogical members [teachers]. I believed that at some point each would need the other.

The principal selected a particular HOD as the IDEAS facilitator because she felt he possessed qualities of a charismatic disposition, as well as the capacity to "speak the language of both management and teachers." His approach was indeed attractive to ISMT members:

> He has the ability to facilitate . . . not tell us what to do, but to ask the right questions to help guide the team to think deeply, share our thoughts, and develop convergence in decision making.

The Organizational Diagnosis

The first formal step in the IDEAS Project at Bellwood involved administration of the Diagnostic Inventory (DI), an instrument that derives from the IDEAS Project's Research-Based Framework for Enhancing Organizational Coherence (RBF, Resource A).

With the statistical and descriptive data from teachers, parents, and students collated in spreadsheet form, the ISMT ran a schoolwide workshop, assisted by external researchers from Nanyang University, Singapore, to identify school highlights and low points and to calculate the overall level of alignment between (a) the five contributory elements of the RBF and (b) the perceptions of the three stakeholder groups. Key findings from the DI revealed a very mixed *index of coherence* and six specific issues:

- The school lacked an inspirational vision.
- Staff were polarized regarding the characteristics of high-quality curriculum and pedagogy.
- Pedagogical practices were not aligned to a clear school purpose statement.
- There were major discrepancies between staff and student perceptions as to the effectiveness of current pedagogical practices.
- Students and staff shared the perception that the wider community did not hold their school in high esteem.
- Teacher morale and student self-esteem were low.

The DI workshops were an eye-opening experience for the staff. It was clear from the results that serious misalignments existed in perceptions of both pedagogical effectiveness and the school's philosophy and effectiveness. But there was also discernible relief when teachers realized that their concerns were widely shared:

> We are hearing for the first time what each other thinks . . . this is different, because we are being welcomed to contribute our views. I didn't realize a lot of us were experiencing the same things.

Teachers were particularly disappointed to receive low DI ratings from students regarding their pedagogical practices, believing this reflected very negatively on them as professionals. Indeed, this aspect of the DI data proved to be a turning point in teachers' decision to look closely at their own practices and to explore teaching, learning, and assessment alternatives. To facilitate this end, the IDEAS Project Protocols of Professional Engagement (Resource A) were posted in staff rooms and became a regular reference point in leaders' efforts to nurture "no blame" relationships and constructive professional dialogue.

Toward Coherence—Four Years On

When the DI was readministered four years later (in 2008), major statistical improvements were apparent in Bellwood Secondary School's perceived effectiveness. These improvements were evident in the five contributory elements and the outcomes element of the RBF (see Resource A).

In the intervening period, a captivating vision had been developed and a schoolwide pedagogical framework created (using the vision as a starting point). A three-year school development plan had been developed and implemented successfully, incorporating the schoolwide pedagogical framework (SWP) and plans for restructured learning environments. A series of action learning projects to transpose the SWP into teachers' classroom practices had also been completed.

By 2008, DI results showed that teachers believed that the school's professional learning community had become more cohesive, respectful, and trusting in its working relationships:

> We have a sense of identity. We thought we had one before, being part of the school, but it's much more than that. . . . I think it's because the meaning of our identity is now different.

The readministered DI also showed that all stakeholder groups perceived major improvements in student achievement levels. Additionally, teachers had come to assume a comparatively high degree of collective responsibility for students' learning and progress. Not unexpectedly, teacher morale had increased dramatically. In the space of four years, Bellwood had transformed from fractured, purposeless, and lacking in confidence to relatively cohesive, purposeful, and characterized by self-belief.

The Importance of Coherence at Bellwood Secondary School

How, one might ask, did Bellwood Secondary School use the dual concepts of organizational diagnosis and coherence to become more effective over a four-year period?

The critical point was undoubtedly the initial step, namely use of the RBF and the staff-administered and -interpreted DI. These conceptual and diagnostic resources enabled teachers to identify for themselves interferences in their professional work. In so doing, they laid the foundations for development of a sense of shared understanding and collective problem solving at Bellwood, out of which a vibrant school vision and SWP (see Table 3.1) were eventually created. The report card that the staff prepared out of the DI in 2004 both distressed and energized the staff. It engendered both a sense of "We're all in it together" and "Who knows what exciting possibilities may lie within our grasp?"

Table 3.1 The Bellwood Vision and SWP Framework

VISION:

Weave—quality teaching, learning, and values

Dream—the best

Lead—to inspire

SWP Framework:

- Provide a conducive learning environment
- Think. Challenge. Question.
- Ensure teacher facilitation
- Impart values through "teachable moments"
- Provide opportunities for a variety of learning models
- Facilitate effective tapping of prior knowledge

It is significant that a new ISMT had to be established at Bellwood in 2007 (year three of the project) because of divisive interpersonal issues that had arisen within the staff. In essence, the concept of teacher leadership had gained currency but was seen as being quashed by actions of the ISMT. With a new ISMT in place, concerted effort was devoted to progressing the notion of three-dimensional pedagogy (Resource A) through the identification of best professional practices across the school. This was a huge step for most teachers. One member shared her anxiety as well as her motivation for volunteering:

> It was scary at first, because we were allowing others to see what we were doing, and this had never happened before. It's not the way teachers in Singapore have gone about their work . . . but I trusted that this would not only help me, but also the school.

In an attempt to begin to embed the pedagogical successes that had been created, the ISMT facilitator undertook in 2008 to conceptualize connections between the school's vision and pedagogical framework on the one hand and the official school development model of the Singaporean Ministry of Education on the other. It soon became readily apparent to both principal and teachers that, in achieving organizational coherence through development of their vision and SWP, they could accommodate ministerial priorities with relative ease:

> We found it surprising but very gratifying that new external dictates could be fitted under our vision and into our SWP. Pressures within the school have decreased immensely as a result. We feel a greater sense of control over our work and our future.

A high level of organizational coherence had been established at Bellwood as the school proceeded to develop a vision and pedagogical framework that were assessed as educationally sound and a source of school pride. By 2008, a critical ingredient of sustained school capacity was firmly in place.

ORGANIZATIONAL COHERENCE

DEEPENING OUR UNDERSTANDING

Contemporary organizational experts have a lot to say about the concept of coherence (or "harmony," or "consistency," or "alignment," or "fit," or "cohesion," to name some commonly used synonyms). Researchers Day, Leithwood, and Sammons (2008), for example, have stated recently,

> A key strategy in . . . endeavours . . . to improve the cultures of teaching, learning and achievement . . . is the alignment of structures and cultures with "vision" and "direction" . . . (p. 84)

In so doing, they have captured the key lesson of the Bellwood case study—in seeking to enhance school success, school leaders should bring the key organizational features of the school into alignment and facilitate a "meeting of minds" about quality pedagogical practice.

Of importance is that coherence has two distinct meanings, the first of which relates to an organization's structures and the second of which relates to processes of cognition.

Coherence as the Alignment of School Structures

As one notable example of the structural perspective, educational researchers Hopkins and Stern (1996) have claimed that schools that are most effective have developed six organizational features and worked to bring the six features into alignment with each other. They note that the six structural features are apparent in varying degrees in every school. The six elements of the IDEAS Project RBF (Resource A) are very similar to Hopkins and Stern's model:

> . . . a clearly articulated and shared vision and values which incorporate a sense of moral purpose; reflected in the way teaching and learning is organized; management arrangements that guide actions of all involved in the school, clarify roles and responsibilities, and promote collaborative action; leadership is dispersed; staff development is a key policy initiative; and schools have powerful links with the community. (p. 508)

All six structural features were worked on assiduously at Bellwood as the school sought to build its index of coherence.

Similar definitions of structural alignment can be found in the world of business. Barki and Pinsonneault (2005, p. 166), for example, describe structural alignment in the corporate world as the "extent to which the integration of distinct and interdependent organizational components constitutes a unified whole, where the word 'components' is in reference to structures, business processes, relationships, people or technologies."

The ready applicability of business definitions of strategic alignment to educational settings is also apparent in the landmark work of Peters and Waterman (1982). These authorities developed what is called the McKinsey 7-S model. It proposes that, when firms achieve harmony among three "hard Ss" —strategy, structure, and systems—and four "soft Ss"—skills, staff, style, and shared values—they become higher performing. According to Peters and Waterman, most attention is directed by organizations in aligning the hard Ss, but successful organizations also address the soft Ss in their developmental processes.

Coherence as Alignment of a School's Processes of Cognition

A quite different perspective on organizational coherence has been proposed by Garvin (1998). Garvin asserted that successful organizational improvement can be traced through three overlapping stages. At the first stage of improvement, development, or revitalization, members of the organization engage in serious collaborative dialogue and intensive reflection. New ideas are created and participants begin to see the potential of their organization through new eyes. Garvin labeled this stage "cognitive." The second stage he labeled "behavioral," where members begin to alter their workplace interactions and behaviors to accommodate their new knowledge. The third stage is performance related, where tangible outcomes are measured and are used to guide further decision making.

The first of Garvin's stages—cognition—seems to us to be particularly relevant in educational institutions. In the Bellwood case study, for example, it manifested in cognitive products (i.e., a new vision, values, and pedagogical framework) that derived from the collective thinking of the Bellwood staff. Most Bellwood teachers agreed when they reviewed their progress in 2008 that it was those products that provided the clarity of purpose that had enabled them to deal successfully with the issue of endemic complacency. The Bellwood case study also illustrates Mohammed's (2001) critically important concept of "cognitive consensus." Essentially, according to Mohammed, a group that is high on cognitive consensus is able to communicate about issues more effectively than is a group with less cognitive consensus. In this way, the foundations are laid for the creation of unique cognitive products such as a distinctive school vision or a highly meaningful schoolwide pedagogical framework. At Bellwood, the staff used the RBF/DI to stimulate cognitive consensus. With a degree of consensus in place, they proceeded to develop important cognitive products. With those products in place, cognitive consensus deepened further.

Thus, school coherence has two distinct meanings, the first relating to organizational structures and the second relating to shared cognition. But it is when the concept acquires both meanings in a school's operations that it is most powerful.

School Coherence as Combined Structural and Cognitive Alignment

The RBF in Resource A manifests both the structural and cognitive approaches to creation of a sense of alignment coherence. As a structural tool, it provides a basis for the calculation of an index of coherence that can be employed to adjust particular school evaluation and development features. As a cognitive alignment tool, it provides a mental model for how the five "contributory" elements of school coherence can be developed and brought into consistency with each other, thereby providing a critically important foundation for enhanced school outcomes.

Thus, in Bellwood, school leaders engaged the teaching and support staff in assessing the school's structural coherence, leading to the understanding that the school was seriously "out of tune." As a consequence, the staff undertook through a range of highly challenging cognitive processes to develop a shared vision, statement of values, and schoolwide pedagogical framework.

The Bellwood case study demonstrates a further key point—that heightened organizational coherence should not be mistaken for enhanced capacity. Rather, development of enhanced school coherence is a prerequisite, or foundation, for building and sustaining capacity.

The definition of *organizational coherence* that we have developed out of case studies such as Bellwood Secondary School, and recent authoritative literature, is as follows:

> **Organizational coherence** in educational organizations occurs when key school features are clearly understood by members of the organization and brought into alignment with each other. The six elements that are essential to enhanced coherence are the following:
>
> - The school's vision and values
> - The school's infrastructural designs (including curricula, time, spatial arrangements, and technologies)
> - Schoolwide pedagogical principles
> - Internal and external stakeholder support
> - Professional learning approaches
> - School outcomes

When these six organizational elements are developed and brought into alignment with each other, enhanced school outcomes are likely to be achieved.

LEADERSHIP FOR ORGANIZATIONAL COHERENCE

In considering the organizational coherence dynamic from a leadership point of view, it is apparent from the Bellwood case study that four broad areas of leadership-related school activity are relevant:

- Access of the school to credible diagnostic "coherence" tools and strategies
- The activation of a representative schoolwide task force to conduct surveys, review school data, and prepare a draft school self-report
- The volunteer effort of committed teachers (potentially teacher leaders)
- "Stepping back" by the principal in order to encourage ownership by the staff of diagnostic survey outcomes

A number of important implications for school-based leadership emerge from these conclusions. But before considering them, we note that, because of its dependence on external support services, the organizational diagnosis and coherence dynamic is in some regards the simplest of the six C-B dynamics for a school to develop. It follows that leadership for the second dynamic should also be relatively simple. However, certain subtleties should be considered before this conclusion is reached.

First, leadership for building school coherence requires that principals and teacher leaders possess, or obtain, mental models of the school as a coherent organization, preferably images that encompass both structural and cognitive features. International researchers Christopher Day, Kenneth Leithwood, and Pam Sammons (2008) make this point in asserting that if successful school improvement is to occur, then the school's structures and cultures must be brought into alignment with the school vision and direction. Once structural alignment is created, they say, school leaders can proceed to build clear pictures of heightened expectations and aspirations, thereby getting the process of enhanced school performance underway. The Bellwood case study illustrates their point very well.

Peter Senge's five disciplines that constitute the core of a learning organization (1990) and that, if in alignment, contribute to enhanced organizational success, represent another very meaningful mental model for school leaders. The five disciplines that school leaders might develop and design are the following:

- *Personal mastery*—continually clarifying and deepening one's vision and seeing reality objectively
- *Mental models*—pictures and images of how we see the world and take action
- *Shared vision*—unearthing shared pictures of the future that foster genuine commitment rather than compliance
- *Team learning*—suspending assumptions and thinking together
- *Systems thinking*—a way of thinking and using language to create holistic change

Second, leadership for building school coherence requires a commitment to distributed leadership. It necessitates that principals be able to step back and show trust in colleagues to assume new levels of responsibility, and accept doubt and criticism when organizational limitations are revealed. This is important because, as Kahrs has observed,

> Any teacher will be reluctant to take on a leadership role without being comfortable with the level of trust received from the school administration. (1996, p. 36, as cited in Murphy, 2005, p. 132)

Third, leadership for school coherence requires that in each school there exists a cadre of prospective teacher leaders. This may appear to be a tall order, but our case studies show that, in fact, it is quite a reasonable expectation. (Note: Of critical importance in our research schools was principals' acceptance at the commencement of the revitalization process of the potential of both teacher leadership and parallel leadership. Thus, principals whom we observed accepted that they might need to reconsider their traditional ways of managing school functions, including their relationships with teacher leaders and potential teacher leaders.)

Renowned leadership authority John Kotter (2001, p. 90) has noted an additional subtlety of leadership that we observed in school-based organizational diagnosis and coherence activities:

> Aligning is different. It is more of a communications challenge than a design problem. Aligning invariably involves talking to many more individuals than organizing does.

This realization enabled principals whom we observed to justify stepping back from activities associated with the ongoing analysis of the school's index of coherence. The net effect was that the newly created ISMTs invariably stepped into the breach to lead schoolwide developmental activities—thereby opening windows of opportunity for potential teacher leaders and the nurturing of embryonic parallel leadership relationships.

Fourth, because of complexities associated with diagnostic data analysis and interpretation, a further school leadership factor relates to the likely need for external consultancy advice. In the research schools, the IDEAS Project consultancy team met this need along with researchers from Nanyang University, Singapore. These credible educational professionals took the position with school staffs that they could be depended on to contribute to all aspects of the three- to four-year revitalization process; assisted with the interpretation of the Diagnostic Inventory data; made clear that the IDEAS Project was grounded in cutting-edge research; asserted that they were advocates for the teaching profession; and reiterated that the concepts of parallel leadership and teacher leadership represented a vehicle for vibrant teacher professionalism and empowerment. (Note: The data that emerge from authentic diagnostic processes are frequently value laden, sometimes provocative, and occasionally explosive. The data must be handled with care. Indeed, if the second C-B dynamic is mismanaged, existing negative mindsets in a school may become entrenched and destructive practices and relationships may intensify. When, for example, the results of a diagnostic survey uncover major issues of teacher morale, of school image, or of dysfunctional decision processes, the expectation that school leaders will trust the revitalization process to proceed may be too great for some. The revitalization process may be abandoned by the principal, and blame, acrimony, and avoidance may result. At junctions such as this, the support and advice of an external agency, in our experience, is therefore essential.)

Fifth, a significant leadership factor in relation to organizational coherence relates to within-school project management. In the research schools, the ISMT served this purpose. The key ISMT position, that of facilitator, was invariably a teacher or middle manager, or combination thereof in several joint appointment instances. The organization of diagnostic surveys, the analysis of the survey data, and the preparation of a school report card represented for many teachers their first taste of schoolwide leadership responsibility. Most facilitators recognized that they were being provided with a unique opportunity to develop personal leadership capabilities and took steps to ensure that they used the opportunity to full advantage.

Thus, leadership for organizational coherence requires a mind-set of circumspection and cautious exploration that may represent a novel experience for many busy school leaders. But this mind-set is essential if the groundwork is to be laid for the creative capacity-building dynamics that follow.

In summary, it can be concluded that leadership for organizational coherence is distinguished by three qualities:

- A strategic quality, particularly in mobilizing data collection, analysis, and reporting procedures
- An organizationwide quality, particularly in the development of schoolwide understandings and shared responsibility
- Broadening out of leadership functions from the principalship to incorporate volunteer teacher leaders

THINKING OUTSIDE THE SQUARE: ORGANIZATIONAL COHERENCE WHEN MEN ARE FROM MARS AND WOMEN ARE FROM VENUS

We have seen that organizational coherence has both structural and cognitive meanings and that it is an essential foundation for sustained capacity building in schools and a very wide range of other human institutions. But what about the most basic of all institutions, adult relationships? Does it apply there? To explore these questions, we investigate the relevance of organizational coherence—both structural and cognitive—in the lives of Michael and Suzie, a young couple who are striving to create a lifelong future together.

To get started consider the viewpoint of well-known social commentator John Gray:

> Michael returns home from work stressed out and eager to kick back on the couch, not talk about his day and watch television. Suzie on the other hand returns home from work stressed out and wants to talk about her day with Michael. What happens? Neither is on the same page—Mars and Venus begin to collide. (2008)

Explore your thinking about organizational coherence by reading and reflecting on the account that follows. As you do, ask yourself these questions:

1. In the Mars–Venus analogy, what is the equivalent of the educational capacity-building concept of "diagnosis"?
2. In the Mars–Venus analogy, what is the equivalent of the educational capacity-building concept of "coherence"?
3. What does the account reveal about the importance of a shared "mental model" for organizational leaders engaged in seeking coherence?
4. Which of the four leadership approaches that we have identified as dominant in educational practice (transformational, advocacy, strategic, organizationwide) do you think is most important in creating and sustaining harmony in the Mars–Venus relationship?

John Gray's popular thesis holds that men and women—Martians and Venetians—are driven in part by different biological needs. This (biological) argument is often accepted as one key reason for variations in gender-related thinking, decision making, and behaviors. It raises a critical question: Can meaningful harmony ever be created and sustained in familial relationships on Earth?

Let's accept, for argument's sake, that a Martian's defining strength is that of *logic.* On the other hand, a Venetian's defining strength is generally asserted to be *emotional strength.* Now let's see if we can find a way of enlightening both men and women as to how each other's planetary strengths (i.e., logic and emotion, respectively) can be seen in a completely new light—one in which strengths are no longer considered mere contributors to differences, but instead are construed as leverages on which to build lasting foundations.

But How?

The mental model that we propose for exploring the Mars–Venus dilemma is a variation of the IDEAS Project's RBF (Resource A). Our research schools used this framework to help them develop a coherent picture of their structural and cognitive coherence before they proceeded to pursue elevated goals and establish schoolwide pedagogical principles.

An adapted version for use by Mars and Venus is contained in Table 3.2. As you will see, the ten questions certainly represent serious challenges for partners—but they are resolvable if Michael Mars and Suzie Venus have the will to explore them together and then follow through with firm action in their daily lives.

Review the ten questions for yourself. What strategy might Suzie and Michael employ to reach shared understanding of them? How might they use their shared understandings to assist each other in pursuing personal goals? How often should they review their relationship, using the coherence framework? At what juncture would a follow-up, detailed review be important? These four questions are integral to use of our construct of combined structural-cognitive coherence.

We believe that variations such as Table 3.2 of the RBF have helpful application in all sorts of human organizations—sports teams, special interest groups, religious groups, service clubs, and volunteer associations. However, the RBF has been developed primarily for use by school-based leaders, and its five contributory elements and outcome elements are of course designed for educational thinking.

Table 3.2 The IDEAS Project Research-Based Framework for Enhancing Organizational Coherence, Adapted for Coherence in Venus–Mars Partnerships

Strategic Foundations

1. What is our shared vision of what we want our partnership to become?
2. Are our decision processes clear and acceptable to both partners?

Cohesive Community

3. How do we want our partnership to be viewed by our communities of support?

Partnership Core Strategies (i.e., schoolwide pedagogy)

4. What functions of our partnership do we pursue in collaboration?
5. What functions of our partnership do we pursue as individuals?

Infrastructural Design

6. Do we use time, space, and technologies to effectively maximize our leisure time in our partnership?
7. Do we use time, space, and technologies to effectively maximize our work in our partnership?

Professional Supports

8. How do we learn from each other's strengths and talents?
9. How do we best learn together?

Outcomes

10. What is our assessment of our achievements together so far?

CONCLUSION

In this chapter we have taken the position that organizational coherence comprises both cognitive and structural components. That is, it requires a meeting of minds as well as the alignment of key structural elements of an organization. In searching to establish it, unique forms of school-based leadership are required of principals, the school's professional learning community, and also trusted external experts. But, once established through carefully designed diagnostic strategies, organizational coherence provides a basis in understanding, trust, and workplace operations that enables the professional learning community to pursue elevated aspirations. In this process, prospective teacher leaders invariably emerge and mature.

Seeking new heights—the third C-B dynamic—is the subject of the next chapter. But before proceeding, explore the meaning of organizational coherence in your own school and your work as an educational leader through a captivating musical metaphor.

COSMIC C-B SIMULATION 2—IS YOUR SCHOOL IN TUNE?

ORGANIZATIONAL COHERENCE: BUILDING PERSONAL CAPACITY

Purpose:

To enable school leaders to explore the concept of organizational coherence through the use of Peter Drucker's "tune" metaphor.

Rationale:

Before proceeding in the next chapter to the "aspirational" capacity-building dynamic—encompassing visioning and schoolwide pedagogical development—it is important that school leaders have a clear image of what it means for their school to achieve the features of a coherent organization. In this simulation, Peter Drucker's tune metaphor—with which we opened the chapter—is used to enable you to experience firsthand what coherence means and how it applies in your school. The materials that are used in the simulation can easily be customized for use with a whole-school staff as the prelude to a real-life organizational diagnosis and coherence process.

Approximate time required: 1.5-hour session

Organization:

Groups of four members are recommended for Steps 1 and 2 and nine members for Step 3.

Materials for each group:

- The RBF (Resource A)
- RBF—Work Copy (Exhibit 3.A)
- How tuneful is your school? (Exhibit 3.B)

Process:

Step 1—Discuss the RBF: What are the core concepts for each element? In what ways does the RBF fit Peter Drucker's tune metaphor? How did Suzie and Michael use it in their Venus–Mars problem solving? Use Exhibit 3A as a working sheet.

Step 2—Use the following abbreviated and customized version of the RBF (Exhibit 3C) to assess the level of tunefulness of your school.

Exhibit 3.A

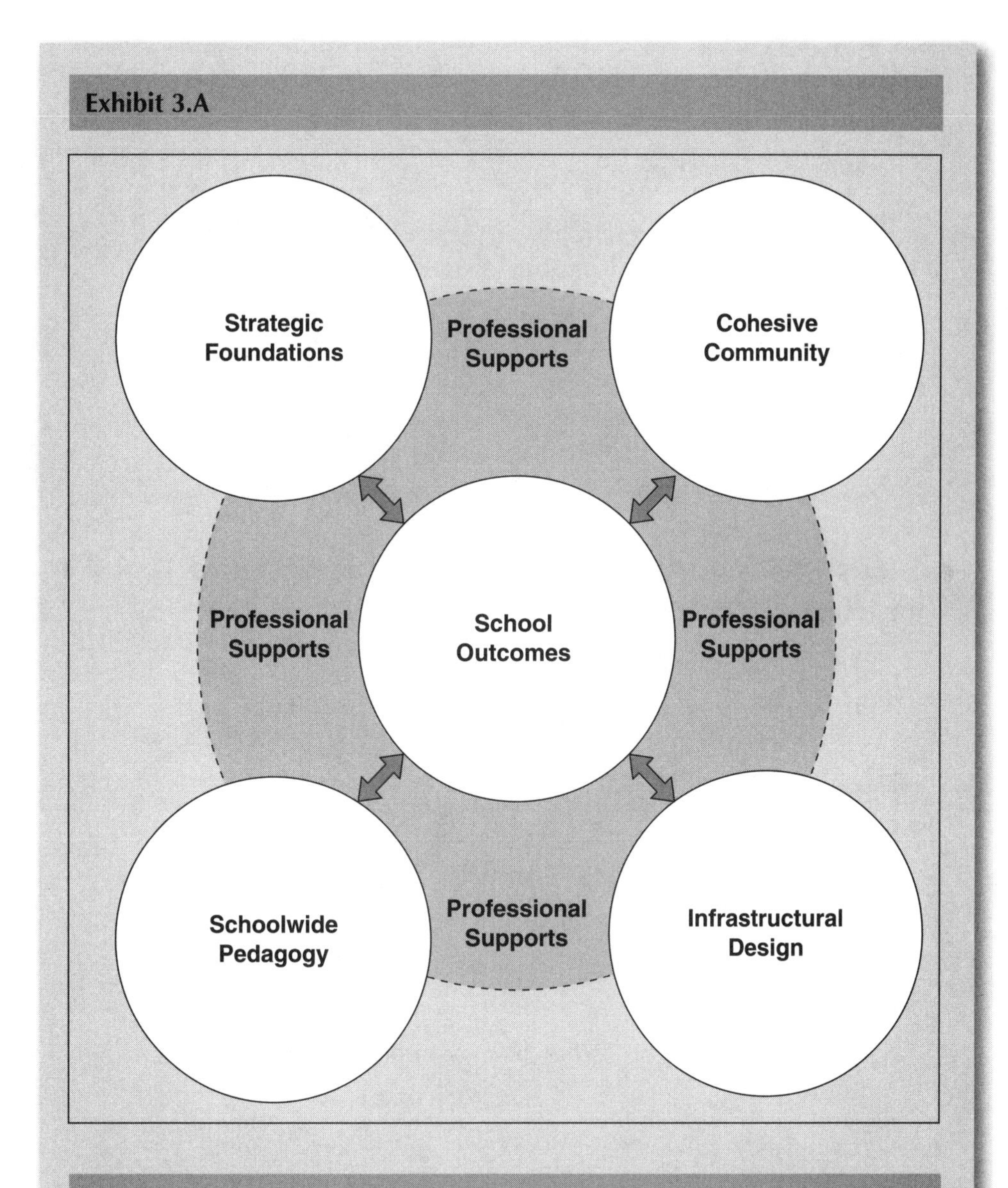

Exhibit 3.B

How tuneful is your school?

Flat?

Discordant?

Melodious?

Lullaby?

Stirring?

Virtuoso?

Exhibit 3.C

STRATEGIC FOUNDATIONS

- ❒ Has your school created its own distinctive musical theme (i.e., vision)?
- ❒ Is your conductor well respected for his or her conductorship?
- ❒ Is leadership within the orchestra encouraged, nurtured, and recognized?
- ❒ Does your school's musical theme inspire you and your colleagues?

COHESIVE COMMUNITY

- ❒ Is your musical theme what your audiences hope your school will perform for them?
- ❒ Is your musical theme what your players want to perform?

INFRASTRUCTURAL DESIGN

- ❒ Are your musical instruments well tuned?
- ❒ Is the auditorium aesthetically pleasing, with acoustics working well?

SCHOOLWIDE PEDAGOGY

- ❒ Are your musicians aware of their individual gifts and proud of those gifts?
- ❒ Are your musicians all playing off the same song sheet?
- ❒ Are your musicians responding sensitively to your conductor and lead players?

PROFESSIONAL SUPPORTS

- ❒ Do you use practice time to fine-tune your instruments?
- ❒ Do you use practice time to refine your specialist skills?
- ❒ Do you use practice time to enhance your orchestral harmony?

Step 3–Assign nine roles: choreographer (1), conductor (1), lead players (2), junior players (2), and audience (3) for the following discussion.

1. What musical descriptor (Exhibit 3.B) best captures your school?
2. Using Exhibit 3.B, and the expanded version of the RBF in Resource A, what developments are needed to become a more tuneful (e.g., entertaining/compelling/melodious) school?
3. How will parallel leadership enable your musical transformation to get started?

4. What well-known tune(s) illustrate(s) your school's current musical image?
5. What musical piece do you aspire to become? Please explain.

Without question, you now have meaningful insights regarding the second C-B dynamic, organizational diagnosis and coherence. You not only understand what coherence means, you know how to go about achieving it. You are ready to commence the process of actual school revitalization, beginning with the complex and essential tasks of visioning and schoolwide pedagogical development.

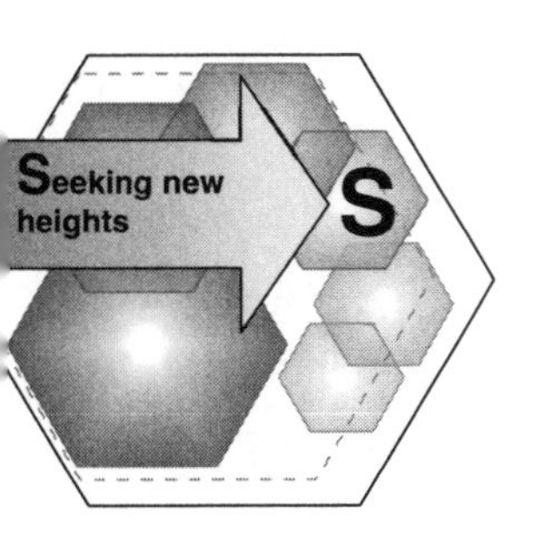

The Third C-B Dynamic

Seeking New Heights

What I do best is share my enthusiasm . . .

—Bill Gates, when asked how he viewed his leadership style (Buchanan, 2010, p. 35)

INTRODUCTION

In writing recently for business, sporting, and educational audiences about Bill Gates's talents, and noting his extraordinary zest for life, international sporting coach John Buchanan (2010) made the statement with which we have opened this chapter. He commented further:

> For Gates, it would seem, there is no task too large or small, only an obvious passion to conquer it so that he can move on to the next. This is one of the true indicators of a high performance team or individual. (p. 35)

Gates's renowned energy and passion for the task ahead sets the tone for our analysis of the third C-B dynamic, seeking new heights.

In Chapter 3 we took the position that developing alignment, or "organizational coherence," is essential if a school's professional learning community is to be given a reasonable chance of generating the mutual trust and they shared understanding that are needed to tackle the challenges of sustained school improvement. *But once a sense of organizational coherence, however preliminary, is in place, what should follow?* Certainly, coherence in and of itself is inadequate to ensure heightened student achievement. We have come to that important realization from our own research and that of a range of reputable international authorities. In this chapter we provide an answer to the *After coherence, then what?* question. In so doing, our focus is the third C-B dynamic, namely, seeking new heights.

Why is "seeking new heights" asserted to be important in creating and sustaining educational capacity building? What does it look like in a school's daily practices? What forms of leadership underpin it? In this chapter, we explore these questions in a school context and in recent educational research. We then consider their applicability in one extraordinary woman's search for new heights in a nonschool setting. Finally, we reflect on the leadership implications of processes associated with the dual aspects of the third C-B dynamic, namely, visioning and schoolwide pedagogical development. To conclude the chapter, we outline guidelines for a professional learning exercise that we recommend you undertake to prepare yourself for a "new heights" project in your own school community.

A SNAPSHOT OF SEEKING NEW HEIGHTS

CARLO MARIA CARAFA HIGH SCHOOL

(Written by Mr. Giuseppe Micciche, principal,
Carlo Maria Carafa High School, Mazzarino, Sicily.
Teacher leader Ms. Rosalia Cutaia also contributed.)

Ancient Ruins, Mafia, Student Apathy

Mazzarino is a town of 11,000 people in central Sicily. Its origins can be traced to a Greek settlement in the sixth century B.C. The hills surrounding Mazzarino contain visible reminders of the Greek, and Roman, invasions and settlement of Sicily. Churches, palaces, castles, and villas, all rich in paintings, sculptures, decorations, fountains, and gardens, still exist in Mazzarino as testimony to the greatness of the golden age of the town, from the 16th century to the first decades of the 19th century. The most important Mazzarino nobleman during this period was 17th-century Prince Carlo Maria Carafa Branciforti. Our school bears his name.

More recently, Mazzarino and its region has been the subject of international bestselling books that have focused on the Sicilian Mafia. Our students and teachers know very well this unsavory aspect of their modern history. It of course impacts on student culture and the school's daily work.

Carlo Maria Carafa High School was established in 2000. There are currently 670 students, ages 14 to 19, divided into 33 classes. The staff comprises the principal and two deputies, 72 teachers, and 15 collaborators.

As principal of Carlo Maria Carafa High School since its inception, I found in early 2004 that I was deeply concerned by issues involving student attitude, behavior, engagement, and morale. The deep history of the town gave our youth no motivation whatsoever to prepare for the 21st-century technological, urbanizing, and highly competitive world. Local jobs and vocational opportunities were few, but most graduates had no real interest in seeking work elsewhere or continuing their studies. Apathy and strong resistance seemed to dominate the school's student culture, manifesting in high levels of bullying, vandalism, and graffiti. The dedication of our teachers seemed to have little impact, resulting in low staff morale and very limited parent involvement in school affairs.

I was in this depressing frame of mind when I participated in an international educational forum in Barcelona in 2004 and was introduced to the IDEAS Project. I found the Project so interesting that I decided to investigate it in detail. Having done so, I presented it to the staff, who were particularly attracted to the *no blame* and *teachers are the key* principles of the project. They established an IDEAS School Management Team (ISMT) and selected two esteemed colleagues as IDEAS facilitators.

Seeking New Heights—Visioning

The IDEAS Project surveys (Diagnostic Inventories) confirmed our school's low staff morale and high student alienation. With these points in mind, I accepted the premise of the IDEAS Project that an inspirational vision should be the starting point in creating a sense of optimism and excitement in our teachers and students. Many hours were spent by me, and by our teachers, juggling historical, geographic, and economic features of our town with the Generation Y features of our students and transposing the jumbled products into images of how we would like to be perceived as a school. Out of these intellectual contortions, eventually, came a moment of revelation in the form of a metaphorical vision statement that was to shape and direct our work as a school for the next several years:

From the Castle to the Network

For us, this school vision statement has immense evocative power, thanks to the two iconographical symbols on which it is based:

- The 15th-century Mazzarino *Castle,* which not only captures the school's roots in the local region but is also a concrete reminder of the region's distinctive cultural features

- The *Network,* which represents global futures, emerging technologies, and our school's desire for engagement with worlds that are very different from our own in Mazzarino and central Sicily

As principal, I have constantly taken the position that the network concept also connotes untried and novel ways of considering relationships between people and political, cultural, and economic systems around the world. Thus, I have used the network aspect of our vision to identify, explain, and justify new forms of school structure to promote an expansion of the way the school sees its boundaries, to encourage new thinking about the natural environment, and to insist that all members of the school community accept their responsibilities as global citizens.

The castle aspect of the vision has proven equally powerful in my work. Most notably, as principal, I have encouraged teachers to use this metaphorical concept to articulate social and historical values that will promote student and parent pride in their very unique community and in themselves. As one particularly important project, the school launched a very successful competition for the town's citizenry to develop the castle metaphor into a visual image and logo for the school.

Seeking New Heights—Pedagogy

The visioning process was completed in 2006. Then, led by our two IDEAS facilitators, teachers undertook to explore the new school vision in their classrooms through a range of action learning strategies. Particularly effective was a teaching strategies analysis in which staff prepared written descriptions of exemplars of the *Castle to Network* vision at work in their individual classrooms. The different meanings of the vision in subjects such as physics, history, philosophy, and so on was illuminating and energizing. Analysis of the almost 100 teacher descriptions revealed extremely rich pedagogy and provided the basis for drafting our priority teaching and learning principles as a school. These pedagogical statements were then transposed into questions by the IDEAS facilitators. Finally, by using three different time frames (an expansion of the Roman god Janus's capacity to look into the past and the future), the ISMT created a series of six focus questions for incorporation in all subjects as well as school welfare policies and student leadership programs. The six questions we regard as a mirror image of our vision (see Table 4.1).

Table 4.1 The Carlo Maria Carafa Pedagogical Framework

<table>
<tr><td colspan="3">From the Castle to the Network</td></tr>
<tr><td colspan="3">Our values:
Hope, personal optimism
• Global peace and sustainability
• Responsible personal actions
• Feeling proud of the school, the town, and Sicily</td></tr>
<tr><td colspan="3">How we learn
(A "Janus" look)</td></tr>
<tr><td>Looking back</td><td>Looking around</td><td>Looking ahead</td></tr>
<tr><td>Where did this idea come from?</td><td>What does this idea mean in my life?</td><td>What might this idea look like in the future?</td></tr>
<tr><td>How has it changed over time?</td><td>How is it used around the world?</td><td>How might it make our world a better place?</td></tr>
</table>

With the six-question "Janus" framework in mind, students are regularly asked their thoughts about the content of their studies and the problems of concern to them in their personal lives. They are thus enabled to reflect upon themselves as individuals and to take into account the viewpoints of their classmates, employing critical and creative thinking skills.

Other extensions of our vision statement into the core of school life include new forms of student participation and negotiation, principal–student contractual agreements, elements of self-governance in class activities, and promotion of the school assembly as a decision forum. It goes without saying that these activities encourage the nurturing of new talents in staff, including forms of teacher leadership.

The school is currently undertaking, with the Sicilian Education Region and the University of Catania, a survey aiming at investigating the existential features, as well as the "life projects," of students in a sample of Italian secondary schools. The intent of this project is to elaborate the needs and aspirations of the Y generation as they apply in Sicilian communities. The results will, we believe, be useful in planning future school approaches to students' intellectual and social growth.

Finally, the school has started various voluntary service projects for the students of nearby schools, establishment of facilities for senior citizens, and home instruction and videoconferencing for students who cannot attend school regularly. Most notably, the school has undertaken contacts aimed at deepening educational and cultural understanding between Sicilian and Australian students.

Each of these activities has been given life and shaped by our *Castle to Network* vision. Each activity has been given additional authenticity because it resonates with the values that derive from the vision, and because it complements and extends the six-question Janus pedagogical framework. In summary, Carlo Maria Carafa High School, through my own work as principal in association with teacher leaders, has employed visioning and schoolwide pedagogical development processes to create powerful new social and intellectual capital within the student body, the professional community, and the local town.

In Retrospect

Positive effects of the educational and organizational processes activated by the school are, in the views of staff and myself, very apparent. Students have become more aware of their rights and their responsibilities and show greater respect toward environmental surroundings and school structures; teacher and student leadership forms are prospering; and episodes of violence, bullying, and vandalism have become rare. Evidence of regeneration in the town of Mazzarino itself can also be traced to our *Castle to Network* vision and our Janus-look pedagogy.

What started out as an intent on my part to do something to make Carlo Maria Carafa High School students feel a sense of belonging in an alienating and negative world has become an exhilarating way of thinking, working, and living for an entire Sicilian educational community.

Postscript

In January 2010, Giuseppe Micciche was awarded the Officer of Merit of the Italian Republic by the prime minister of Italy, Mr. Berlusconi, and the president of Italy, Mr. Napolitano, in recognition of the exceptional achievements at Carlo Maria Carafa High School.

SEEKING NEW HEIGHTS: DEEPENING OUR UNDERSTANDING

The seeking new heights C-B dynamic has both visionary and pedagogical dimensions, as the case study of Mazzarino High School illustrates. The two dimensions are characterized by common qualities. First, they provide the means for school leaders to inspire school community members—teachers, students, parents—to more focused and energized work. Second, they provide a means for school leaders to generate a powerful sense of belonging and school identity.

Seeking New Heights Through School Visioning

In our view, establishing elevated aspirations and heightened expectations in the daily work of a school necessitates a two-pronged developmental approach. The first developmental approach is strategic, usually undertaken through creation of a school vision statement. Our nine criteria for a school vision that will engender a sense of future-oriented confidence and enthusiasm are contained in Table 4.2. The second developmental approach is pedagogical, usually undertaken through creation of a schoolwide pedagogical framework (SWP). Our definition of an SWP is in Table 4.3. It goes without saying that a school's statements of vision and SWP should be very closely linked, as they clearly are in Carlo Maria Carafa's *From the Castle to the Network* vision and Janus-look pedagogical questions. It also goes without saying that the leadership processes for the respective approaches should be closely linked—in fact what we call "parallel."

Table 4.2 IDEAS Project Criteria for a School Vision

- Inspirational
- Educational
- Ethical
- Futuristic
- Memorable
- Vivid
- Achievable
- Based on shared values and beliefs
- Developed within the school community

Table 4.3 A Definition of Schoolwide Pedagogy

Schoolwide pedagogy
A schoolwide pedagogy (SWP) is an agreed set of pedagogical principles that reflect the distinctive qualities of a school community.

(Continued)

(Continued)

SWP enables a teaching staff to

- emphasize agreed priority strategies for teaching or learning (or both) in the diverse curricular and extracurricular practices of a school,
- reinforce each other's strengths in their core work, and
- grow professionally through a collaborative professional learning approach.

Our position regarding the importance of a powerful school vision in motivating a school community to heightened aspirations and expectations is well captured by Choi (2006, p. 27):

> Envisioning involves creating an overall picture of a desired future state with which people can identify and which can generate excitement.

But how, one might ask, does the creation of a school vision begin to engender a sense of shared identity and excitement in teachers' work as well as in the mind-sets of students and parents? Choi explains further:

> In addition to formulating a vision, they (i.e., leaders) are adept at communicating the vision and infusing day-to-day work with a larger sense of purpose and greater intrinsic appeal. (p. 27)

Licata and Harper (2001) endorse this point, noting that an inspiring, creative vision can place everyday routine, with its implicit drudgery, in realistic perspective in teachers' work lives:

> Teachers who share a relatively robust school vision may be more likely to implement their imagined possibilities and less likely to be distracted by some of the more tedious routines and conflicts that tend to be part of everyday life in schools. (p. 5)

Some observers argue that it is more difficult today than it has been historically for school leaders to facilitate processes for heightening teachers' aspirations. These observers quite rightly make their point because the past decade has seen a trend toward centralized educational decision making that some regard as an overimposition of top-down authority. As one recent instance, the chancellor for schools in New York recently made the following statements about how high expectations for enhanced school improvement should be created:

> When you set high expectations, give schools the authority and resources to meet them, and then hold them accountable for results, schools respond in a positive way. (Klein, 2010, p. 14)

Such a statement clearly reflects a genuine commitment from a system educational leader. But in our view, it may underestimate both the need for schools to establish their own aspirational goals and the capacity of school leaders to provide high levels of motivation to their school communities. Leading international change agent John Kotter has posed what we regard as a valid criticism of the top-down imposition of aspirations and goals (2001, p. 93):

> Achieving grand visions always requires a burst of energy. Motivation and inspiration energise people, not by pushing them in the right direction as control mechanisms do but by satisfying basic human needs for achievement, a sense of belonging, recognition, self-esteem, a feeling of control over one's life, and the ability to live up to one's ideals.

Without a highly meaningful, contextually relevant school vision in place, we believe, the task of raising the aspirations and expectations in teachers' work is extremely difficult. But with a meaningful vision in place, heightened aspirations can follow quite naturally, opening the door to pedagogical enhancement.

Seeking New Heights Through Schoolwide Pedagogy

But, one might ask, how do heightened aspirations and expectations that are manifested in a school vision statement contribute to enhanced classroom practice? This highly complex and extremely important question has two answers, both of which are inseparable from human motivation. First, we know from our own research (see Resource B) that when teachers' sense of professional well-being is enhanced, through strategies such as inspirational visioning, their perceptions of the efficacy of their pedagogical practices also increases. Importantly, students' perceptions of the efficacy of pedagogical practices also increases. Highly authoritative recent research has also shown that, when teachers work collaboratively as a professional learning community to establish high expectations across the school, schoolwide achievement can improve significantly and gaps in student achievement on socioeconomic grounds can be significantly reduced (Newmann & Wehlage, 1995). Based on internationally renowned research such as that of Newmann and Wehlage, Ross and Gray (2006, p. 182) make the decisive point that the key to schoolwide pedagogical enhancement lies in "collective teacher efficacy." They explain that:

> Teachers with high expectations about their ability produce higher student achievement. Collective teacher efficacy refers to the perceptions of teachers in a school that the efforts of the faculty as a whole will have a positive effect on students.

This brings us directly to the our critically important concept of schoolwide pedagogy (SWP), which we interpret as an agreed statement of pedagogical principles that reflect the distinctive qualities of a school community and that provide a framework for teachers to support each others' instructional priorities, reinforce each other achievements, and learn from each other. City et al. (2009) make a very convincing case in support of this concept:

> Repeatedly, district and school practitioners tell us that one of the greatest barriers to school improvement is the lack of an agreed-upon definition of what high quality instruction looks like . . . a set of protocols and processes for observing, analysing, discussing, and understanding instruction that can be used to improve student learning. (p. 3)

Bryk (2010) is similarly adamant:

> Schools in which student learning improves have coherent instructional guidance systems that articulate the what and how of instruction . . . the efficacy of individual teacher effort depends on the quality of the supports and the local community of practice. (p. 24)

Because a school's SWP derives from a vision that meets daunting criteria (Table 4.2), and from synthesis of best practices, it asks teachers to pitch their expectations at a level that is both highly challenging and achievable. Thus, in the Mazzarino case study, the six Janus-look questions became the platform that enabled teachers to transpose an inspirational vision into highly stimulating pedagogical practices and, in so doing, to reinforce each other's efforts and learn from each other.

Based on the various authoritative contributions that we have considered, and research-based case studies such as Carlo Maria Carafa High School, we offer the following definition of *seeking new heights* in the C-B process:

Seeking new heights involves creation of a projection of the future that is grounded in responsibility, confidence, and hope. This projection manifests in two interrelated forms–a vision statement and a schoolwide pedagogical framework.

LEADERSHIP FOR SEEKING NEW HEIGHTS

The construct of schoolwide leadership takes on a new and distinctive form in the third C-B dynamic, with the roles of principals and teacher leaders being of equivalent importance.

The importance of the principal's leadership is readily apparent in the Mazzarino thumbnail. That is, at the point of creating a school vision, it helps immensely if the principal has particular qualities—such as deep conviction for the school and students, a high energy level, sophisticated communications strategies, and creative flair—that will captivate and energize colleagues. According to Leithwood and Jantzi (2006, p. 233), qualities such as these constitute the heart of "transformational" leadership and are inseparable from establishing heightened aspirations and collective motivation in a school community. Leithwood and Riehl (2005) explain further that the first function of educational leadership is that of establishing a shared vision. If that is to happen, principals must themselves be visionaries who can inspire others to go beyond what they would otherwise do.

Giuseppe Micciche, principal of Mazzarino High School, clearly illustrates Leithwood and Riehl's intent. But how does passion and energy in the principal's office become passion and energy in teachers' work? Cross, Baker, and Parker (2003, p. 52) explain the flow-on effects of a principal's transformational leadership this way: "energizers" in an organization can inspire others to go beyond what they would otherwise by initiating interactive aspirational processes and by enthusing others with their own passion, dynamism, and charisma. (Note: Cross, Baker, and Parker note that the converse, relating to de-energizer principals, regrettably also holds true).

That said, heightened passion and energy in teachers' work is not necessarily synonymous with enhanced school pedagogy. Bryk, Easton, Kerbow, Rollow, and Sebring (1993), for example, have written of "Christmas tree schools" where immense energy is exerted by individual teachers, or small teams of teachers, resulting in flashing lights, shining bulbs, and glittering tinsel, but the net effect is one of debilitation—when the power source is unplugged, what remains is a dead tree. This colorful analogy poses challenges for educational leaders at all levels, but we believe those challenges are in fact resolvable. The obvious answer, to us, lies in two critically important concepts—parallel leadership and schoolwide pedagogy. That is, if a teaching staff has developed an SWP as an extension of an uplifting school vision (in the case of Mazzarino, the six Janus-look questions constituted their SWP), then the chances of idiosyncratic pedagogical proposals taking up immense quantities of teacher energy, and creating contradictions and confusion within the school, are substantially reduced. Peter Senge made the following telling comment on this point:

> You cannot implement "learner-directed learning," for example, in one classroom and not others. It would drive the kids nuts, not to mention the stress on the individual teacher. (as cited in O'Neill, 1995, p. 21)

It goes without saying that the principal–teacher leader relationship is of the utmost importance in ensuring that such breakdowns, inconsistencies, and interferences do not occur.

Of major importance is that an SWP, in our experience, cannot be developed without a mature form of teacher leadership in place in a school. By maturity in teacher leadership, we mean that teacher leaders demonstrate the following attributes:

- A high degree of pedagogical credibility and expertise
- A capacity to assume independent organizational responsibility in the school
- Sophisticated skills in synthesizing meaning out of group products that may appear on the surface to be disparate, divergent, or even chalk and cheese
- A trusting and respectful professional working relationship with the school principal

The personal and professional challenges for teachers who rise to serious pedagogical leadership challenges are indeed daunting:

> Teacher leaders begin to recognize that their focus must move from a single innovation or from their own classroom to a wider, whole-school perspective. Teacher leaders with influencing skills begin to see that their voices are heard by their colleagues, by the parents, and in the community. The influence of teacher leadership can make the difference beyond the individual grade level or team. (Katzenmeyer & Moller, 2001, p. 91)

In tracing the development of the third C-B dynamic in the research schools, it is apparent that school-based leadership was characterized by three very important qualities:

1. A transformational principalship quality, particularly in mobilizing visioning processes and energizing teachers to become optimally involved

2. A transformational teacher leadership quality, particularly in facilitating and shaping the development of creative schoolwide pedagogical frameworks

3. A highly respectful and trusting principal–teacher leader relationship

Thus, without parallel leadership, we conclude, the achievement of philosophical and practical consistency between a school's vision and pedagogy is virtually impossible.

THINKING OUTSIDE THE SQUARE: MOTHER TERESA AND SEEKING NEW HEIGHTS

The concept of seeking new heights is of course not unique to educational institutions. Mother Teresa's legacy of achievements in our strife-ridden world illustrates that point. A great deal is to be learned from Mother Teresa's life and example, as the following description illustrates. As you review it, ask yourself four questions:

1. In Mother Teresa's life work, what is the equivalent to the educational concepts of vision and schoolwide pedagogical framework (SWP)?
2. How did Mother Teresa communicate her vision, both internally to her Order and externally to the world, to enable her to have an amazingly uplifting effect on people across the boundaries of nations, cultures, and religions?
3. Which of the four leadership approaches that we have identified as dominant in educational practice (transformational, advocacy, strategic, organizationwide) do you associate most with Mother Teresa's work?
4. How was parallel leadership a part of Mother Teresa's leadership approach?

A former high school teacher, Mother Teresa was inspired to join the Sisters of Loreto but left her convent to work directly with the poor. She established the Missionaries of Charity and began the process of working with lepers and orphans in Calcutta and, subsequently, other Indian cities. The Missionaries of Charity affiliated with a range of lay groups, and by 1979, when she received the Nobel Prize for Peace, she and her affiliated groups comprised a network of more than 200 different organizations in over

25 countries. She had confronted seemingly insurmountable difficulties in a wide range of forms—in organizations, in cultures, and in human nature—and enabled millions of people to see beyond the obstacles in their lives.

Mother Teresa created her own personal vision—*Understanding Love*—and, over the course of her lifetime (and beyond), transposed that vision into "work" that continues to be lived every day through the Missionaries of Charity's value-based practices of *feeling, giving,* and *believing.* Her work exemplifies what we mean by the aspirations C-B dynamic. In her Nobel Prize speech, she summed up her view of her world, her personal response to it, and her role as a leader:

> There is so much suffering, so much hatred, so much misery, and we with our prayer, with our sacrifice, are beginning at home. Love begins at home, and it is not how much we do, but how much love we put into the action that we do . . .
>
> And with this prize that I have received as a prize of peace, I am going to try to make the home for many people that have no home. Because I believe that love begins at home, and if we can create a home for the poor—I think that more and more love will spread. And we will be able through this understanding love to bring peace, be the good news to the poor. The poor in our own family first, in our country and in the world. (Montefiore, 2005, p. 190)

A world-renowned sportsman who visited Mother Teresa's mission in a Calcutta back street demonstrated the way that her extraordinary work influenced people beyond the boundaries of her missions. He described his experience this way:

> It was a very uplifting moment. When she came towards me I didn't know what to do or say. But when she got there I suddenly felt relaxed. She has a very calming aura about her. She handed me her business card, which read: *The fruit of silence is prayer, the fruit of prayer is faith, the fruit of faith is love, the fruit of love is service.*
>
> The mood of the place was very serene and relaxing. By devoting her life to charity she has proved herself to be a totally selfless person. It makes you feel guilty when you think of the sacrifices she has made. (Craddock, 1996, p. 1)

NOTE: The elite sportsman in question, the Australian cricket captain Steve Waugh, subsequently chose to contribute to the work of the Missionaries of Charity and to establish missions in India on his own behalf.

We believe that the Mother Teresa story exemplifies the essential features of the third C-B dynamic in schools—namely, creation of a deeply inspiring vision and development of workplace practices that reflect the integrity and dynamism of that vision. Although of course none of us would claim to operate on or near Mother Teresa's pedestal, she herself would most certainly encourage us to endeavor to do so. That, in essence, is what seeking new heights is about.

Mother Teresa's leadership was world changing. Known for many years as the "Saint of the Gutter," she was beatified in 2002.

CONCLUSION

In this chapter we have asserted that seeking new heights is fundamental to sustained school success. We say this because the construct of aspiration is grounded in purpose and enthusiasm, energizing people in organizations and stimulating them to heightened goals and ongoing effort. We have established from our research that aspiration in highly successful schools manifests in two critically important forms—in a statement of vision that provides hope, purpose, and direction at the level of strategic management and in a schoolwide pedagogical (SWP) framework that provides hope, purpose, and direction at the level of classroom practice.

We have established also that, as the seeking new heights C-B dynamic unfolds, teacher leadership assumes unequivocal importance and identity in school operations. Indeed, we know of no instance where the SWP dimension of the third C-B dynamic has been developed without concerted teacher leadership. That said, we assert also that it is parallel leadership as an integrated principal–teacher leader relationship that underpins the aspiration dynamic.

With this understanding firmly established, we can now proceed to explore the essence of school capacity building, namely, the micro-pedagogical deepening dynamic. But before doing so, we encourage you to undertake a simulated activity to enhance your personal capacity as a leader of the first aspect (i.e., school visioning) of the third C-B dynamic.

COSMIC C-B SIMULATION 3—SCHOOL VISIONING THROUGH ENVIRONMENTAL SCANNING

SEEKING NEW HEIGHTS: BUILDING PERSONAL CAPACITY

Purpose:

To enable school leaders to experience firsthand a creative environmental scanning approach to school visioning.

Rationale:

As is indicated throughout Chapter 4, visioning is a values-based process that enables a school community to explore and agree on elevated educational goals. In so doing, it comprises the key launching pad for the development of a school's pedagogical framework. It is inseparable from the principal's leadership responsibility, but in order to engender schoolwide commitment, it is best undertaken as a collaborative process that involves teacher leaders working hand in hand with the principal.

Simulation Three provides school leaders with a tried-and-true approach to school visioning. The materials that are used in the simulation can easily be customized for use with a whole school staff as the preparation for an authentic school visioning process.

Approximate time required:

Two 1-hour sessions

Organization:

Groups of six are recommended.

Materials for each group:

- A copy of The 7 Foundations for Visioning for each work group (Exhibit 4.A)
- A copy of the Principal's Memo to Elizabeth Vale SMT for each individual participant (Exhibit 4.B)
- The *VISIONING AT______* design copied onto a large sheet of paper for each work group (Exhibit 4.C)
- A copy of the criteria for a school vision for each work group (Chapter 4, Table 4.2)

Exhibit 4.A

The 7 Foundations for Visioning

1. **Community beliefs and values**
   - Does the school have particular religious or spiritual traditions that the school should sustain and enrich? If so, what are they?
   - Does the school have particular communal, cultural, ecological, or other quality-of-life values that the school should sustain and enrich? If so, what are they?
   - Does the school or community have particular international links (e.g., a sister city relationship)?
2. **Historical antecedents and key artifacts**
   - What key events and patterns of growth have shaped the community's history?
   - What dominant figures, artifacts, and achievements stand out in the community's history?
   - What historical logos, slogans, missions, and visions should be remembered as part of a process of school revitalization and renewal?
3. **Geographic features and landmarks**
   - What topographical features dominate the local landscape?
   - Are there prominent local landmarks?
   - Is the region noted for particular geographic features?
4. **Demographic trends and patterns**
   - Is the community in a period of population growth, stability, or decline?
   - Is the local population dominantly permanent? What is the level of transience?
   - What social, cultural, ethnic, religious, indigenous, or other groups give the community its makeup?
   - What is the socioeconomic status cross section of groups?
5. **Economic characteristics**
   - What industries (primary, secondary, service) dominate?
6. **School-based organizational dynamics**
   - What is the size of the school population?
   - What grade levels does the school comprise?
   - What subject specializations are offered? Centers of excellence?
   - What academic/nonacademic emphases are valued?
   - Does the school have distinctive design features? If so, what are they?
7. **Futuristic goals and aspirations**
   - What aspirations for the future of the school have been identified based on a consideration of students' futuristic needs?

Exhibit 4.B

PRINCIPAL'S MEMO TO ELIZABETH VALE C-B SMT

ELIZABETH VALE PUBLIC SCHOOL

EST. 1928

210 Boundary Ave
Elizabeth Vale 1234
Phone: (00) 4321 5678

Re: Visioning at Elizabeth Vale.

Dear Colleagues:

Like myself, I suspect you were not surprised to read our *survey* results and to learn that our longstanding school motto of ***Labor Omnia Vincit*** is not regarded by our staff as adequate to serve our professional goals.

I have read the "7 Foundations for Visioning" for schools engaged in capacity building. For the benefit of SMT members who are new to the school, or who have not previously thought about such matters, I offer the following comments on the seven Foundations as they relate to Elizabeth Vale Public School. You may have additional insights that should be added to the details that follow. If so, please do so.

I am asking that we develop a list of up to six priority features of Elizabeth Vale School to guide our Visioning process. Once we have reached agreement about the priorities, we should lead the staff, and perhaps interested parents and students, in a process of identifying possible new vision statements. I would hope that we will have to eventually select from amongst at least twenty different ideas.

I will of course take an active role in that process, but would not wish to impose my own particular views on either our staff or the community.

- *Community beliefs and values*

  Elizabeth Vale residents are proud of their Sister City arrangements with Monte Fedici in Italy and Tho Chinh in Viet Nam. Our elected politicians are noted for their tolerant outlooks on multiculturalism and also environmental issues. Very regrettably, the indigenous history of the area seems to now be lost. This is very unfortunate in that we have over 40 students who claim an indigenous heritage.

- *Historical antecedents and key artifacts*

  James and Elizabeth Graham were one of the original pioneering pastoral families to settle here in the 1870s. The statue of Elizabeth Graham in the town center attests to her pioneering spirit, sense of adventure and love of rural life. In the 1970s the area was the focus of a minor tourist boom, setting in motion the break up of farms into acreages and small lots. With the establishment of a hydro plant just outside the city in the 1980s, and then the paper manufacturing plant, the historical origins of the community began to dim in people's memories. This has accentuated with the creation of the Elizabeth Vale Industrial Estate over the past decade.

- *Geographic features and landmarks*

  Elizabeth Vale is an historical suburb, located about 40 minutes from the main city center. The term "Vale" derives from the low-lying "valley" in which our suburb is set (and sometimes floods severely, because of its location at the confluence of our two local streams).

- *Demographic trends and patterns*

  With the growth of the Industrial Estate, there has been an influx of new families into the area. Many of our new residents are recent arrivals in our country and State, giving the school a rich cultural mix.

- *Economic characteristics*

  I would anticipate that new industries will emerge over the next decade, because of our geographic location. The Chamber of Commerce is currently pursuing ways of encouraging e-industries to set up here.

- *School-based organizational dynamics*

  Our total population is 950 students, K–12. We reached a low enrollment point of 850 in 2005, and are now growing steadily. A new Performing Arts Center will be built next year, with close links to the community's Arts Theater.

- *Futuristic goals and aspirations*

  I believe that it is clearly apparent that the air of optimism and inquiry that began with Elizabeth Graham and her fellow pioneers is alive and well, 130 years later.

I hope that these details will prove helpful as we commence a most exciting stage in the history of our school and community.

Sincerely,

Geoff

Exhibit 4.C Visioning at Elizabeth Vale

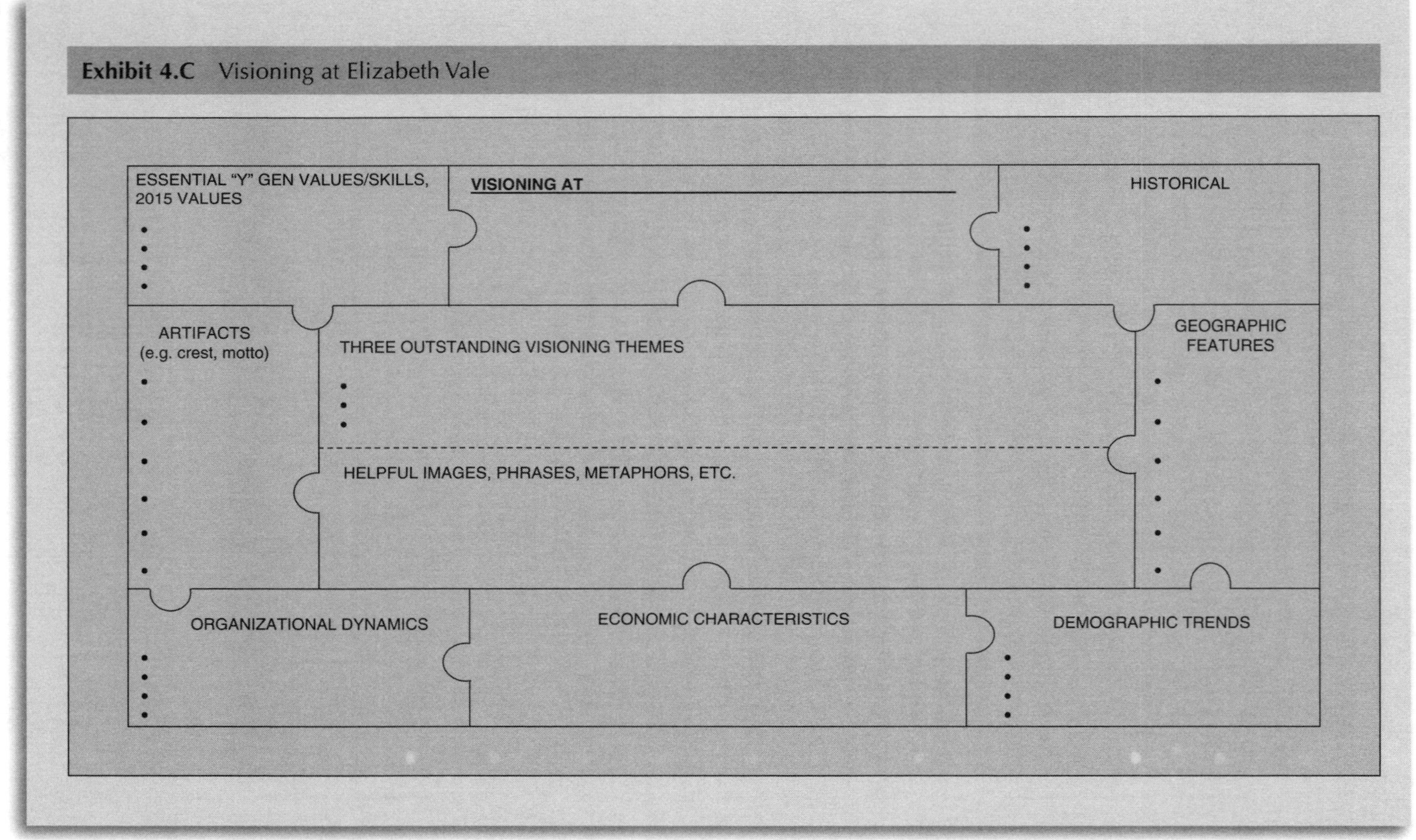

Process:

First 1-hour session

Step 1—Assign roles: principal, middle manager, two teacher leaders, parent, and student.

Step 2—Read the principal's memo to the Elizabeth Vale School Management Team individually.

Step 3—Discuss the seven possible foundations for a school vision as they relate to Elizabeth Vale Public School. Complete Exhibit 4.C individually. As a group, complete the seven Foundations sections of the *VISIONING AT ELIZABETH VALE* work chart (Exhibit 4.C), using the foundations descriptions that individuals have created.

Step 4—Complete the top middle section of the *VISIONING AT ELIZABETH VALE* work chart. That is, identify three strong themes for a future Elizabeth Vale Public School vision, taking into account the relative importance of the seven foundations at Elizabeth Vale.

Second 1-hour session

Step 1—As a group, create an agreed-on Elizabeth Vale vision. The proposed vision can be in the form of phraseology, imagery, or metaphor, and may have associated diagrammatic or aesthetic features. Once developed, place it in the center of your chart. Check it against the nine criteria in Table 4.2.

Step 2 (optional)—Once your vision statement is completed, place the chart on the wall for members of other groups to view. One person from each group should remain alongside the chart to explain to others the thinking and conversations that lie behind the vision.

Step 3—Review your experience with this simulation. What do you regard as the necessary role of the principal in a school visioning activity? Teacher leaders?

Step 4—Develop a strategy for visioning at your own school, based on your experience with the Elizabeth Vale simulation and your views regarding leadership roles and responsibilities in school visioning.

Having immersed yourself in this chapter, and completed the visioning simulation, you can consider yourself well qualified to proceed to lead a visioning activity in your school.

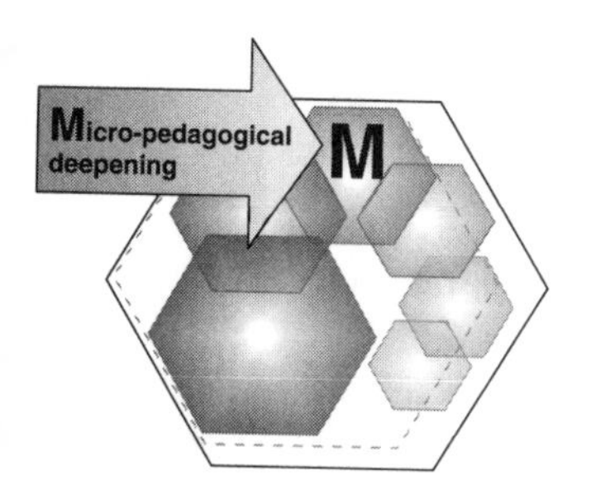

5

The Fourth C-B Dynamic

Micro-Pedagogical Deepening

(Prepared in collaboration with Dr. Dorothy Andrews and Ms. Lindy Abawi)

Teaching holds a mirror to the soul, [therefore] knowing myself is crucial to good teaching.

—Parker Palmer (1998, p. 2)

INTRODUCTION

In the previous chapter, Elizabeth City and her colleagues drew to our attention the importance in school improvement of "an agreed-upon definition of what high-quality instruction looks like." With this somewhat novel but important thought as our guide, we proceeded to discuss our construct of SWP—schoolwide pedagogy. We showed how it can be developed out of an inspirational school vision and how it can provide the basis for consistency and refinement in teachers' work and transferability in students' learning.

But how does City's idea of an "agreed-upon definition of what high quality instruction looks like" facilitate what Palmer Parker (in our opening quote) calls "teaching that mirrors the soul"? That is what every dedicated educational leader wants to know. That is what every professional teacher aspires to. These questions are the focus of our attention in this chapter, the fourth C-B dynamic, *micro-pedagogical deepening.*

Before getting underway, we note that deepening pedagogical practice is not to be confused with professional activity associated with the third C-B dynamic—seeking new pedagogical heights. The third dynamic is dominantly organizational in focus and is quite often achieved without the fourth being attempted, let alone accomplished. Stated differently, the creation of an inspirational school vision and associated schoolwide pedagogical framework constitutes an essential requisite to deepened pedagogical practice—but does not in and of itself guarantee transformations in teachers' work. Following his recent research into a large-scale school improvement project, Andy Hargreaves succinctly captured the very substantial difficulties that are involved in proceeding from the organizational to the deep pedagogical transformation stage of school improvement. He observed,

> Schools were spectacularly successful in improving in the short term, but few had begun to engage in long-term improvement processes. Dialogue about deep transformations in teaching were largely yet to occur. (2008, p. 184)

The subject of this chapter is micro-pedagogical deepening—*micro* because it is focused on concentrated detail, *pedagogical* because it is about teaching and learning, and *deepening* because it emphasizes rich meaning and significance in teachers' work. It is a topic that may be new to many educators, is critically important to 21st-century school improvement and capacity building—and is very challenging.

As a starting point in getting a sense of the meaning of this critically important concept, we look inside a school where it was nurtured, facilitated, and practiced, with transforming effects on teachers as well as students and their community.

A SNAPSHOT OF MICRO-PEDAGOGICAL DEEPENING

GREENFIELD ELEMENTARY SCHOOL

A Bang or a Whimper?

The story of Greenfield Elementary School is an educational success story. It is the story of a school that transformed its sense of identity, culture, and student outcomes over a four-year period. It is a story that reflects the power of teachers as leaders but also the power of deep pedagogy.

Greenfield Elementary, catering for 4- to 12-year-old students, was identified in 2004 as one of the most socioeconomically disadvantaged urban schools in the nation (Australian Bureau of Statistics, 2006). It was located in a highly multicultural community, dominated by recently arrived immigrants and refugees with little to no English, as well as students from highly transient families that had experienced generational unemployment. At least 80 percent of the families in the school were recipients of educational maintenance allowance.

The Greenfield teaching staff considered themselves competent professionals, but their dedication and skill proved inadequate in meeting the expectations of either system supervisors or parents regarding literacy and numeracy outcomes. Consequently, system officials designated Greenfield as an "at risk" or "targeted" school. Although teacher morale sank to an all-time low level with this decision, the principal retained a passionate desire to move the school to an image of success, and several staff indicated that they shared her dream.

The principal summed up her perspective at this juncture:

> We were at rock bottom. We were told we had failed. We had to do something to refresh, to test just how good we could be.

Accordingly, the principal made two very significant decisions. The first was to commit to a formal school revitalization process and the second was to "tap on the shoulder" an individual member of staff whom she perceived to be the right person to co-lead the revitalization process with her. That "right" person was Marilyn, a very well-respected teacher in the school community, known for her skills in conceptualizing and articulating big-picture explanations of complex situations and for her versatility in leading group activities.

An environmental scan that was undertaken (i.e., the IDEAS Project Diagnostic Inventory) to get the revitalization process underway led the staff to the inexorable conclusion that their school lacked a meaningful vision, was disconnected from its community, and did not possess a shared understanding of high-quality teaching and learning. How, they asked, could they drag themselves out of their mire in the face of such odds? Then, not long after the scan was completed, and a self-report card prepared by the staff, it was announced that Greenfield School would cease to exist within four to five years as part of a regional merger. The staff might have given up completely at this point but, with the encouragement of the principal and Marilyn, decided to proceed with their revitalization project. The principal wrote in her journal,

> This decision was possibly our first big step in the journey to revitalize. As a staff, we made a commitment to go out with a BANG, not a whimper! The school vision that was developed over the coming months—*Learning Together to Build a Bright Future*—attempted to convey the sense of hope that the staff were beginning to feel and that they wanted to convey to their communities, as well as their system supervisors.

Micro-Pedagogical Deepening at Greenfield

With the *Bright Future* vision in place, Marilyn organized a range of "Successful Greenfield Teaching and Learning" activities to enable her colleagues to transpose the new school vision into model classroom practices. The Greenfield SWP (Table 5.1) was synthesized out of teachers' descriptions and endorsed at a faculty meeting. Staff began almost immediately to feel that they were "on the same page" in their daily pedagogical work. Discussion—sometimes very intense—regarding the best ways of addressing the six core pedagogical concepts and 13 SWP questions (Table 5.1) ensued. Over the coming semester, the teachers explored a number of topics that were largely new to them, including *Which strategies work well with each of the six concepts? How do we build from one year level to the next with each concept? Which questions are most relevant in individual subjects? Which questions and concepts do I personally have a gift for?*

Table 5.1 The Greenfield SWP Principles

<table>
<tr><td rowspan="6">C
E
L
E
B
R
A
T
E</td><td>**INCLUDE**</td><td>• What do we know about each child's needs and gifts?
• How do we embrace our school's diversity?</td></tr>
<tr><td>**COLLABORATE**</td><td>• How do we make best use of our individual strengths and ideas?
• How does this experience enable us to learn from each other?</td></tr>
<tr><td>**CONNECT**</td><td>• How does this learning experience connect to real life?
• How can this experience connect to the future?</td></tr>
<tr><td>**BUILD**</td><td>• How does this experience build on what students have previously learned?
• What supports are needed to facilitate new learning?
• How does this new learning encourage us to think in new ways?</td></tr>
<tr><td>**REFLECT**</td><td>• What opportunities have I provided for reflection?
• What have I personally learned?
• How can I apply this learning in my future teaching?
• Where to go from here with my new understandings?</td></tr>
</table>

At this juncture, buoyed by their two semesters of developmental success, the Greenfield staff decided to undertake a comprehensive progress review. They concluded from the review that their SWP was too "teacher-centric" and pondered what a "student-centric" SWP would look like.

The *Bright Future* Learning Framework in Table 5.2 was developed in the ensuing months out of a particular concern that students were not engaging sufficiently in learning processes. The Learning Framework represented an advanced level of development and pedagogical understanding at Greenfield. It proved successful almost immediately, encouraging students to become more involved in goal setting; to conference with teachers and parents about their learning; and to reflect on their progress, their challenges, and their successes. It proved to be a turning point in transforming the mindset of Greenfield students from "We can't do it and don't want to" to "We can do it and want to."

Table 5.2 The Greenfield *Bright Future* Learning Framework

CELEBRATE		
C E	**INCLUDING**	• What do I know about myself? • What do I know about my fellow students?
L E	**COLLABORATING**	• How am I using my ideas to help others? • How can I use others' ideas with this challenge?
B R	**CONNECTING**	• How does this idea connect with what I already know? • How might this idea connect to real life?
A T E	**BUILDING**	• What help do I need to continue my learning? • How does my new learning encourage me to think in new ways?
	REFLECTING	• When and how do I reflect on my learning? • Where to go from here?

With their two learning frameworks in place, and led by Marilyn and two volunteer colleagues, the Greenfield staff set themselves an even greater challenge—to explore each of their six pedagogical concepts in depth. They did so in two ways. First, they developed a comprehensive Greenfield description of each pedagogical principle. A thumbnail description of one concept is in Table 5.3. The simplicity of this brief description, particularly the three unusually titled core strategies, masks the deep meaning that it held for those who created it.

Table 5.3 A School-Developed Description of the Principle of Collaborative Learning

Collaborative Learning

Our definition: "Learning from other people while helping other people learn!"

Our educational justification:

- Y Gen's preferred learning approach
- 1 + 1 = 3
- Collective intelligence, shared cognition

Our core strategies:

- Engaged listening
- Mentors and mentees
- Learning circles

Second, the ten Learning Framework questions were modified to apply to a systemic priority, student literacy. The resulting questioning framework became the basis for the school's approach to literacy development for the next three years, assisted by an external literacy expert.

In reflecting on their intensive literacy work, in the context of their *Bright Future* Learning Framework (Table 5.2) over a three-year period, Greenfield teachers made a number of observations that provide helpful insights regarding micro-pedagogical deepening:

- Exploring personal beliefs that underpinned literacy practices was helpful in strengthening staff relationships.
- The staff underwent a total rethink of the way they approached all aspects of literacy.
- Teachers developed a concern for *all* students in the school—their welfare and achievement—not just the students in their own classes.
- Students began to talk about their own literacy learning.
- Mechanisms to spend productive time with the previous year's teachers of a class of students emerged naturally.
- Conferences of parents, students, and teachers provided opportunities to give and receive literacy feedback.
- Some individual teachers became expert in an area of literacy that they valued.

It is therefore apparent that micro-pedagogical deepening must be grounded in a concern for individual student welfare and learning, but can only be achieved if teachers enhance their self-understanding and professional skill, individually and collectively.

The research database in Resource B indicates that the Greenfield teachers were successful in creating enhanced achievement in student literacy and in sustaining those improvements over at least a further two-year period. By the time the school was amalgamated, the staff were no longer designated targeted or failing. They could hold their professional head high, and did so.

MICRO-PEDAGOGICAL DEEPENING: DEEPENING OUR UNDERSTANDING

Micro-pedagogical deepening is a new term, coined as a result of our research into pedagogical processes in schools that enhanced their levels of achievement and set in place systems that they believed would sustain their success. Of the six dynamics that our research uncovered as fundamental to successful school C-B, micro-pedagogical deepening is the newest in terms of educational thinking. It is also the most complex. And we believe it may be the most important.

The concept of micro-pedagogical deepening that was fundamental to the success of Greenfield Elementary School teachers encompassed three levels of professional development and application, namely a teaching framework, a learning framework, and a literacy framework. As the Greenfield teachers worked through the three levels—both individually and collectively—their teaching became focused, diagnostic, and individualized, and their work became more meaningful. But what does "meaningful work" in 21st-century schools mean and does it really matter if teachers' work is "meaningful"? Answers to these questions are fundamental to our understanding of the highly challenging fourth C-B dynamic.

Meaningful Work in 21st-Century Schools

> Teaching is one of those rare jobs whereby on any given day you can literally change someone's life. This sense of calling compels educators to persist through difficult times, cope with stressful situations, and often succeed despite trying environments. (Eklund, 2009, p. 26)

Meaningful work is asserted by some authorities to have five characteristics, all of which we believe are part and parcel of teaching as a vocation. They come into particularly sharp focus in the fourth C-B dynamic, micro-pedagogical deepening. The characteristics are

- *authentic human activity*—i.e., work that contributes to human survival;
- *productive outcomes*—i.e., work that enhances the quality of life of societies and communities;

- *social relatedness*—i.e., work that adds a warmth and sociability to people's lives;
- *political expression*—i.e., work that allows people to articulate and assert their values and sociopolitical goals; and
- *shaped by those who do it*—i.e., work that enables workplace participants to design their vocational practices (Crowther, 1994).

The Greenfield case study reveals the presence of all five qualities in the work of Greenfield teachers, no doubt explaining the vast increase in staff morale that occurred over the period of their revitalization process.

Micro-pedagogical deepening also reflects three themes that renowned sociologist Chalofsky (2003) has asserted are essential to work in 21st-century knowledge societies, namely,

- knowing one's purpose in life and how one's work fits that purpose;
- having autonomy, empowerment, and a sense of control over one's work environment; and
- having a balance of work self and personal self.

Teachers in the Greenfield case study, confronted by debilitating accusations of failure and the prospect of their school's closure, determined to go out with a bang. And they did so. In the three-year period of time remaining to them as the Greenfield School staff, they created an inspiring vision for a better world, engaged collaboratively to enhance their workplace relationships, shaped new and dynamic pedagogical processes, and took advocacy action. In so doing, they transformed themselves as professionals and enhanced the achievement levels of their students. It can be said that they were enabled to do so to some extent through the incorporation of principles of meaningful work in their approach to pedagogy.

Two additional constructs have emerged during the past decade and a half to impact significantly on micro-pedagogical deepening practices. The first construct is e-technology, which many observers believe is beginning to have the effect of democratizing teaching practice in ways never before seen. That is, learning is becoming increasingly participatory, since, with the use of blogs and wikis, for example, students can interact with peers in a very diverse range of locations and in forms over which teachers have limited control. Thus, Warner (2006) argues, Gen Y students' access to knowledge has created a "power shift," with students no longer reliant on their teachers in ways that they were in previous historical contexts.

The second construct to emerge as a pivotal influence on micro-pedagogical deepening is that of the professional learning community, or "PLC," as it is increasingly described. The concept of PLC was perhaps first explored in the mid-1990s by prominent American researchers Louis, Marks, and Kruse (1996) and Shirley Hord (1997). Their research provided evidence that enhanced student achievement can occur when teachers explore their practice as a schoolwide, shared experience and learn collaboratively. Subsequent research by King and Newmann (1999); Bryk, Camburn, and Louis (2000); A. Hargreaves (2003); and Bolam et al. (2005) has indicated that the most effective professional learning communities—that is, those that create enriched pedagogical practice—focus simultaneously on the dual concepts of successful student learning and trust in teachers' professional relationships.

It can only be concluded from an analysis such as this that the work of today's teachers is more complex than it has ever been and more important than it has ever been. But it is meaningful, and more transparent and intelligible than it has ever been. The fourth C-B dynamic is situated in this challenging context.

Expertness in Pedagogical Practice

Our analysis of policy documents drawn from state and district sources in North America, Europe, Eastern Asia, and Australasia reveals that "expertness" in the work of teachers is regarded internationally as possessing at least three characteristics: depth in individual teachers' knowledge and skills (as opposed to surface understanding); reflection-on-practice (as opposed to innate, uninformed practice); and specialized skill (as opposed to "one size fits all" notions of professional capability). Micro-pedagogical deepening, we assert, should involve the pursuit of all three forms of expertness.

Very helpful additional insights can be gleaned from the work of education sociologists and psychologists. Garmston, for example, has differentiated between novices and experts, asserting that classroom experts "know more than novices and organize that knowledge differently, retrieve it easily, and apply it in novel and creative ways" (1998, p. 1). Pedagogical expertness, according to Garmston, incorporates five requirements:

- In-depth knowledge of what to teach
- Understanding of complex pedagogical strategies
- Practical knowledge of how to engage a diverse range of students in learning
- Profound understanding of self
- Constructive engagement in the activities of a PLC

Expertness in pedagogical practice has also been asserted by leading global educator Max Van Manen to have a quality of "mindfulness": a unique relationship of practical learning action between an adult and a young person on his or her way to adulthood (Van Manen, 2002, p. 30). Van Manen's process-oriented concept of professional expertness is also evident in Leech and Moon's (2008) assertion that meaningful pedagogy

> acknowledges teachers as intellectuals, requires teachers to be researchers of their own practice and is a complex interplay between theory and practice. (pp. 28–29)

Palmer's "mirror to the soul" perspective on pedagogical expertness (with which we opened this chapter) also captures the essence of Van Manen's "mindful" understanding of self and students in mature teacher professionalism.

A third perspective on pedagogical expertness has emerged from recent analyses of research into student achievement. Pedagogy researcher John Hattie (2003, p. 9) has differentiated between surface and deep learning as follows:

> Surface learning is more about the content (knowing the ideas, and doing what is needed to gain a passing grade) and deep learning more about understanding (relating and extending ideas, and an intention to understand and impose meaning).

Hattie proposes three dimensions of expertise that relate to highly successful teaching:

- *Challenge:* the provision of challenging tasks, rather than "do your best" goals for students
- *Deep representation:* making lessons unique by changing, combining, and enriching activities, according to students' needs and teachers' own goals
- *Monitoring and feedback:* monitoring student problems and assessing their level of understanding and progress, and providing relevant feedback (2003, p. 15)

We suggest that the eloquent description of deep mathematics pedagogy in Table 5.4 captures conceptions of expertness as described by authorities such as Garmston, Van Manen, and Hattie. Judge for yourself. What might an equivalent statement in another subject or discipline look like?

Table 5.4 The Beauty of What I Teach

Mathematics is the basis of our 21st-century lives and our worlds, just as it was two millennia ago.

It explains the way things change, and all movement in the cosmos.

Mathematics is the one universal language. It can tell the story of every shape and size, it can symbolize the simplest and most abstract relations between all things living and theoretical and it provides the magic in describing place and space.

Mathematics is the basis of the work that each of us does and every school subject that we study. And it enables us to balance our budget so that we can vacation using transport and technologies that also depend on it.

Mathematics is surely the supreme human triumph!

(With thanks to Frank Hainsworth, 2008, Gold Coast.)

Thus, a great deal is known about expert pedagogy, though it might be argued that few education systems and schools currently make as much use of the available insights as would be desirable. To do so, they would need to acknowledge and apply a number of fundamental principles of micro-pedadogical deepening, each of which is apparent in the Greenfield case study as well as in recent educational research on expert pedagogy:

- Many teachers have the potential to be expert practitioners, but don't see themselves that way or appreciate that possibility.
- Expertness in pedagogical practice begins with detailed self-knowledge and necessitates "holding a mirror to the soul."
- Expert pedagogy is inseparable from the pursuit of high expectations and grandiose aspirations in both teaching and learning.
- Expert pedagogy requires that one view one's chosen specialization as a "supreme human triumph."
- Expertness is not only an individual teacher function but also a schoolwide function.
- Expertness implies a continuous search for personal gifts and specialized expertise.

Based on this range of practical and scholarly considerations, we conclude that it is possible to define *micro-pedagogical deepening:*

Micro-pedagogical deepening happens in a school when teachers engage in three forms of pedagogical inquiry and application:

- Personal reflection on, and nurturing of, their gifts and talents in relation to their teaching
- Conceptual development of the school's pedagogical principles
- Streamlining of individual and schoolwide strategies for teaching, learning, and assessment to accommodate students' needs as 21st-century learners

LEADERSHIP FOR MICRO-PEDAGOGICAL DEEPENING

Micro-pedagogical deepening, as we have seen in the Greenfield case study, can have transformative impacts on teachers' work and on students' achievements. What kind of leadership, one might ask, is needed for a school's pedagogical practices to have such effects?

This question, we believe, has a three-pronged answer.

First, leadership for the fourth C-B dynamic is inseparable from mature teacher leadership, with all six elements of our Teachers as Leaders Framework (see Resource A) clearly in evidence in case studies such as that of Greenfield Elementary School. The six elements are as follows:

- Convey convictions about a better world
- Facilitate communities of learning
- Strive for pedagogical excellence
- Confront barriers in the school's culture and structures
- Translate ideas into sustainable systems of action
- Nurture a culture of success (Crowther et al., 2009, p. 3)

Second, the role of the principal in the successful operationalization of the fourth C-B dynamic is background, facilitative, and supportive rather than up front, organizational, and directive.

Third, the fourth C-B dynamic requires a degree of intellectual analysis and critique that some will find difficult to connect with the everyday routines of a school, and some may think is better undertaken by external experts, supervisors, and consultants.

Regarding the first of our three points, we note that pedagogical deepening activities at Greenfield and other schools in our research were undertaken through at least five different mechanisms, all of which incorporated teachers as significant leaders:

- A school management team (ISMT) as a collaborative unit
- One or more teacher leaders, with ISMT support

- The ISMT and one or more heads of departments
- Teacher leaders and principal
- The ISMT and principal

Solansky (2008, p. 338) notes the benefits of shared leadership of this type for organizational productivity:

> Shared leadership provides team members with confidence, satisfaction, and ownership. . . . Even though a leader is not designated within a team, one person may still take on this role with or without the overall team's approval and this impacts critical processes within the team that likely impact team performance.

Although the ISMT emerged during the fourth C-B dynamic as the core leadership agency, the structure and function of ISMTs changed regularly at this time in response to changing school circumstances. Some schools made the ISMT an official teaching and learning committee, charged with implementing the SWP, while other schools engaged the deputy principal, and/or the curriculum coordinator, and HODS, to work with the ISMT to develop and implement their SWP framework. Regardless, the capacity of the full professional community of the school to work effectively together, led by the ISMT, invariably matured during this C-B stage.

It is apparent that, for pedagogical deepening to occur successfully in a school, teacher leaders must be involved in very basic ways, encompassing a range of motivational, organizational, intellectual, and mentoring functions. In essence, they need to have well-developed organizational skills, clear convictions regarding the best interests of their students, a capacity to motivate and inspire others, recognition as highly competent classroom practitioners, and, last but not least, special talents in synthesizing a wide range of school-developed ideas into meaningful new constructs. It is a very tall and very important order, but it is possible and carries with it a new sense of professional efficacy. Katzenmeyer and Moller (2001) sum up our position accurately:

> The sense of efficacy encourages teachers to move the locus for student results back into the teaching profession and to place less blame on factors beyond their control, such as the students' home environments. If teachers feel confident in their abilities to be leaders, they will assume responsibility for the learning of all students. (p. 32)

Regarding the second of our three points about leadership for the fourth C-B dynamic, the principal was actively involved in micro-pedagogical deepening in about 50 percent of the research schools, and relatively uninvolved in the remaining cases. In only one instance did the principal assume a superordinate responsibility for directing pedagogical deepening activities. It is also significant that, as pedagogical deepening activities evolved, middle management staff (i.e., HODs, deputies, coordinators) frequently became part of the school's pedagogical leadership team, motivated by their interest in the development of schoolwide accountability systems and the integration of SWP principles with their curriculum subjects. It was very apparent to the researchers that, by this stage of the school development process, both principals and staff had become very familiar with IDEAS Project definitions of parallel leadership and teacher leadership. At IDEAS Project forums, it became the norm for them to describe their "parallel" experiences and recommend for distributed leadership concepts and strategies to colleagues from other schools.

Of importance is that, while principals were not noticeably visible in pedagogical deepening processes in the 13 research schools, it would be wrong to conclude that they were not influential. In most cases, they chose to remain in the background but took an active role in ensuring that teachers followed up on the visioning and SWP outcomes of the previous (third) C-B dynamic. Blasé and Blasé affirm this observation:

> Talking with teachers to promote reflection and promoting professional growth are the two major dimensions of effective instructional leadership. (2000, p. 135)

Regarding our final point about leadership for the fourth C-B dynamic, teacher leaders in the research schools drew on external expertise, networked with other IDEAS facilitators in their region, and accepted opportunities to enhance their leadership and facilitation skills in public forums. As they gained new knowledge from their micro-pedagogical explorations, they used it to design creative workshops, develop classroom action plans, work as mentors, and prepare brochures and media presentations. Murphy (2005, p. 58) cites fellow researchers LeBlanc and Shelton in making a point that we have observed in numerous schools where teachers were provided opportunities to develop their pedadogical expertise and leadership talents simultaneously:

> Teacher leadership is also often associated with *enhanced* creativity: "traditional thinking is challenged and new ways of rethinking old concepts occur . . . the collaboration that results from teacher leadership breaks teachers out of . . . common ruts." (LeBlanc & Shelton, 1997, p. 33, as cited in Murphy, 2005)

The challenge of leadership for micro-pedagogical deepening is therefore certainly substantial. As we have shown, it involves motivating colleagues to undertake personal pedagogical critiques, sharing pedagogical practices and preferred ideas; organizing pedagogical development workshops; synthesizing outcomes for schoolwide application; and integrating schoolwide pedagogical principles with systemic priorities. Is successful school capacity building possible without authentic teacher leadership? The micro-pedagogical deepening research data suggest that the answer to this important question is an unqualified "No."

In summary, leadership for micro-pedagogical deepening requires a trust and belief in both teacher professionalism and teacher leadership that was not part of 20th-century education workplaces, or 20th-century educational leadership thinking. It can be concluded that leadership for micro-pedagogical deepening is distinguished by three qualities:

1. A strategic quality, particularly in mobilizing professional learning experiences that enable serious critique of practice to occur
2. An educative (advocacy) quality, particularly in the brutally honest search for personal values, gifts, and talents in personal and schoolwide pedagogical practices
3. An intellectual quality, particularly in refining original school-based knowledge

To a degree that was not apparent in earlier C-B dynamics, with micro-pedagogical deepening the demands for leadership are centered squarely on teacher leaders. We go so far as to say that, without teacher leadership, the fourth C-B dynamic is not achievable.

THINKING OUTSIDE THE SQUARE: THE GRAMEEN WAY AND MICRO-PEDAGOGICAL DEEPENING

The concept of "deep" professional activity is of course not unique to educational institutions. It is part and parcel of practice in medicine, law, engineering, and, perhaps, all professions. Thus, a great deal is to be learned from exploring deep practice in settings other than education. Here, we consider the extraordinary example of the Grameen Bank in third-world countries such as Bangladesh, where banking practice has been elevated to a level of moral action that many will find surprising. As you review it, ask yourself four questions:

1. To what extent do the Grameen Bank's "Decisions of Commitment" meet the criteria for "meaningful work" (Crowther, 1994)?
2. What is the equivalent of the Grameen Bank's three-level micro-banking system in Greenfield Elementary School's micro-pedagogical deepening work?

3. What lessons for school-based pedagogical development are to be learned from the case of the Grameen way?

4. Which of the four leadership approaches that we have identified as dominant in educational practice (transformational, advocacy, strategic, organizationwide) do you think are most relevant in creating and sustaining depth in the work of the Grameen Bank?

The entrenched poverty and associated lack of quality of life for people in third-world countries are sources of widespread global concern. But glimmers of hope do exist.

The Grameen Bank is one such glimmer. It is a micro-credit/microlending process that was developed in Bangladesh about 30 years ago by economist Muhammad Yunus. Yunus's goal was to create a bank that would increase opportunities for people in impoverished communities to enhance their individual and collective well-being. The highly inspirational vision of the Grameen Bank—*Creating a world without poverty: social business transforming lives*—derives from a banking philosophy that some would regard as revolutionary: removal of collateral requirements and creation of a finance system built on mutual trust, accountability, participation, and creativity (United Nations Educational, Scientific and Cultural Organization, n.d.).

The Grameen Bank rejected conventional banking methodologies and created its own, based on five beliefs:

- The bank should go to the people.
- Credit is a human right.
- Credit should be based on trust, not on legal procedures and systems.
- The poor have unutilized or underutilized skills.
- The poor, particularly women, need help to help themselves.

Charity is not part of the Grameen way, since the bank asserts that charity "creates dependency and takes away an individual's initiative to break through walls of poverty. Unleashing of energy and creativity in each human being is the answer to poverty" (Grameen Bank, n.d.).

In Grameen projects, borrowers engage with a local group that is committed to growing their entrepreneurial capacities together. They aspire to become self-employed, generating income, building savings, and obtaining quality housing.

The Grameen Bank's operating principles, or "protocols," are in Table 5.5. The "16 Decisions of Commitment" can be regarded as the equivalent of principles of teaching and/or learning of the type developed by Greenfield Elementary School. Borrowers are encouraged to use the 16 Decisions of Commitment as a philosophical and practical guide in their involvement with Grameen Bank agents, as well as in their work in their communities and in their personal development.

"Micro-pedagogical deepening" of the 16 decisions or protocols in the work and lives of people in their communities is fundamental to the Grameen Bank's philosophy. It is a highly complex process that can be construed as encompassing three levels of activity. At the *surface* level, the bank trains field-workers to become expert change agents, providing support in village workplaces. Many field-workers begin their training as interns, developing new skills to meet specific objectives and engaging in "prac" visits to field sites. The expert field-workers are trained to identify and develop natural talents in their clienteles.

At the *middle* level, individuals are encouraged to explore ways to utilize the Grameen 16 Decisions to their individual entrepreneurial advantage. At this level, borrowers endeavor to turn basic knowledge and talents into the

Table 5.5 The Grameen Bank's 16 Decisions of Commitment

The Healthy Living Principle:
• We shall plan small families. • We shall look after our health, and build and use pit-latrines. • We shall always keep our children and environment clean. • We shall drink water from tubewells (or boil water or use alum).
The Collective Responsibility Principle: • We shall take part in social activities collectively. • We shall collectively undertake bigger investments for higher incomes. • We shall always be ready to help each other. • We shall minimize our expenditures and save.
The Courage and Social Justice Principle: • We shall not practice child marriage. • We shall not permit injustice. • We shall keep our centre free from the curse of dowry. • We shall all maintain center discipline.
The High Expectations Principle: • We shall seasonally plant as many seedlings as possible. • We shall not live in dilapidated houses. • We shall ensure our children are educated. • We shall grow, eat, and sell vegetables all year round.

SOURCE: Modified from www.grameen-info.org/.

ability to become self-sufficient. Borrower status invariably rises accordingly, dependence on male-based cultural norms diminishes, and improved housing quality as well as enhanced nutrition and education begin to move families out of the cycle of poverty. "Conversations" facilitated by field-workers nurture preparatory communication and leadership capabilities of the type that are fundamental to individual self-actualization.

At the Grameen way's *deepest* level, adherence to the 16 Decisions enables borrowers to become "mindful" of their work practice and the effects of their practices on their personal and collective self. At this advanced stage of development, involving intensive micro-analysis of individual and collective action, decisions are viewed as a group responsibility. All 16 criteria associated with the four principles are used to critique actions and decisions. Highly successful new entrepreneurs are encouraged to become Grameen way mentors and role models.

Thus, "deepening" in the Grameen way encompasses individual and collective consciousness raising and problem solving through three distinct levels. Is such a process applicable in the work of schools? We believe so. We call it micro-pedagogical deepening.

TWO POSTSCRIPTS

Detailed research by Larance (1998) in Grameen way communities identified more than 20 important transformations, including the following:

- Seventy-eight percent of participating citizens felt much more valued.
- The majority of borrowers' families crossed the poverty line.
- Economic partnerships developed between people of different religious and social backgrounds.
- As trust developed, borrowing and lending practices increased.
- Many women developed a new sense of individual identity.
- Collective responsibility for child welfare increased.

Second, in 1996, the founder of the Grameen way, Muhammad Yunus, and the bank itself were awarded the Nobel Prize.

CONCLUSION

In this chapter we have established the critical importance of a radical new concept—micro-pedagogical deepening—and outlined its key characteristics from both practical and scholarly perspectives in successful C-B. We have taken the position that pedagogical deepening constitutes the core work of expert teachers. It is the micro-pedagogical deepening dynamic where the growth in schoolwide teacher excellence and expertise achieve full maturity. Without pedagogical deepening, we believe that school quality cannot be enhanced on a sustained basis. Thus, the micro-pedagogical deepening dynamic is the locus of our C-B framework.

The leadership implications of pedagogical deepening are also readily apparent. For pedagogical deepening to occur, teachers who either are or aspire to become expert practitioners must be accorded opportunities to engage in processes of reflection, creation, exploration, application, and critique. This can only occur if the facilitators of the school's developmental work are themselves committed, practice oriented, contextually sensitive, and highly professional—in other words, teacher leaders. But without the support and encouragement of competent school principals, it is doubtful if prospective teacher leaders will volunteer their time and energy, or whether they will seek the sort of mature expertise that is contained in our Teachers as Leaders Framework (Resource A). Thus, the concept of parallel leadership emerges as fundamental to the micro-pedagogical deepening C-B dynamic.

COSMIC C-B SIMULATION 4—DIVING DEEP INTO YOUR PEDAGOGY

MICRO-PEDAGOGICAL DEEPENING: BUILDING PERSONAL CAPACITY

Purpose:

The purpose of this exercise is to provide the opportunity for school leaders to explore the meaning of micro-pedagogical deepening through a simulation bearing analogous resemblance to pedagogical deepening, namely deep sea reef diving.

Rationale:

Micro-pedagogical deepening is a very powerful—but also very new—educational concept. It can be argued that "depth" is central to the work of any mature profession. How do you make it a part of your professional profile? How can you contribute to it across your school? As a result of your experience with this deep sea diving simulation, you will be better prepared to lead the way into the world of 21st-century enriched educational practice and sustained capacity building.

But, you may ask, how is that possible—how could deep sea diving possibly be used to illuminate micro-pedagogical deepening?

Consider this scenario.

Five members of the Green Reef Scuba Diving Instructional Team (GRIT), of which you are a member, are planning a deep sea reef dive off the eastern shoreline of Kaneohe Bay in Oahu, Hawaii. Their purpose is to gain hands-on experience before leading their own dives in the coming weeks. The team is affiliated with the United Team Diving organization, and in accordance with their strict certification process, all team members possess open water diving certification. (The open water certification is the "beginner diving instructor classification" and indicates competency to dive to depths of 18 meters). Three levels of skill are present in your five-member team:

- **Open Water Diver–Level Instructors (i.e., beginner diving instructors)** have participated in multiple dives elsewhere but have never led a dive beyond 18 meters and are unfamiliar with diving as a team endeavor. In preparation for the team dives to come next week, they have learned diver signals and how to air-share if necessary and have refreshed their understanding of diver decompression tables.
- **Advanced Diver–Level Instructors (i.e., proficient diving instructors)** have experience diving beyond 18 meters, and in Kaneohe Bay waters, but have not led dives in here. They have certification in safety and equipment management and are used to diving in teams, using buddy systems. In preparation for the dive to come, they have identified and logged the essential components of the dive in order to ensure all safety procedures are in place, weather conditions have been taken into account, and contingency plans have been formulated in the event of an encounter with the many reef dangers that abound.

- **Dive Master–Level Instructors (i.e., lead diving instructors)** have led deep sea diving sessions around the reefs in Kaneohe Bay and in similar locations off the Hawaiian Islands and internationally. Possessing dive master certification means that a diver has also undergone intensive training in rescue and emergency diving situations, has dived at great depths, and has shouldered the responsibility of ensuring quality instruction for less certified divers.

Dive masters have the expertise to deal with stress in others and the inner strength to assist others when the unexpected occurs. They are experts who wish to share their excitement and love of the underwater wonderland with other GRIT team members, while aiming to develop in their less-experienced colleagues an understanding of the exciting Kaneohe Bay reef area and the confidence and skill to lead dives of their own in the weeks ahead.

Drawing on knowledge from the United Team Diving guidelines (www.unifiedteamdiving.com/), GRIT team members have developed their own principles of practice (Exhibit 5.A).

Exhibit 5.A

The GRIT vision:

Diving together–

- Exploring our waters
- Enjoying our diving
- Protecting our depths

The GRIT principles of practice:

- **Inclusion**–catering for all levels of scuba diving abilities
- **Collaboration**–mentoring and challenging dive members to build personal diving capabilities
- **Connection**–networking with marine authorities and reef-centered industries to maintain the health of the waters and reefs
- **Understanding**–developing deep knowledge of the cartographic features of the underwater worlds around the Kaneohe Bay Islands
- **Reflection**–reviewing dive experiences to enhance proficiency from each new diving experience

It is the agreed view of the team that the GRIT principles of practice are essential to guide all dives, regardless of the level of certification of the formal leader. Thus, in today's Keneohe Bay trial dive, all participants will have the principles in mind.

The rationale for this micro-pedagogical deepening simulation lies mainly in the first requirement of deep pedagogical practice—developing personal gifts and talents to become an expert practitioner.

Organization:

Teams of five

Approximate time required:

Allow 1.5–2 hours, preferably in two sessions.

Materials for each individual:

- Exhibit 5.A—The GRIT vision and principles of practice
- Exhibit 5.B—The GRIT diving talents list
- Exhibit 5.C—GRIT Learning Log

Session One

The Day Before the Dive

Step 1—*Assigning roles for tomorrow's dive.* Place yourself in the role of one of the five-member GRIT team. Assign instructor-level roles on the following basis: one dive master–level instructor (whose name is "Mac"), two advanced-level dive instructors, and two open water–level dive instructors.

Each individual diver selects specialized talents and expertise from the GRIT diving talents list (Exhibit 5.B). Note: The dive master–level instructor selects *five* talents from the list, the two advanced-level dive instructors select *three* talents, and the two open water–level dive instructors select *one* talent.

With the Kaneohe Bay GRIT Team trial dive to take place tomorrow, your dive master, Mac, has asked all team members to commence a new entry in their GRIT Learning Log (Exhibit 5.C). Please complete 1 through 6 of the log now. Some negotiation within the team may be needed to ensure that all ten GRIT diving talents (Exhibit 5.B) are assigned. Mac should facilitate this decision process.

Exhibit 5.B

GRIT diving talents:

- Endurance swimming
- In-depth knowledge of the Kaneohe Bay Islands coastline and reefs
- Nautical mechanics skills
- International diving experience

- Small-group leader experience
- Deep sea diving expertise
- Emergency deep sea experience
- Kaneohe Bay Islands diving experience
- Marine geology knowledge
- Knowledge of marine poisons and experience with treatments

Exhibit 5.C

My GRIT Learning Log—Contributions and new skills:

(i) My current certification level
(ii) My aspirational certification level
(iii) My special expertise(s)
(iv) My aspirational expertise(s)
(v) Colleague(s) with expertise I aspire to achieve
(vi) A personal challenge during the dive
(vii) New learning as a result of the dive

Step 2—*Mac's expectations.* The dive master, Mac, reiterates the importance of improving team practice by reminding the team of the following:

1. Without the skills and knowledge of expert instructors, diving students (your clients) run the risk of being inadequately skilled to face the turbulent currents and other dangers they may encounter off the reefs surrounding Kaneohe Bay. Thus, team members should aim to (a) enhance their personal capabilities and (b) learn from each other's diving talents. (The dive master acknowledges that the goal for him relates to an internal quest for greater expertise as a leader.)
2. It is the responsibility of each team member to enhance his or her personal talents in at least one of the ten talent areas in order to pursue the next level of certification while also contributing to the growth of one or more colleagues.

Mac invites all team members to reflect on and share the talents, gifts, and needs that they bring to the diving team and to the dive. During the discussion, he periodically refers to the GRIT vision and principles of practice as well as to team members' established talents and current levels of proficiency.

Session Two

The GRIT Team Dive

Step 1—*Your dive.* Embellish the description that follows, using your assigned talents, your imagination, details in the dive master's account, and whatever actual diving expertise you have. Also take into account your assigned instructor level. Each diver should try to make three or more entries.

Each of us has slipped over the side of the boat and entered our special world. I share this world with my colleagues while sparkling, elongated shapes flash past and a deep sea turtle glides effortlessly toward me. We are at one with each other and our world. I am at peace—and feel safe and secure in this world of unknowns.

Mac, our dive master, has asked us to note that on our return to shore we will reflect on how we managed the challenge and see where improvements can be made before we lead our formal dives next week.

Already I can clearly see how worthwhile it was to check on the cartographic maps for this dive as it has made it clear that the drop off the reef into the deep boat channel is incredibly sharp. The overhang from the reef edge from where we are diving hides that to some degree because of the kelp build-up that seems to go hand in hand with destruction of the coral.

I am close to my next level of certification and will be able to note signal directions if need be. That is just as well because right now I sense danger of some sort. I mustn't panic, but where is help if I need it?

Here comes someone to see if I am okay—I can see her signalling Mac to check where the rest of the divers are. He glances quickly around and sees one of the team going right out of reach. In no time at all, the diver who had checked on me swims straight out to him or her and is able to stop the wandering diver from going over the drop.

I wonder whether this is really what she should have done! After all, I could be dying!

___

___

___

I can see she needed to go—but perhaps we need some other method of alerting others to an emergency situation because the rest of the team are just going about their business unaware of what is happening.

Ah-h-h! Someone has checked and seen that the danger point has passed. She alerts the rest of us that all is okay. Good! She is a new member of our team and it is obvious that she has remembered our GRIT principle of "never losing sight of the diver on either side of you." There is our newest diver now and he is tiring. He is using hand signals to indicate that he wants to return to the boat. We all go, as we stick together, no matter what.

I think I may be struggling a little too—I feel as if I have lost strength.

Step 2—*The debrief.* Back at shore and after a warm shower and a drink, each team member reflects on the dive and writes up their log (Exhibit 5.C, item 6). Each team member shares what he or she has written and discusses what worked well for him or her and what did not. Mac leads discussion of the following questions:

- How did you use your talent(s) to contribute to the dive?
- What new insights do you now have about yourself as a diver?
- What is the deepest level of diving expertise that you need in order to meet your aspirations for successful diving? What must you do in order to achieve that level? How did this dive help (or not help)?
- What of importance have we as a team learned about the GRIT principle of "collaboration"? How was the intent of that principle evident during the dive? What refinements are needed?
- What additional understanding do we need before next week's official dive?

Step 3—*Back to pedagogical deepening.* As a group, complete the following chart:

Comparing "Deepening" in Recreational, Human Service, and School Context

Context	*Level One*	*Level Two*	*Level Three*
Grameen	*16 Decisions*		
Greenfield			*Literacy applications of learning framework*
Kaneohe		*(i) Instructor level capabilities* *(ii) Personal talents*	

- What is your definition of each level of deepening?
- What balance do you think is desirable in your school among the three levels?

Step 4–*Pedagogical deepening and your school.* Complete the Step 3 "Deepening" chart as it applies specifically to your school. What developmental work is required at each of the three levels? What leadership role do you see for yourself in getting an appropriate three-level developmental process underway?

Step 5–*Congratulations!* You have developed a working knowledge and understanding of micro-pedagogical deepening, the most complex of the C-B dynamics and a critically important construct for the 21st-century teaching profession.

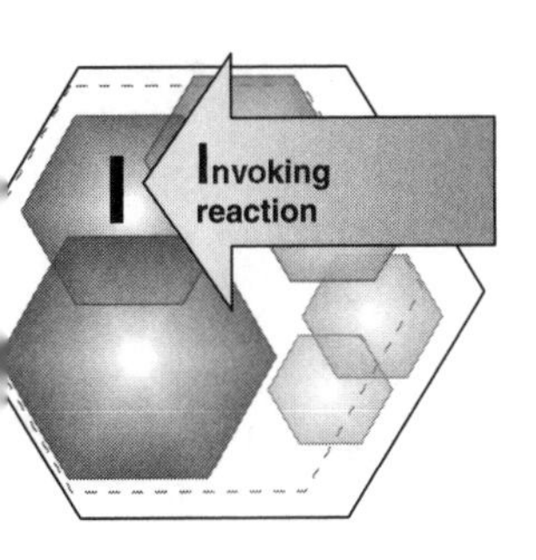

6

The Fifth C-B Dynamic

Invoking Reaction

(Prepared in collaboration with Dr. Joan Conway and Ms. Shauna Petersen)

> *During my lifetime I have dedicated myself to this struggle of the African people. . . . I have cherished the ideal of a democratic and free society. . . . It is an ideal which I hope to live for and achieve. But if needs be, it is an ideal for which I am prepared to die.*
>
> —Nelson Mandela
> (Pretoria, April 20, 1964, quoted in Montefiore, 2005, p. 133)

INTRODUCTION

In previous chapters we have seen how schools seeking to improve the quality of their outcomes must first establish that they are "in tune" and then create significant new educational knowledge, preferably incorporating an inspiring vision and a highly meaningful schoolwide pedagogical framework. Those tasks accomplished, they can approach the challenge of classroom-based pedagogical enhancement with a sense of mutual trust, shared understanding, and collective motivation. But that is not the end of their school improvement journey. To the contrary, for sustained improvement to occur, a school must subject its educational products to intense internal and external scrutiny.

The intent of the *invoking reaction* C-B dynamic is captured dramatically in our compelling opening statement from Nelson Mandela, made at his trial for sabotage and attempted violent overthrow of the South African regime in 1964. In his speech, he affirmed his deep convictions; outlined how he had acted upon those convictions; and appealed for widespread support for the work of the "spear of the nation" movement.

Mandela's speech "invoked reaction" that was extraordinary in terms of law, politics, and public consciousness. Government apartheid policy in South Africa subsequently became more intense and more insipid—though temporarily so. And, within the country's population, the speech inspired a range of extraordinary responses, including deep fear, intense anger, and fervent hope, as well as new consciousness of the intolerable injustices of political, economic, and social life in South Africa. It may well be said, in retrospect, that Mandela's speech proved a turning point in the history of South Africa. Such is the potential power of a carefully articulated statement that has been developed in response to a matter of societal or community importance.

We of course do not envision educational leaders confronting circumstances as challenging, or consequences as daunting, as those that confronted Nelson Mandela. But the invoking reaction dynamic has much deeper meaning and greater importance in the world of educational leaders than has historically been presumed. Thus, in this chapter, we examine some of the core processes associated with it. We proceed to do this through three steps: exploration of a case study from our research schools, discussion of the meaning of invoking reaction in educational literature and research, and discussion of the fifth C-B dynamic's school-based leadership implications. That done, we proceed to explore a non-educational exemplar of invoking reaction, namely the work of MSF (Médecins Sans Frontières, or Doctors Without Borders), and provide an exercise to assist you to develop invoking reaction leadership capabilities for application in your school context.

A SNAPSHOT OF INVOKING REACTION

EACHAM HIGH SCHOOL

When Creativity Becomes a Bore . . .

Eacham High School is a single-campus school with an enrollment in 2008 of 1340 students, mostly from English-speaking backgrounds, and a teaching staff of 82 full-time and 20 part-time professionals. Founded in 1926, Eacham is located in leafy environs 17 km northeast of a major city.

In the 1960s and 1970s, the area was home to enclaves of creative artists and performers who sought alternative lifestyles. While the local population today is more mainstream, values of social justice, creativity, and individual expression are still evident and reflected in the school's long-standing "Deeds Count" motto.

But by 2004, Eacham High was a school in the doldrums. While student achievement levels were relatively high, serious issues were identified from IDEAS Project diagnostic surveys in early 2005:

- Teachers were tired and felt overly burdened by systemic change.
- With an inordinate proportion of teachers about to retire, there was a danger that much of the school's accumulated expertise would be lost.
- While the culture was regarded as unique, with its origins in 1970s artists, performers, and cultists, no one in 2004 could explain or justify it clearly.
- Teacher professionalism was neither valued nor encouraged, resulting in low professional morale.
- Constructive, systematic use of student data in teachers' planning and decision making was rare.

Responding Pedagogically

When the Eacham school improvement journey formally commenced in 2005, the project facilitator (the deputy principal) immediately established a committed school project management team. This team led the school staff and students through a series of team-building and values-clarification workshops that resulted in the development of a new statement of purpose:

> At Eacham High School each person feels safe to be themselves and challenged to think critically, work in teams, show leadership, and achieve success along many pathways.

As described by members of the school project management team,

> The purpose statement has crystallized our unique culture for newer staff, provided a framework for discussing behavior with students, provided a framework to align school procedures and processes, and formed the basis of a different style of communication to portray Eacham's culture to the community.

What had been tacit became explicit. The purpose statement was printed in student diaries and school publicity brochures, posted on the walls in all rooms of the school, and used by the principal to demonstrate aspects of school practice at meetings with parents and students. The project facilitator explained the next stage of the process (i.e., pedagogical development) this way:

> We spent nearly 10 months investigating our personal pedagogies in relation to our statement of purpose and also exploring a number of authoritative pedagogies that seemed relevant to us. We then distilled six principles of teaching and learning that were based on our priority concepts of best practice in teaching.

To facilitate the implementation of the Eacham schoolwide pedagogical framework (Figure 6.1) in classrooms, the school management team worked with the learning areas' heads to devise a Unit Planning Template (Figure 6.2). The aim of this resource was to provide professional stimulus for groups of teachers who worked closely together but might not otherwise see themselves as having common interests:

> It (the Planning Template) encouraged teachers to consider multiple aspects of the six Eacham teaching and learning principles within their individual subjects. Then, by sharing their individual approaches in teaching a principle, the foundations were laid for consistency, transfer, and reinforcement in the learning experiences of students. (Project Facilitator)

Over the next year, the Unit Planning Template came to be used to plan and review all new units of study in Eacham High School. It also became the framework for a wide range of other planning activities, including facilities construction, professional learning, and staff recruitment.

When the IDEAS Project diagnostic surveys were readministered in years three and four of the improvement project, teacher morale had increased dramatically, as had student and parent perceptions of the significance of their school in their lives.

Invoking Reaction, the Eacham Way

Intertwined with the developmental process at Eacham is a complex perspective on the invoking reaction C-B dynamic.

First, the concept of organizational critique was used comprehensively, particularly through the Unit Planning Template, to build accountability into teachers' initiatives to enhance their individual and schoolwide pedagogical development. Teachers used the template to critique their personal pedagogy and to share pedagogical ideas. Self-critique, public accountability, and mentoring were equally prominent features of this process. As described by one teacher leader,

> The template makes professional learning a joy while also retaining for me as a teacher the intellectual challenge of creating new ideas and the satisfaction of knowing you are visibly accountable.

Another significant organizational critique emphasis at Eacham, as a result of their vision and pedagogical developments, related to school-based leadership: parallel leadership was formally endorsed as a process and was extended to incorporate student leadership roles and functions, individually and in teams. Most particularly, students engaged on a regular basis in analysis of the pedagogical framework as it related to their learning processes.

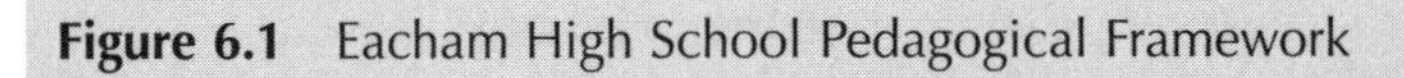

Figure 6.1 Eacham High School Pedagogical Framework

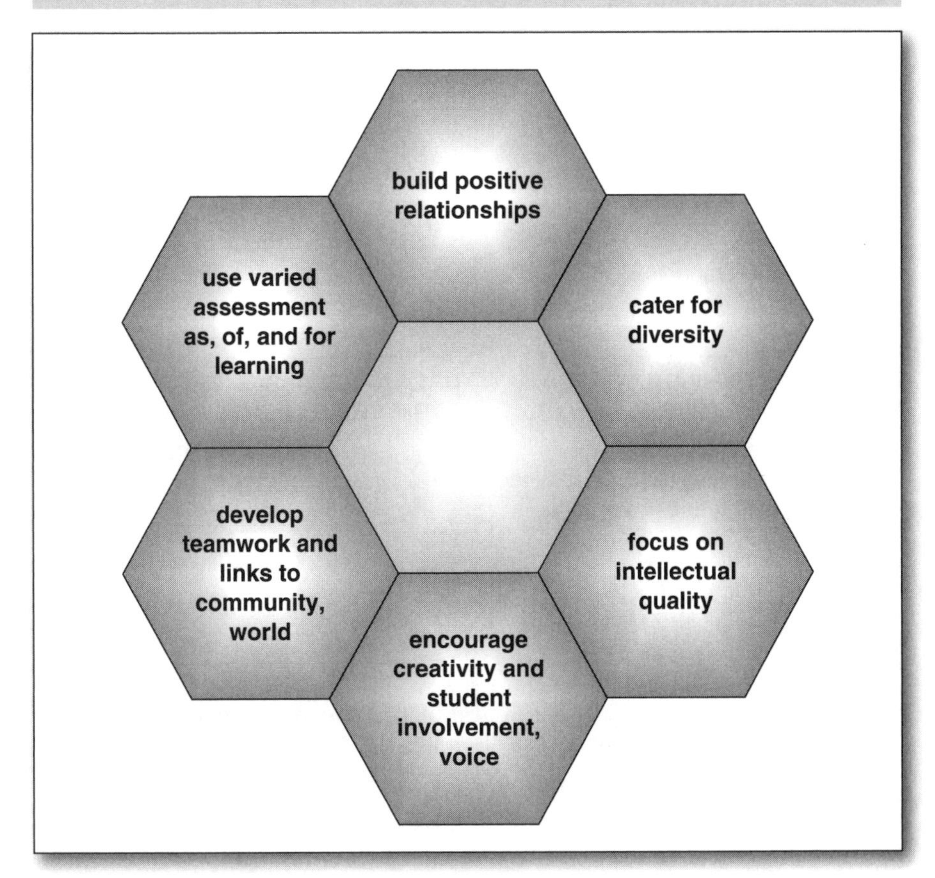

Figure 6.2 Unit Planning Template

<table>
<tr><th colspan="2">EACHAM PLANNING TEMPLATE</th></tr>
<tr><td>UNIT DESCRIPTION:</td><td>BUILD POSITIVE RELATIONSHIPS:
What interactive strategies do I need to focus on?</td></tr>
<tr><td colspan="2">FOCUS ON INTELLECTUAL QUALITY:
What are the deep understandings (key concepts) that need to be gained?
What skills and processes will be taught?
What thinking skills will I focus on?</td></tr>
<tr><td>CATER FOR DIVERSITY:
How will we determine students' special needs and talents?
How will students' different learning styles be catered for?
What enrichment/enhancement opportunities will I provide?
What modification will I make for special needs students?</td><td>ENCOURAGE CREATIVITY, STUDENT INVOLVEMENT, & VOICE:
How will creativity be encouraged?
What choices will students have within the activities and assessment tasks?
How will students' learning goals be negotiated, monitored, and evaluated?</td></tr>
<tr><td>DEVELOP TEAMWORK & COMMUNITY & GLOBAL LINKS:
Why will students see this unit as relevant now and in the future? What real-life issues or problems will be explored?
How will students be able to show leadership, work in teams?
How can we link the students to the community?</td><td>USE VARIED ASSESSMENT STRATEGIES "AS, OF, & FOR":
What samples and modeling need to be provided for the tasks?
How will students demonstrate their knowledge and skills
• as they are learning (formative)?
• of the learning (summative)?
• for future learning (metacognitive)?
How will success be celebrated?</td></tr>
</table>

Third, heads of departments used the template to build schoolwide understandings and applications of the school's schoolwide pedagogical framework (SWP):

> Linking teachers in multidisciplinary groups to complete the Unit Planning Template and compare their products had the effect of inspiring them in their work—it facilitated formal and informal professional development from different perspectives, a new experience for most. (Project Facilitator)

Fourth, the internal emphasis on teacher leadership led to a major new external networking role for teacher leaders:

> Previously, I would never have put myself forward to be a public face for the school. However, speaking on several occasions about the work we've done with our school improvement process and the template has given me confidence. So when the principal asked if I'd like to attend a certain conference, I found myself thinking, "Yes, I can do that." Sharing in a public arena seems to create a type of backwash for refining what we've done and what we're doing, and then an assurance that we've got more to share.

Finally, the Eacham principal, deputy, and teacher leaders joined a national school improvement network and became heavily involved in professional advocacy of the IDEAS Project. Student leaders also participated in activities of these types, joining staff in explaining their vision, values, and schoolwide approach to pedagogy to state, national, and international visitors to the school. In responding to questions, comments, and critiques of their presentation, they engaged in forms of invoking reaction not previously contemplated and in so doing had significant influence on state and national policy agendas.

Eacham's 1960s image of cutting-edge educational leadership has been largely restored, and continues to grow.

INVOKING REACTION: DEEPENING OUR UNDERSTANDING

We saw in the opening quote for this chapter what can happen when leaders with deep convictions regarding a cause, a capacity to mobilize human and material resources, and a flair for passionate communication decide to take their ideas into public arenas. Worlds can change as a result.

We saw in the Eacham case study that school leaders—the principal, deputy principal, and teacher leaders—brought about significant educational enhancements by placing their school's newly created knowledge in public arenas and engaging with a range of communities to critique, refine, and enrich that knowledge. Based on our own research, supplemented by the considered views of a range of international authorities, we conclude that the fifth C-B dynamic, invoking reaction, is essential to sustained capacity building and has three components: organizational self-critique, strategic networking, and professional advocacy.

Organizational Self-Critique

Understanding of the construct of organizational self-critique in school revitalization has evolved largely from the pioneering work of Argyris and Schon in the 1970s. To these theorists, successful organizational learning is inseparable from ongoing reflection and challenging of basic workplace assumptions. Argyris and Schon's distinction between single- and double-loop learning captures the difference between systematic, surface evaluation on the one hand and deep, values-based interrogation on the other. They state that double-loop learning in an organization is possible when

> individuals within an organization experience a problematic situation and inquire into it on the organization's behalf. They experience a surprising mismatch . . . and respond to the mismatch through a process of thought and further action that leads them to modify their images of organization. (as cited in Robinson, 2001, p. 60)

Parker Palmer (2007, p. 11) also notes the power of double-loop-type learning in consciousness raising in organizations such as schools:

> A disciplined process of group reflection—whether that means a team working on a long-term problem or two people assessing a crisis—can help us distinguish between the emotions that illuminate our environment and those that simply reveal our shadows.

The teachers at Geographe School who critiqued their personal values and their professional practice to create the Pedagogical Leadership Charter that is in Figure 6.3 engaged in a form of double-loop learning. That is, they examined deep-seated personal values, linked their convictions to their students' needs, placed their pedagogical practices under a microscope, and then went public with their shared commitments, inviting reaction from their school community.

In the case studies that provided the basis for our research, both forms of "loop learning" were used to invoke audience reaction. Single-loop learning

Figure 6.3 The Geographe Elementary School Charter for Educational Success

Our Pedagogical Leadership Charter

In our school we want our students to become active, well-informed thinkers who question, take an ethical stance, and engage creatively in their communities.

To do this, our students will engage in learning experiences where they learn how to discover, how to reflect, how to analyze, and how to express themselves.

Our teachers will assist by modelling our learning approach, designing experiences for students, and engaging collaboratively across the school.

(Printed with permission of Mr. Tim Baker, principal, Geographe Elementary School)

was evident when, for example, feedback at cluster meetings resulted in adjustments being made to the detail and format of pedagogical principles. Double-loop learning was evident when, for example, the values underpinning a vision statement were challenged on social justice grounds and subsequently rethought by the IDEAS school management team of the school in question.

Sharing and Refining New Knowledge Through Strategic Networks

Strategic networks in modern organizations can be either internal or external (Limerick, Cunnington, & Crowther, 2002, p. 62). Internal networks enable the various components of an organization to manage themselves as autonomous parts, while collaborating with other components of the organization. Internal networks are particularly important in knowledge organizations such as schools because they enable synergies to evolve in relatively natural and unforced ways (Limerick et al., 2002, p. 63).

External networking is important in modern organizations because of the increasing difficulty of doing everything in-house (Limerick et al., 2002, p. 68) and because the fact of discontinuous change places huge demands on organizations to learn from the best practices of others, using a range of strategic alliances. Thus, a recent international report highlighted that the "best leaders take responsibility for improvements in weaker schools" and asserted that, generically speaking, schools should take responsibility for each other's improvement through sharing their own successes, engaging collaboratively in problem solving in relation to site-specific issues, and establishing ongoing cluster dialogue (National College for Leadership of Schools and Children's Service, 2009, pp. 30–32). It goes without saying that this concept represents a dramatic departure from standard practice in most school systems. Michael Fullan (2005a, p. 17) has summed up this point as an element of what he calls "lateral capacity-building":

> Such purposeful interaction accomplishes two things: Quality knowledge is shared and sorted; and mutual commitment is generated. Mobilizing the minds and hearts of people across the district is the key to deeper, lasting reform.

Louise Stoll (2009, p. 123) has also recently made pointedly clear both the power and changing meaning of external networking as an educational concept:

> Networking knows no borders. School leaders, teachers, students, and whole schools in different countries now link up with each other, sharing across cultural boundaries.

External networking was readily observable in cluster activities in the IDEAS Project where some schools undertook continuous joint developmental work and borrowed from each other's pedagogical experiences. Also very important was the role of the university project team. Perhaps most notably, information systems have been built to create "diasporas" that extend from Sicily to Australia, from public to Catholic schools, and from early years to postcompulsory levels. What participants have in common, as they come together through teleconferencing, chat rooms, Skype, e-mail, and short message service, is their common interest in "invoking reaction" to their school-based developmental work.

As a final word, it would be wrong to assume that networking is an unproblematic concept. Karen Seashore Louis (2008, p. 53) summed up the internal–external networking functions of PLCs (professional learning communities), as representing a major ongoing challenge for school leaders:

> PLCs need both to look inward, taking advantage of the unexplored talents of staff members and creating cohesiveness around the goal of student learning, and to look outward. The strain between focusing on the individuals who want to participate in professional groups outside the school . . . and the need to create internally focused work groups is a persistent issue for PLCs.

Professional Advocacy of Newly Created Ideas and Values

At the invoking reaction stage of the C-B process, leaders in the research schools believed they had something important to share with the educational world, something that would inspire other educators but that would itself benefit from the considered analysis and critique of other professionals. As powerful new networks developed, some participants undertook to speak out on issues of importance to them, having influence that extended widely, including to the publication of this book.

Advocacy is linked to the exercise of power in that it can be used either to work in the favor of individuals or to influence a system in ways that will benefit disadvantaged groups in society (MacBeath, 2006a, p. 7). When renowned U.S. leadership philosopher William Foster spoke of educational administrators' moral obligation "to develop, challenge and liberate human souls" (1986, p. 18, in Lindle, 2004, p. 169), he clearly had the notion of professional advocacy in mind. That said, Kathleen Brown (2004, p. 96) has noted the extreme difficulty of advocacy for some educational leaders, pointing out that "establishing a dialogic context can be complicated, difficult, and frightening." Bill Mulford has also acknowledged such difficulties but has proposed a purposeful response: "Rather than rely on bureaucracy or new public management, schools need to become professional learning organizations, consciously and continually pursuing quality improvement" (2004, p. 633). Terry Wrigley (2006, p. 11) notes the power of collective professional engagement when educators contemplate advocacy of a cause:

> Together, our voices will be stronger and our efforts will bear fruit. We can overcome the limitations of today's schools. Through collective struggle we can fulfil our dreams of a better education and a better world.

The concept of teacher leadership as we have conceptualized it has a strong advocacy dimension, as reflected in the fourth element of our Teachers as Leaders Framework (see Resource A):

Confront barriers in the school's culture and structures by

- standing up for children, especially disadvantaged and marginalized individuals and groups
- working with administrators to find solutions to issues of equity, fairness, and justice
- encouraging student "voice" in ways that are sensitive to students' developmental stages and circumstances (Crowther, Ferguson, & Hann, 2009, p. 3)

Finally, Judyth Sachs's (2003) concept of "activist teacher professionalism" focuses on a number of key principles that resonate with the advocacy aspect of the invoking reaction dynamic: fostering inclusiveness, encouraging collective and collaborative action, communicating effectively, recognizing the expertise of all parties involved, creating an environment of trust and mutual respect, behaving with ethical practice, being responsive and responsible, acting with passion, and, last but not least, experiencing pleasure and having fun.

In summary, the understandings that we have developed from the literature and from our research lead us to the following definition:

Invoking reaction involves the refinement, validation, and dissemination of significant new school-based knowledge through organizational self-critique, internal and external strategy networking, and professional advocacy.

- *Organizational self-critique* is undertaken through processes of single- and double-loop learning. It involves the sharing and affirmation of newly created knowledge for purposes of the affirmation and/or critique of that knowledge.
- *Strategic networking* can be both internal or external to an organization. It enables synergies to be developed through communications strategies, ongoing sharing of professional practices, and refining through feedback mechanisms.
- *Professional advocacy* involves taking a principled stance in support of a relatively powerless, marginalized or deprived group or individual, and then taking action on behalf of that group or individual.

LEADERSHIP FOR INVOKING REACTION

In considering the invoking reaction C-B dynamic from a school leadership point of view, it is apparent that four broad areas of leadership-related activity are involved:

- The activation of internal networks (i.e., PLCs) to facilitate intradepartment and cross-grade critique and implementation of schoolwide pedagogical principles
- The mobilization of external forums, clusters, and networks to enable dissemination of school-developed products, and critique of those products (particularly visions, values, and schoolwide pedagogical frameworks)
- The articulation of newly created knowledge—in public forums and media presentations—to clarify and refine the school's vision, pedagogy, and cultural values for the school community

- Advocacy for enhanced school improvement processes and teacher leadership opportunities with system officials

A number of important implications for school-based leadership emerge from this analysis.

First, leadership of the invoking reaction dynamic locates school leaders squarely in public arenas, with a range of attendant challenges. To Thompson (2004), this necessitates that leaders understand that the exercise of "social power" is fundamentally a moral responsibility. Effective leaders, he says, always keep in mind the "right and good":

> They engage with others in building, by example and constructive effort, an environment within which individuals and groups are free and encouraged to discern and actualize the right and the good in fulfilment of shared goals, values and purpose. (p. 28)

In similar vein, Munby (2009, p. 30) has noted a new "ethical" responsibility of school leadership as a result of growing understanding of the interrelatedness of networking and accountability:

> There is an increasing expectation that the best leaders will take responsibility for improvements in weaker schools. This represents a fundamental change in the responsibilities of senior school leaders.

Fullan has also addressed this point, following his research into highly successful school districts:

> District leaders constantly communicate the moral purpose. They make it clear that everyone has a responsibility for changing the larger education context for the better. (2005b, p. 68)

When Eacham's principal and teacher leaders undertook to place their developmental work in national and international arenas, explicating for diverse audiences how their Deeds Count motto, pedagogical framework, and Unit Planning Template had rejuvenated not just their school but their community, it could be said that they were directed by a clear sense of "moral purpose."

Second, leadership for the fifth C-B dynamic is inseparable from advanced forms of accountability. Wood and Winston (2005, p. 86) have noted that accountability in 21st-century contexts has three components, all of which are discernible in the Eacham case study—acceptance of responsibility, voluntary transparency, and answerability. Bottery (2008, p. 18) makes a similar point regarding school leadership and what he calls proactivity and reflexivity:

> Educational leaders . . . need to work towards developing proactive and reflexive forms of accountability, ones which are not simply of the form which are "done" to them, but to whose definition and scope they contribute.

When the Eacham principal and key teacher leaders encouraged the school's seven heads of department to use the school's Unit Planning Template to explore their new SWP in all seven disciplinary areas, they can be said to have entered the advanced accountability territory proposed by Wood and Winston and Bottery.

Third, invoking reaction is distinguished from earlier (20th-century) forms of networking and public sharing of information because it is focused on the dissemination and critique of knowledge that has been created within the school. The Eacham school leaders knew that their SWP constituted powerful intellectual property, and had to decide whether to keep it to themselves. They took what might be called a moral leadership response. A. Hargreaves and Fink (2006, p. 257) have discussed this issue as a particular 21st-century educational challenge and have suggested that the best way of addressing it lies in processes of proactivity:

> The most resilient schools don't just react . . . they engage assertively. . . . Activist leadership influences the environment that influences it by activating personal and professional networks, forging strategic alliances with the community, influencing the media by writing articles for newspapers, appearing on radio and television programs, and protesting openly against misconceived policies.

Fourth, it is very important for our purposes that parallel leadership appeared to consolidate and take on a life of its own at the invoking reaction stage of the C-B process. Without exception in the research schools, principals and teacher leaders—comprising individual teachers in about half the research cohort, and teams of two to five members in the other half—demonstrated the core values underpinning our definition of parallelism (that is, shared trust, mutual respect, and allowance for individual expression) as they engaged in invoking reaction activities. In one instance, the *Jan and Dan Show* acquired a degree of celebrity status across the immediate cluster of schools and beyond, with both the principal and teacher leader working interactively and interchangeably in public forums, critiquing Project products, mentoring potential teacher and student leaders, and hosting national and international visitors.

Thus, self-understanding and self-confidence appeared to us to transpose during invoking reaction C-B activities into an elevated sense of empowerment and professional esteem in the mind-sets and presentations of teacher leaders. Barth (2001) has also noted links between assertive empowerment and "better schools":

> We are most likely to find rich conceptions of a better school and inventive ways to attain it when teachers step into leadership roles and articulate for the public and for the profession just what school and teaching might become. (p. 447, cited in Murphy, 2005, p. 58)

It can be concluded that leadership for invoking reaction is distinguished by three qualities:

- An organizationwide quality, particularly in the mobilization of networks and forums to garner double-loop reaction to school-created pedagogical knowledge
- A strategic quality, particularly in the utilization of double-loop feedback in ongoing school-based pedagogical development
- An educative (advocacy) quality, particularly in the promotion of the construct of teachers as leaders in public forums and with system officials

In reviewing these three qualities, we conclude that leadership practices in relation to the invoking reaction dynamic were characterized by a newfound maturity in teacher leaders' mind-sets, sense of self, and behaviors. That is, teacher leaders who engaged in invoking reaction C-B activities demonstrated noticeably high levels of aptitude in articulating complex processes of knowledge creation, sophisticated skills in public presentation, a capacity to accommodate negative and cynical feedback without rancor, and a readiness to provide facilitative assistance to needy colleagues in other schools.

Leadership as an "organizational quality" is the dominant form of leadership that we observed in conjunction with the invoking reaction C-B dynamic. It has been asserted as a particularly mature and advanced form of school-based leadership (Pounder, Ogawa, & Adams, 1995), a claim with which we largely agree. While the practical meanings of organizationwide leadership remain relatively undeveloped in the literature, we conclude our discussion by noting that, at the invoking reaction stage of capacity building, leadership as an organizational quality appears to us to begin to manifest in a form that is very distinctive—and that we call parallel leadership.

THINKING OUTSIDE THE SQUARE: MÉDECINS SANS FRONTIÈRES AND INVOKING REACTION

The following account is offered as a classic example of the invoking reaction dynamic at work in an organization. The account illustrates that, when an organization's work is grounded in deep values that are publicly visible, processes of marketing and image building largely take care of themselves. Thus, there is much for school leaders to learn from the wonderful example of Médecins Sans Frontières (www.msf.org), a leading international aid organization that does very little advertising, promotion, or formal image building. As professionals in their various fields, MSF staff advocate for the best possible treatment for people afflicted by crisis, independent of political power. They may be said to "invoke reaction" in four ways that are consistent with the functions of educational institutions:

- Through speaking out on behalf of marginalized citizens
- Through advocacy for law, processes, and resources to address emerging issues of human need
- By being able to provide quality human care wherever disaster strikes
- By building powerful international networks of support within their individual professions.

Explore your thinking about invoking reaction by reflecting on the account that follows. As you review it, ask yourself four questions:

1. In the work of MSF, what is the equivalent of the educational concept of invoking reaction?
2. How did MSF reach its underlying convictions? What special qualities drive MSF to transpose those convictions into action?
3. Which of the four leadership approaches that we have identified as dominant in educational practice (transformational, advocacy, strategic, organizationwide) do you think is most relevant in the MSF case study as a way of successfully invoking reaction?
4. How is distributed leadership a part of the MSF leadership approach?

Médecins Sans Frontières, commonly known as MSF, or Doctors Without Borders, was created by doctors and journalists in France in 1971 in response to a perceived global need for humanitarian medical service that is free of political and military influence. In the 40 ensuing years, MSF has developed into an extraordinary global network, with an ever-increasing body of volunteer personnel, ranging from doctors and nurses to administrative, logistical, and technical staff. MSF may be said to epitomize the construct of sustainable organizational capacity.

As an organization, MSF has developed a unique capacity to respond to a crisis, as indicated most recently in Haiti and Chile following devastating natural disasters, and in the face of ongoing unrest in countries like Bangladesh, Pakistan, and Somalia. Because of successes such as these over several decades, the Nobel Peace Prize was awarded to MSF in 1999 in recognition of its continuous effort to provide medical care in acute crises and for raising awareness of humanitarian disasters.

MSF as an ever-expanding organization brings to life aspects of the invoking reaction C-B dynamic as we have defined it. We say this because MSF does very little in the way of public advertisement, or commercial marketing, for funds, personnel, or political approval. And yet its momentum, integrity, influence, and image grow and expand each year.

The following explanation is very relevant to our purposes with the fifth C-B dynamic—MSF uses its established success, its universally respected values, and the dedication of its staff to attract volunteers from all countries, cultures, and creeds; to build new international networks; and to advocate its core humanitarian values with governments of all political persuasions. Resource contributions from governments and private agencies invariably follow. And, as one successful venture after another unfolds, MSF itself becomes more influential in global politics, more mature in service delivery, more attractive in the eyes of potential volunteers, and more respected in most, if not all, nations.

In accordance with the MSF Charter, participating employees agree to honor four principles:

- Médecins Sans Frontières staff provide assistance to populations in distress, to victims of natural or man-made disasters and to victims of armed conflict. They do so irrespective of race, religion, creed, or political conviction.
- Médecins Sans Frontières observes neutrality and impartiality in the name of universal medical ethics and the right to humanitarian assistance. It also claims full and unhindered freedom in the exercise of its functions.
- Members undertake to respect the code of ethics of their professions and to maintain complete independence from all political, economic, or religious powers.
- Members understand the risks and dangers of the missions they carry out and make no claim for themselves, or their assigns, for any form of compensation other than that which the association might be able to afford them. (Médecins Sans Frontières, n.d.).

As part of its charter, MSF advocates for increased aid, awareness, and improved medical treatment and protocols. However, it is the manner in which it does this—by networking across the globe, by attracting people committed to its values, and by responding to crises without intervention from political, racial, economic, or religious barriers—that epitomizes the invoking reaction C-B dynamic.

In essence, MSF may be said to invoke reaction in four different ways as a means of building and sustaining its "capacity":

- **Advocacy**—MSF critically assesses new situations in detail, makes public statements regarding them, and endeavors to provide treatment that meets the needs of the situation.
- **Consciousness raising**—MSF draws attention to forgotten crises, alerts the world to looming crises, criticizes the inadequacies of global aid programs, and advocates for the dignity of all humans.
- **Building quality medical care**—MSF campaigns for access to essential medical resources and treatments, and builds the associated skills and talents of its participating medical staff.
- **Emphasizing international networks**—MSF uses its organizations in 19 countries to access financial, human, and logistical resources and thus enable it to respond with relative ease and speed in an emergency.

Each of these four MSF strategies implies a specific form of the C-B dynamic invoking reaction. Each is authentic in ways that corporate advertising and media-based promotion generally are not. Each has proved immensely successful in the work of MSF. Each has value in demonstrating the meaning of the fifth C-B dynamic in school settings.

CONCLUSION

In this chapter, we have taken the position that the benefits of a school improvement process will be enhanced if the products of the process, in the form of new knowledge, are publicly shared, critiqued, and refined. We have revealed that the invoking reaction dynamic is constituted of complex processes of single- and double-loop critique, various forms of internal and external networking, and assertive advocacy for both ongoing school revitalization and the teaching profession. We have noted that, as these processes unfold, the maturity of the concept of teacher leadership is revealed in a new light and the legitimacy of parallel leadership is affirmed. With this in mind, we proceed to our final C-B dynamic: consolidating success. But first we encourage you to undertake a professional learning exercise to assist you in your efforts to become an invoking reaction C-B leader in your school, and possibly others.

COSMIC C-B SIMULATION 5—SCHOOLS WITHOUT BORDERS

INVOKING REACTION: BUILDING PERSONAL CAPACITY

Purpose:

In this activity, school leaders and aspiring leaders unpack the invoking reaction dynamic, developing clear pictures of what their school might achieve through strategic networking, advocacy, and organizational self-critique. To do so, they role-play a team of MSF (Doctors Without Borders) volunteers who have come together to review their most recent assignments and develop strategies for the expansion and ongoing promotion of MSF.

Rationale:

The invoking reaction C-B dynamic encompasses three core constructs—strategic networking, advocacy, and organizational self-critique—that are all of major importance in schools that have created significant new knowledge and wish to consolidate that new knowledge in the long-term future. Engagement with these constructs in this simulation of the work of 4 third-world MSF volunteers will enable principals and teacher leaders to develop understanding and skills in relation to the three constructs and to share insights beyond the borders of their own classrooms and schools.

Two respected group "shared cognition" strategies—*think, pair, share* and *1:4PCR* (Frangenheim, 2006)—are used in the simulation.

Approximate time required:

Two 60-minute sessions

Organization:

This activity is intended for use by school leadership teams.

Materials for each group:

- Prerequisite reading—Chapter 6
- Exhibit 6.A—Four MSF Volunteer Roles

Exhibit 6.A

FOUR MSF VOLUNTEER ROLES

Volunteer One: A midwife from Brussels, Belgium, who has returned from a posting in the town of Wardher, Ethiopia, where she was involved in identifying problems relating to women's health. Wardher, situated in the largest zone of the conflict-affected Somali region, sits amid dry scrubland dotted with small, remote villages and nomadic settlements.

> *As part of my job, I worked closely with the health center's staff, sharing knowledge and expertise. . . . Before I left, I stood back and observed my team successfully responding to a complicated case. I knew at that moment that I had achieved what I had come to Ethiopia to do. I am sure that our Ethiopian staff will do a good job providing medical care for the women of the Somali region in the future.* (Ebrahami, 2010)

Volunteer Two: A doctor from the north coast of New South Wales, Australia, who has been working for Médecins Sans Frontières in China. She has been based in the city of Nanning, in Guangxi province, in a project providing health care for HIV-positive patients. The project was opened by Médecins Sans Frontières in 2003, and despite the wealth and economic progress that is apparent in some of China, rural communities, migrant workers, and the marginalized still require international aid.

> *My role is to supervize the three national doctors, to coordinate . . . and to assist with their education and training. . . . My lovely translator is constantly at my side, . . . and corrects me when I am about to make a culturally insensitive faux pas. . . .*
>
> *My next challenge will be to document the impact of the HIV project, . . . from the perspectives of the patients, the staff, and our partners. What are the lessons we have learned and how will this shape what we do in the future? This is a critical component of any field project. In the process I am sure I will do plenty of self-reflection on my experiences and the lessons I have learned, and maybe will bring a new set of skills and ideas with me to the next project!* (Spillane, 2010)

Volunteer Three: A nurse from Connecticut who has just returned from working with Médecins Sans Frontières in southern Sudan. As supervisor of the therapeutic feeding center, her focus has been on providing care for malnourished patients. She had worked previously with MSF in Ethiopia; this was her second placement with Médecins Sans Frontières in Ethiopia.

> *A significant part of my job was to provide training for the national staff. . . . I found the staff enthusiastic to learn and they were always grateful for any guidance I could give them. When I reflect back . . . remember the most difficult and*

> *challenging times. . . . hearing a mother's wails, . . . knowing that if we had reached her a day earlier the outcome could have been different . . . having to choose which child should be given priority for oxygen therapy. . . . I'm sure I learnt something new every day I was there. The intense teamwork that is part of life in the field has given me friendships that I will treasure for the rest of my life.* (Mowat, 2010)

Volunteer Four: An epidemiologist from California who has recently gathered information on the medical needs and issues MSF teams are encountering in post-quake Haiti. The data help create a bigger picture of people's health care needs and how they may evolve. This knowledge enables MSF staff to continue to effectively treat survivors and to plan for the critical medical work ahead.

> *In the days after the earthquake in Haiti, the media were filled with images of massive destruction. . . . They showed an alarming number of dead bodies, leading some to worry that those bodies would spread disease . . . but from an epidemiological point of view they are not a priority.*
>
> *Every natural disaster unfolds a bit differently and the priorities in Haiti are evolving . . . so we've really got to get out there and treat people who are not able to come to us. MSF is trying to get out into the community.*
>
> *The risk of outbreaks of disease is of course elevated. In Haiti two things have happened as a result of the earthquake. First is that a lot of the infrastructures that keep infections at bay have been disrupted or destroyed. . . . The second is that the population is greatly weakened.*
>
> *MSF is trying to meet the immediate medical needs of our patients while taking into account these evolving concerns. It's a fluid situation. . . . Haiti's recovery is a long-term one. . . . Even after the current media spotlight on Haiti fades, there will be patients with extensive needs as a result of the earthquake.* (Reilley, 2010)

- Venn diagram for each group (as below, drawn on large sheets of paper)

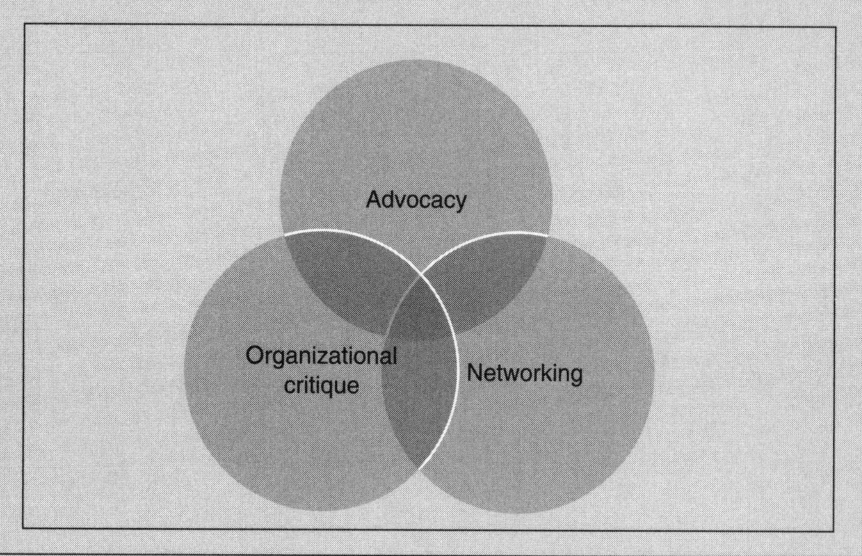

Process:

Session One

SHARING MSF UNDERSTANDINGS OF THE THREE INVOKING REACTION CONSTRUCTS

The four-member team of returned MSF volunteers has come together, with the guidance of a facilitator, to share the experience of their most recent assignments and to develop a position statement for the promotion of MSF.

Step 1—Arrange groups of five—a process facilitator and four MSF volunteers. Assign roles using the four scenarios outlined previously. Create a role description for yourself as a returned MSF volunteer, using your scenario description and by calling on your imagination and other MSF knowledge that you may have.

Step 2—The facilitator guides you through the think, pair, share strategy:

- **Think:** What made you join MSF? What do you strongly believe in as part of the MSF organization? What was achieved by MSF during your most recent assignment? What was your personal contribution? What should the world know about MSF's efforts? How might you use this experience in other aspects of your personal and professional life?
- **Pair** with the "MSF volunteer" next to you and think aloud, together.
- **Share** reflections with your group of four MSF volunteers. Develop two to three dot points for each circle: Organizational Critique, Networking, and Advocacy.

Step 3—What do Venn diagram overlaps mean to you? What core message for MSF emerges from the triple overlap in the center of the diagram? Consider the strength of the invoking reaction dynamic—when each of the constructs supports the others in the MSF organization.

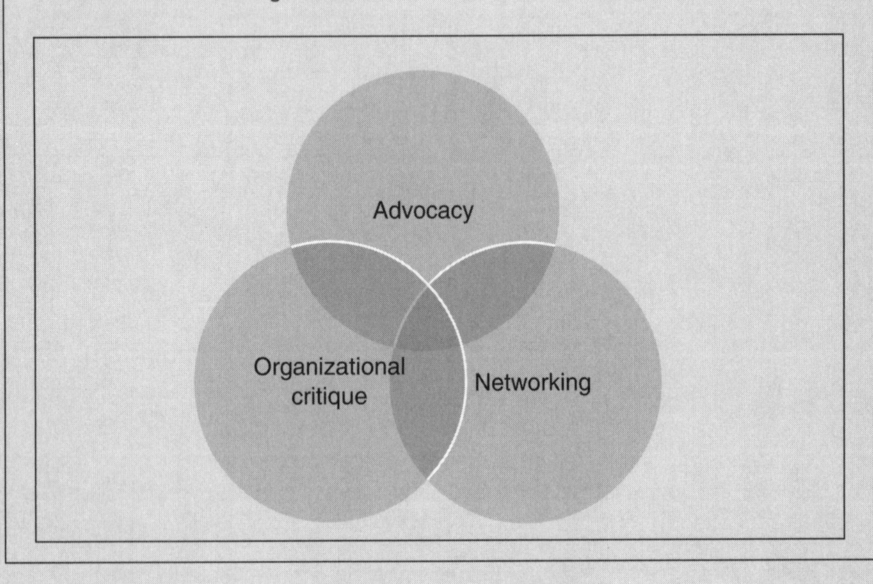

Session Two

REFINING THE THREE INVOKING REACTION CONSTRUCTS FOR YOUR SCHOOL WITHOUT BORDERS

Step 1—Following reflection on your experience with the MSF simulation, think about what each of the three invoking reaction constructs of networking, advocacy, and organizational self-critique means in the Eacham High School case study. (There are, in fact, at least two instances of each of the three constructs represented in the Eacham snapshot.) Discuss these. What would the fundamental points in an Eacham invoking reaction school plan be, if you were an Eacham school leader?

Step 2—Choose a recent successful outcome in your school's ongoing development process. This might be an aspect of student achievement, or attitudinal development, or perhaps teacher professional growth.

Step 3—In groups of four, use the 1:4PCR strategy (synthesis, critique, and version adapted from Frangenheim, 2006) to complete the same Venn diagram that was used for the MSF simulation.

Successful school outcome: ______________________________

1 Individual	Reflect on how each of the constructs might look in your school. Make notes to record your thinking.
4 Share with group of 4	Share your ideas with the other three in your group and discuss the different responses. Synthesize your thinking into key statements.
P Publish	In your group of four, record your synthesis in the Venn diagram.
C Circle	Post your Venn diagram on a wall and leave one group member as the "explainer" of your product. The other group members circle around the room and note what other groups have recorded, discussing the content with the various "explainers," and making notes as they go.
R Refine	Back to your home group of four, discuss any new understandings. Now refine your Venn diagram as necessary and share with the whole group.

Step 4—What core message for your school emerges from the detail in the center of this diagram? Consider the strength of the invoking reaction C-B dynamic when each of the constructs supports the others in the work of your school.

Step 5—How might your school use the construct of parallel leadership to ensure that the fifth C-B dynamic—invoking reaction—has maximum effectiveness in your school? What do you envision as the key functions of the principal and teacher leaders in implementing the invoking reaction dynamic?

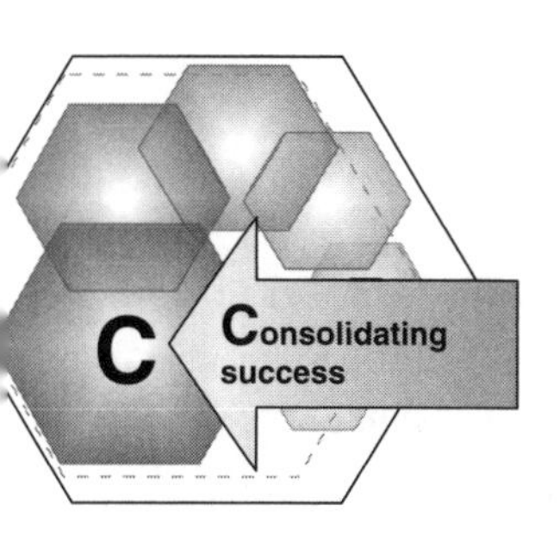

7

The Sixth C-B Dynamic

Consolidating Success

(Prepared in collaboration with Dr. Allan Morgan)

Sustainability is a meal, not a menu. You can't pick and choose. All the principles go together. You have to eat all your "greens."

—Andy Hargreaves and Dean Fink (2006, p. 251)

INTRODUCTION

The past decade has seen the emergence of a range of exciting models for school improvement. But many teachers and principals remain unconvinced of their worth, questioning whether they can be sustained in the face of challenges such as constant staff turnover, inconsistent supervisor expectations, and seemingly cataclysmic systemic priorities. Added to that is the "new broom principal" mind-set—"I'm the new broom, sent here to sweep the place clean. I'll let you know when I have decided what is best for you and how to proceed from there."

In such contexts, the consolidation of hard-earned successes and achievements has not been a topic of major importance in most schools in recent years.

But times are changing. Schools in the 2010s are part of a new world, one where they are being exhorted to not only achieve more but also to sustain those achievements into the future. Leaders of the schools in our research recognized the vulnerability of what they had achieved, especially pedagogically, and took deliberate action to embed the processes that they believed had generated their successes. Insights regarding their work provide the basis for our analysis of the sixth and final C-B dynamic, consolidating success. This dynamic is essential, we assert, if schools are to break "boom and bust" cycles of school improvement and sustain their achievements for the benefit of future generations of students, teachers, and communities.

Thus, we take the clear position that whatever successes are achieved must be sustained if they are to have significant educational value. But how, one might ask, are the processes that result in enhanced school outcomes most successfully consolidated in a school's structure and culture? As a first step in answering this critically important question, we look inside the workings of a school where hard-earned successes were indeed embedded for the benefit of future generations of students and teachers.

A SNAPSHOT OF CONSOLIDATING SUCCESS: ALL HALLOWS CATHOLIC ELEMENTARY SCHOOL

All Hallows Elementary School is a medium-size Catholic elementary school in a mid-socioeconomic area within a large city. It has outstanding harbor views that include a series of old naval docks with deep historical significance.

Standardized test results in recent years have indicated well above average achievement levels in literacy and numeracy. Annual surveys have also shown that All Hallows has an enthusiastic and highly supportive parent community. It has had no visible issues for at least the past decade.

In 2006 the school began engagement with a whole-school improvement process (the IDEAS Project) for the specific purpose of refining its core pedagogical processes and embedding those processes in the school's culture, strategic planning, and core classroom activities. Over a three-year period, the school, through the facilitation of the IDEAS school management team (comprising six teachers and the principal), created a new school vision that captured the particular spiritual traditions and historic surroundings of the school, developed a schoolwide pedagogical framework (see Figure 7.1), and began implementation of the SWP in a range of curriculum areas.

Figure 7.1 The All Hallows Vision, Values, and SWP

All growing . . . All together . . . All Hallows

The Five Docks of Learning

At All Hallows Parish School, our vision for learning encompasses the following key principles:

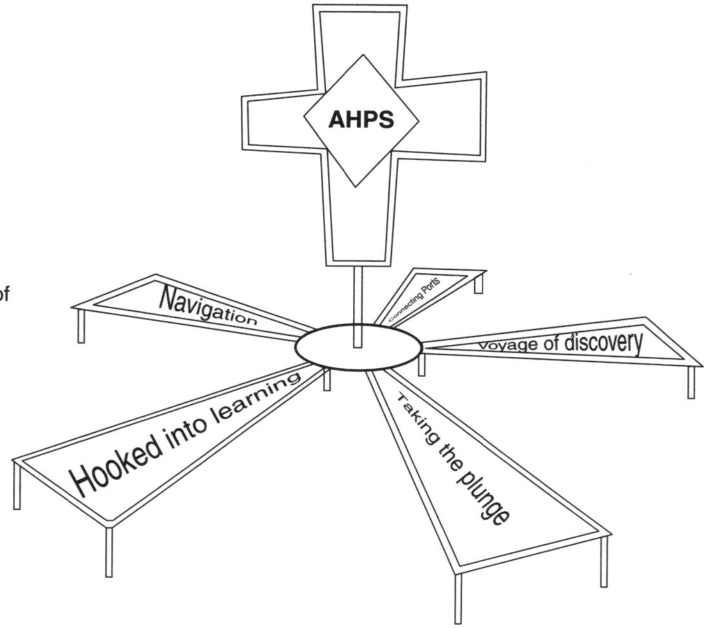

Hooked into Learning

Learners at All Hallows will:

- Be active participants in their faith development
- Be motivated using a variety of learning strategies
- Be encouraged to build on prior knowledge and experiences
- Be involved in the decision making, planning and goal setting of their learning
- Be engaged in using a variety of resources and technology

Taking the plunge

Learners at All Hallows will:

- Challenge themselves to take risks in a safe and positive learning environment
- Have access to a range of multimodal media
- Develop the skills and attitudes to be able to achieve their personal best
- Engage in open-ended activities that encourage higher order thinking

Voyage of Discovery

Learners at All Hallows will:

- Seek understanding of their faith
- Share knowledge
- Investigate, inquire and research
- Engage in open-ended tasks
- Use problem solving skills
- Maintain motivation

Connecting Ports

Learners at All Hallows will:

- Make connections with their faith community and Catholic traditions
- Make real connections with Catholic beliefs and respond with action
- Make real world connections
- Share their ideas and learn from each other
- Use a range of technologies
- Make connections with other learners in the wider community
- Apply knowledge and understanding across subject areas

Navigation

Learners at All Hallows will:

- Evaluate and reflect on their learning
- Use feedback to set future direction
- Be acknowledged for their achievements

Then, in mid-2009, the school was advised that a change of principalship was planned for 2010. The question of the sustainability of the newly developed vision and SWP became a very practical concern.

The accounts that follow outline the actions that were taken to consolidate successes for the benefit of future cohorts of All Hallows students.

The Principal's Perspective

From my viewpoint as principal, student academic achievement in 2004 was sound. However, the school lacked coherence and "spice." A majority of staff had been teaching at the school for three years or fewer, so there existed limited shared understanding of the school's purposes and no obvious consistency, reinforcement, or transfer of learning across the grade levels and subject areas. Our good outcomes seemed vulnerable.

Immense energy went into creating the new *All Growing—All Together—All Hallows* vision and the "Five Docks of Learning" SWP. I considered that my role during these lengthy, time-consuming, and complex processes was to keep enthusiasm high, resource the various activities, and encourage teachers to "have a go," as well as ensure that we were complementing the values of our Catholic system. That was particularly important when we analyzed our staff, student, and community surveys and found that there were some areas of values-related disagreement that could cause breakdowns in relationships.

But as a result of our serious analysis of who we are and want to become combined with the ingenious creativity of the teacher leaders on our ISMT, we have created a school that has become more self-critical and a school community that has come to appreciate the idea of continuous school improvement as a planned process. I say this because our school survey data tell us so. Thus, to embed our achievements by consolidating our core developmental processes is absolutely essential to me, since I am in the process of leaving the school for another position. But I leave feeling confident, with five strategies in place.

First, the IDEAS school improvement process is so ingrained in teachers' thinking that it will undoubtedly continue to guide school development processes. Second, our staff understand the fundamentals of parallel leadership, with a cadre of about six teachers being perceived by themselves and others as teacher leaders. Third, the teaching staff have made a schoolwide decision that numeracy development will be the school's curriculum priority for the next one to two years. The Five Docks of Learning pedagogical umbrella will ensure that new teachers joining the staff, and the incoming principal, are provided with a framework that will ensure a coherent approach to developmental work in numeracy. Fourth, the assistant principal and I met with the regional curriculum advisor and explained the school's

SWP development process and Five Docks of Learning framework. The advisor endorsed our work and is ensuring that the new principal appreciates our SWP. Fifth, we have developed a Five Docks brochure to communicate our identity, especially our pedagogical distinctiveness. It is colorful, compelling—and ours. Students love it; parents admire it. It leaves no doubt about what we have created as a school, what we value, or what we insist must be sustained into the future.

Additionally, I will take specific steps to induct the new principal into our vision, SWP, and developmental processes. The regional consultant will be involved in the selection process for the new principal and will continue to follow the development of our school's improvement processes in the coming year.

By consolidating our developmental processes and outcomes in this way, sustainability of our successes, I believe, is reasonably assured.

A Teacher Leader's Perspective

As the facilitators for the IDEAS school improvement process, Suzanne and I worked with our principal to coordinate the development of the *All Growing—All Together—All Hallows* vision. We then facilitated the creation of the Five Docks of Learning pedagogical framework. We took the position that the products we were creating must be able to describe to future cohorts of parents and students our goals, values, and distinct pedagogical priorities as a faith community. We are convinced that they do. Now, we have to ensure that what we have created is sustained into the future.

To show our commitment to what we had created, we launched our vision on the occasion of our 90th school birthday, thereby attempting to embed it symbolically in the minds of our community members. The students' involvement in the visioning process helped them get excited about it, but, more important, it helped give the vision a practical importance. As a result, even our six-year-olds use the language of the vision in their daily dialogue. Our SWP was launched 12 months later at the same annual event. To highlight its symbolic importance in our school, students were involved in scripting and performing a play that animated the Five Docks of Learning. They were superb!

In the two to three years ahead, we will "unpack" specific pedagogical strategies for each of the curriculum areas, commencing with numeracy. Specifically, in the coming year, we as a teaching staff will look at how our students learn math using the Five Docks of Learning as our framework for cross-school complementarity in practice and understanding:

- Why do I love the way All Hallows math works?
- What math will I explore this week that is new for me?
- How can I share my new math learning with other people?

- Where do I see math alive in my worlds?
- What am I learning about myself from All Hallows math?

This student-focused process will be our most important step in embedding our vision and SWP in our classroom practices. Should the impending change in principalship worry us? It doesn't, for several reasons. First, the ISMT will continue to function as the school's key committee, with Suzanne and I as the facilitators, guiding professional learning and keeping us focused. Second, teachers were consulted about the preferred talents of a new principal and, in doing so, highlighted our commitment to both parallel leadership and the school's vision and Five Docks schoolwide pedagogy. Third, we believe that the new principal has special gifts that will enrich our SWP work, and we are excited about benefiting from that.

We are therefore very confident that what we have created will be sustained—and in fact become richer with the passage of time.

CONSOLIDATING SUCCESS: DEEPENING OUR UNDERSTANDING

Our research schools achieved "success," as defined by gains in student achievement, student and teacher well-being, and school image in the community. But our research also revealed that success in a school's work over time is very seldom clear-cut. For example, success may be achieved in one area of school activity but not others. Or it may be achieved across a period of time—say, four years—but not in each and every one of those years. Or it may be achieved in a particular year and that success maintained, but not increased, in subsequent years.

We have taken these complex subtleties into full account in generating our definition of success. We have concluded that if, in the views of a school staff, or community, increases in student achievement in an area of agreed priority meet expectations that were stipulated in advance, and are maintained over a period of several years, in the face of changing people, systemic goals, and contextual factors—then an important school success has been achieved and sustained.

Our definition of success carries with it the clear position that enhanced outcomes without sustainability have limited value in the ongoing work of a school. But how, one might ask, are the processes that result in enhanced school outcomes most successfully consolidated so that the successes can be sustained in the long term? The All Hallows snapshot provides a range of insights that we have found convincing, and plausible. Authoritative commentators also hold a range of viewpoints on this critically important question, leading us to look at the meaning of the sixth C-B dynamic—consolidating success—from four different perspectives: systematic, metanoiac, cultural, and leadership.

The Systemic Perspective on Consolidating Success

Whose responsibility is it to consolidate and sustain hard-earned educational success? Does accountability reside primarily with leaders at the system or school level? Unfortunately, there is limited agreement on this fundamental issue relating to the final C-B dynamic. Consider, for example, the recently expressed viewpoint of heads of a national educational system:

> Achieving universally high outcomes is only possible by putting in place mechanisms to ensure that schools deliver high-quality instruction to every child. (Barber & Mourshed, 2007, p. 25)

It is clear in this account that Barber and Mourshed view system-level leadership as inseparable from the achievement and sustainability of school-level success, a seemingly laudable stance on their part. Indeed, important short-term gains were achieved through the national "mechanisms" that they initiated (including highly prescriptive curriculum, comprehensive student assessment, and regular formal school evaluations). Yet that same national system has recently been charged by authoritative international observers with contributing to diminished student standards over the longer term, largely as a result of overprescription of the centrally driven reforms and consequent interferences with teachers' schoolwide pedagogical functions (Ferrari, 2009, p. 1). How, then, to proceed in endeavoring to consolidate short-term gains into long-term successes?

Michael Fullan's view is that consolidation and sustainability are in fact inseparable constructs and that it is the system that should take the onus of responsibility for consolidation strategies that will generate long-term sustainability in and across schools. Fullan's logic is convincing—the key to sustainability is the "skillful and balanced management of energy" (2005b, p. 37) and, since systems control "energy" (in the form of school resources, staffing, curricula, and educational policy generally), it follows that responsibility for the consolidation of successes should begin at the system level. Fullan also contends that sustainability is the "capacity of a system to engage in the complexities of continuous improvement consistent with deep values of human purpose" (2005b, p. ix). Following his research into schools that achieved short-term success, he posed an important question, "Are the good results sustainable?" and then proceeded to answer his own question:

> In a word, NO. The strategies have required tremendous energy and supervision, which in their own right cannot be sustained for long (burnout, turnover, overload take their toll). . . . There is no chance that the strategies . . . could result in widespread, sustainable reform. (2005b, p. 6)

But Fullan is also careful to note that the consolidation of success is inseparable from a number of constructs that focus directly on individual school leaders, including "lateral capacity-building through networks" (2005b, p. 14). Barnes, Camburn, Sanders, and Sebastian (2010, p. 274) support the intent of Fullan's view:

> Sustaining . . . structures, incentives, and resources would require broad, sustained support from knowledgable district leadership that could withstand staff or superintendent turnover, support coherent guidance for the principal group, and buffer their communities of practice from strong undermining forces.

Capra (2002) goes further, both philosophically and practically. He asserts that sustainability is a property of an entire system, not of individual units therein (p. 215), and that responsibility for sustainability must reside explicitly with the system or the meaning of both the system and its component parts will be lost. Viewed this way, sustainability begins to take on a radically different form, one that might be labeled "ecological." Bottery (2008, p. 282), has taken this values-based stance, asserting that educational leaders should view their school development work in the broadest possible systemic context—because, in the final analysis, it is biospheric sustainability that matters most in their work: "the sustainability of life itself, and not just the anthropocentric concern for human sustainability, for it is that within which humanity has to survive."

Is it realistic to link the sustainability of a school initiative to the sustainability of the biosphere? Bottery clearly sees a connection. For example, he emphasizes the importance of processes of international networking and shared decision making about planetary issues ahead of parochial issues and site-based concerns in the work of 21st-century school leaders. Those principals and teacher leaders in our case studies who developed visions and pedagogical frameworks that reflected concern for global values associated with continuity, balance, connectedness, and hope could, we think, be regarded as capturing Bottery's intent. A. Hargreaves and Fink (2006, p. 9) also regard sustainability as a multilevel, interconnected issue:

> Public education should not be treated as a temporary business that is looking to produce quick returns . . . it should learn from the environmental movement. . . . Sustainability isn't just a metaphor borrowed from environmental science. It's a fundamental principle for enriching and preserving the richness and interconnectedness of all life.

Thus, it is readily apparent that the concern of school leaders for the sustainability of their hard-earned school success is increasingly regarded as inseparable from systemic processes and from questions of deep human and philosophical value.

The Metanoia Perspective on Consolidating Success

Peter Senge's concept of "metanoia" provides a second perspective on how the consolidation of a hard-earned school success can be effectively sustained. Metanoia, as described by Senge, is a continuous process of learning within the professional community of the school, beginning with the decision to commit to revitalization, extending throughout the life of the revitalization process, and continuing beyond the point of formal consolidation into the school's future life. Senge (1990) justifies his concept of metanoia on the basis of its inherently human quality:

> Through learning we become able to do something we never were able to do . . . through learning we extend our capacity to create, to be part of the generative process of life. (p. 14)

It follows from Senge's postulation that if "real learning" within the school's professional learning community ceases, then the possibility of sustained school improvement diminishes dramatically. It might be argued that the All Hallows ISMT was aware of this potential threat when they stated,

> In the coming year we as a teaching staff will look at how our students learn math using the Five Docks of Learning as our framework for cross-school complementarity in practice and understanding. Should the impending change in principalship worry us? It doesn't . . . the school project management team will continue to function as the school's key committee guiding staff learning and keeping us focused.

Three consolidating constructs are implicit in the All Hallows' teacher leaders' analysis: a clear, ongoing focus in teachers' ongoing professional learning; teacher leadership roles and functions; and strategic continuity through an effective ISMT. Murphy, Elliott, Goldring, and Porter (2007) provide a helpful explanation of how and why the consolidation of these concepts can provide the basis for continued and sustained success:

> In working with colleagues, instructionally centred leaders establish an expectation that the continual expansion of one's knowledge and skills focused on helping students succeed is the norm of the school. (p. 187)

At this juncture the reader might well ask, "At what point do the C-B dynamic of consolidating success and the ongoing process of sustaining success become one?" The complexity of the *consolidating-sustaining* relationship is among the most perplexing issues in 21st-century educational leadership debates. We will return to it shortly.

The Cultural Perspective on Consolidating Success

To some authorities, the organization "is" a culture (Smircich, 1983, as cited in Limerick, Cunnington, & Crowther, 1998). To other authorities, culture is but one element within an organization. Limerick et al. (1998, p. 168), for example, assert that "like variables such as strategy and structure, culture can be shaped or managed by those within the organization."

It follows from both lines of thinking that an organization's members, particularly its leaders, can create meaning out of their culture to fashion public perceptions, to frame members' understandings of themselves and of their organization, and to shape futuristic direction. This can be said to have happened at All Hallows Catholic School, where the Five Docks of Learning brochure that grew out of the IDEAS Project developmental work was used to engender a deep-seated sense of pride, special belonging, and energy in the school and broader community. Indeed, the All Hallows brochure can be viewed as a "consolidating" action that captures the intent of all three of Edgar Schein's (2004) levels of culture:

- Artifacts—photos show students viewing their school with pride, confidence, and enthusiasm
- Values—the brief pedagogical descriptions incorporate Diocesan religious values
- Assumptions—teachers (who created the brochure) are portrayed ingeniously and implicitly as intelligent, creative professionals

One might ask, "Why not simply employ a marketing agency to create such artifacts?" Many organizations, including schools, in fact do. But could a marketing agency capture the All Hallows achievements and ethos as effectively as the teacher leaders and principal have done in their Five Docks brochure? And would next year's teachers, students, and parents at All Hallows be as convinced of the authenticity of the school's achievements and successes if the brochures were produced by a commercial firm? Our experience is definitively *no*. In our view, cultural artifacts such as the All Hallows brochure have extraordinary power to contribute to continuity in the ongoing work of a school, but to do so they must first and foremost be authentic. And it is teacher leaders, not commercial marketing agencies, who are best able to ensure that authenticity and therefore set the stage for continuity.

Mitchell and Sackney (2009) also highlight the importance of cultural artifacts, particularly language, in managing school development processes successfully. They assert,

> By being present to a new set of root metaphors and a new set of images for schools, educators can let go of old identities, release the need to control, participate in a larger field for change, and construct schools as living systems. (p. 8)

Indeed, the importance and role of language in effecting change and sustaining school improvement is acknowledged by virtually all change authorities. Bucholtz and Hall (2004, pp. 369–370) note that a group's process of establishing identity involves the invention of similarity in descriptions by downplaying difference. The relevance of Bucholtz and Hall's point is apparent in the All Hallows brochure, where carefully selected language, photographs, and metaphoric description, combined with ingenious layout and design, were used to nurture an overall image of the school as an integration of religious, educational, and community values.

Mitchell and Sackney (2009) assert that when school activities and curricula are built around communications strategies in ways such as these, they both align and energize the lives and learning of people within the organization. Such is the power of comprehensively developed and refined school culture in the fifth C-B dynamic.

The Leadership Perspective on Consolidating Success

Implicit in the previous section is that a growing number of authoritative educational commentators regard the issue of sustainable school improvement as inseparable from sustainable leadership. A. Hargreaves and Fink (2004), for example, point out that leadership sustainability and leadership succession are inextricably linked and part and parcel of continuous school improvement. They argue that sustainability is not the same as making things last; rather, it is about creating a culture in which the focus is on planning for the continuance of learning beyond the principal's tenure at the school. These authors assert that, when sustainability is at the forefront of thinking in a school, principals plan for their departure by championing the spread of influence of the professional community and appropriating resources to develop the talents of teachers across the school so as to "stimulate continuous improvement on a broad front" (p. 9). In essence, A. Hargreaves and Fink (2006, p. 251) view the *consolidation* of school success and the *sustainability* of success as conceptually distinct but as closely interrelated, with leadership providing the glue. In similar vein, Leithwood, Day, Sammons, Harris, and Hopkins (2008) have provided compelling evidence that leadership is closely linked to school improvement and that a change in school leadership has the potential to abort successful change faster than any other factor. They conclude that leadership provides the means through which school successes are embedded and therefore may be viewed as the thread of sustainability.

In summary, three conclusions emerge from this brief literature analysis of the sixth C-B dynamic. The first conclusion relates to the consolidation-sustainability question. *Consolidating* involves the application of a range of concerted actions, at a particular point in time, or points in time, to officially endorse a proven process of school revitalization and to orient new staff, including principals, regarding the school's priority pedagogical processes and their meaning. *Sustainability,* on the other hand, is a long-term process that begins with the commencement of a school improvement initiative and extends beyond the formal completion of the initiative to provide ongoing feedback about the effectiveness of the school improvement process, to contribute to maturation of teachers' expertise and professionalism, and to ensure the distribution of leadership across the school.

Second, both consolidation and sustaining of school success can be viewed from multiple perspectives, including systemic, metanoiac, cultural, and leadership. All have important contributions to make to our understanding of the core constructs.

Third, sustained school success is vulnerable. Thus, the issue of leadership is essential, with important roles for principals, teacher leaders, and system supervisors.

Based on our literature review, and our consideration of the All Hallows thumbnail, the following definition of consolidating success is proposed:

Consolidating school success involves the embedding of those core processes that have contributed to the enhancement of school outcomes. The processes have strategic, professional learning, and enculturation applications:

- *Strategic*–incorporation of the school's vision, values, and SWP as the centerpiece of annual/triennial school program plans; use of the school's vision and pedagogical priorities as a reference point in selecting new staff
- *Professional learning*–continuous deepening of professional expertise relative to the school's pedagogical priorities and practices
- *Enculturation*–induction and orientation of staff, including the principal, into the school's vision, values, and SWP; and use of creative communications to build student and community pride in the school

LEADERSHIP FOR CONSOLIDATING SUCCESS

We commenced this chapter with a colorful metaphor in which A. Hargreaves and Fink suggested that sustainability is a meal, not a menu, and not to be picked from. You have to eat all the greens to be healthy, they insist. What, then, are the implications for school leaders concerned for the sustained health of their diners? We believe that four important implications are apparent in the consolidating/sustaining work of our research schools, and also in the perceptions of a range of authoritative commentators.

First, although consolidating can be viewed as point-in-time action, whereas *sustaining* is an ongoing process that begins with a commitment to revitalization, consolidating, sustaining, and leading are inseparable and mutually reinforcing constructs in successful school improvement. It follows that school leaders must take responsibility for ensuring that all six C-B dynamics—the six greens on the school improvement menu—are well prepared and attractively presented and that their diners are encouraged to partake enthusiastically of them (as opposed to picking at them or pushing aside those that they may not particularly like). Our observation is that in the All Hallows thumbnail, all six C-B greens were indeed enthusiastically savored by teachers and students, at the direct encouragement of the principal and teacher leaders. Linda Lambert (2007, p. 312) has captured the spirit of the leadership for the consolidating/sustaining relationship as we observed it at All Hallows:

> Sustainable schools are those with high leadership capacity, defined as broad-based skillful participation in the work of leadership. In other words, sustainability is a function of leadership, a particular kind of leadership.

Muijs, Harris, Chapman, Stoll, and Russ (2004, p. 167) have made an important additional point regarding the special challenge of catering to the consolidation/sustainability needs of diners who have special needs:

> While many schools can make short term improvements, sustaining improvement is a big challenge, particularly for schools in economically deprived areas.

Our research is conclusive that school improvement is indeed very feasible in disadvantaged schools—provided that school leaders understand the concepts of consolidation and sustainability and work assiduously toward them.

Second, we have noted previously the regrettable, contentious, and largely unresolved tension between school- and system-level authority in matters relating to the consolidation of school success. The complexity of this tension was made apparent recently when the head of the largest school system in the United States stated,

> In New York City . . . we have taken . . . steps . . . over the past several years to evaluate schools and hold them accountable for results. One of the most transformational accountability tools we created is progress reports, which assign an A to F letter grade to schools each year. . . .

These reports compare school outcomes with those of similar schools citywide, and are posted online. (Klein, 2010, p. 14)

Just six months later, a critic of top-down imposition of educational change noted that

> just released research from New York shows the Klein initiatives . . . have led to falling standards, a dumbed-down approach to the curriculum and a host of unintended consequences. (Donnelly, 2010, p. 21)

What, then, is the preferred allocation of responsibilities to school and system leaders for sustaining school success? Leithwood, Seashore Louis, Anderson, and Wahlstrom (2004) have addressed this question, suggesting that the two most important system leadership functions are those of "providing direction" and "exercising influence" (p. 20). Barnes et al. (2010, p. 274) go further:

> Sustaining . . . require[s] broad, sustained support from knowledgable district leadership that could withstand staff or superintendent turnover, support coherent guidance for the principal group, and buffer their communities of practice from strong undermining forces toward the status quo.

It follows from arguments such as these that the responsibility of district supervisors in contributing to, facilitating, and assessing school success is very considerable indeed—but this should not negate or interfere with the need for schools to create their own sense of purpose, their own learning communities, their own self-imagery, and their own procedures for passing on accumulated wisdom to new principals, new generations of teachers, and new cohorts of students. The chef (school principal) and master chef (district superintendent) have to have clear lines of communication and complementary objectives, as was clearly the case with All Hallows succession planning.

Third is the thorny question of the form of leadership that is most suited to the consolidating dynamic. It is now a decade and a half since the concept of leadership as an organizationwide quality was introduced into the education literature by Pounder, Ogawa, and Adams:

> The concept of leadership as an organisational quality suggests that the total amount of leadership found in schools will have a positive relationship to their performance. . . . Furthermore, it suggests that all members of schools—including principals, teachers, staff members, and parents—can lead and thus affect the performance of their schools. (1995, p. 567)

In the intervening years, distributed leadership has become an institutionalized feature of the educational leadership literature, if not educational practice. Thus, Bennett, Wise, Woods, and Harvey (2003) have suggested that distributed leadership constitutes multiple functions, three of which would appear to be particularly relevant to the embedding and consolidation of school success:

- "Letting go" by senior staff, thus facilitating easy transitions in management of innovations underway or recently established
- Extending the boundaries of leadership, thus engendering a culture of shared ownership
- Seeing leadership as fluid, with blurred leader–follower distinctions, thus encouraging a willing volunteer leadership outlook at junctures at which the need for consolidation of successes is greatest

More recently, Ingvarson and Kleinhenz (2006, as cited in Mulford, 2008, p. 43), have concluded from their detailed research analyses that improved schooling over time requires the enhanced capacity not just of one person but of many and a broad distribution of leadership functions, talents, and responsibilities also. In the All Hallows thumbnail, serious leadership functions were assumed by the principal, by the two key teacher leaders, by the ISMT, and by system officers. Ensuring that all greens get eaten, it follows, is not just the responsibility of the cook.

Fourth, there is no single leadership style or approach that is singularly suited to consolidating success. To the contrary, our research data show that three different approaches—strategic, organizationwide, and advocacy—were all evident in the consolidating strategies of the research schools. Our conclusion in this regard is supported by Maden's studies of effectively functioning schools:

> No one leadership style was found to be present. Notably schools where improvement was sustained had strong external networks and connections and tended to interpret rather than be run by national initiatives. (2001, as cited in Muijs et al., 2004, p. 167)

Our research is also supported by Feiler, Heritage, and Gallimore (2000, p. 67) on the question of the role of teacher leaders in the sixth C-B dynamic:

> Leadership roles need not become institutionalised. Although teacher leaders need time to mature in their roles, to develop leadership skills, and to become effective agents of change, the school can

create leader roles to meet its needs and terminate them as a need diminishes or as other needs take on higher priorities.

Multiple cooks in the school kitchen, it follows from the analysis, don't necessarily spoil the broth (or the broccoli).

It can be concluded that leadership for consolidating success is distinguished by three qualities:

- A strategic quality, particularly in futuristic planning and succession planning
- An organizationwide quality, particularly in the mobilization of a school management team to provide the glue in the school's past-present-future professional learning activities
- An advocacy quality, particularly in the work of the school management team as custodian of the school's vision and SWP

Before concluding this chapter, we consider a compelling illustration of consolidating success from the world of environmental conservation to see what lessons might be learned from it for school leaders.

THINKING OUTSIDE THE SQUARE: STEVE "CROCODILE HUNTER" IRWIN AND CONSOLIDATING SUCCESS

When Steve Irwin was tragically killed in a marine accident in December 2006, his death was described as one of the most widely reported events ever, other than acts of terrorism. This was no wonder—the notorious "Crocodile Hunter," who had captured the imaginations of millions across the globe through his infectious enthusiasm for animal conservation, left behind an extraordinary legacy of environmental achievement. But would that legacy be sustained? The answer, four years later, seems to be a definitive *yes.* Indeed, the Crocodile Hunter's work continues on much as it did during his lifetime. And therein lie important insights for educational leaders who are interested in sustaining their achievements.

As you review the description that follows, ask yourself three questions:

1. What is the meaning of "consolidating success" and "sustaining success" in the world of the Crocodile Hunter?

2. What lessons for school-based sustainability are to be learned from the example of the Crocodile Hunter?

3. What forms of leadership—Strategic? Transformational? Organizationwide? Advocacy?—are readily apparent in the description?

Steve Irwin grew up with wildlife, helping his parents who in 1970 had established a reptile and fauna park. He revealed at an early age an uncanny gift with animals. Taking over the management of his parents' small wildlife park in 1992 (and renaming it Australia Zoo) coincided with his marriage to Terri Raines, a wildlife enthusiast visiting Australia from the United States. It became Steve's vision to develop the world's best zoo. In less than 20 years, Australia Zoo, particularly through its ingenious website access, has gone some way toward becoming that. Today, it acts as an important global conduit for the "conservation message" and for coherent management of a complex web of environmental, educational, and humanitarian interests.

Under the combined leadership of Steve and Terri, the zoo operations grew quickly to include a television series (*The Crocodile Hunter*), the Steve Irwin Conservation Foundation (renamed Wildlife Warriors), and the International Crocodile Rescue. The Australia Zoo, which began as a two-acre park in 1970, now encompasses 1,500 acres and employs over 600 staff. It is a multifaceted and extraordinary achievement, and it continues on after Steve's tragic death.

Steve Irwin exploded onto the wildlife documentary scene with an exuberant "Crikey!" when the *Crocodile Hunter* was first broadcast on television in 1992. Subsequently, his infectious enthusiasm, boisterousness, and apparent rugged fearlessness were easily aped by talk-show hosts who scrambled to include him on their programs. But he defied caricature. Moreover, prominent naturalists praised him for introducing millions to the natural world; Sir David Attenborough said after Irwin's death that "he taught them how wonderful and exciting it was, he was a born communicator" ("Terri Irwin Presents," 2006). One might well ask, Can the achievements of highly charismatic and transformational leaders such as Steve Irwin be sustained beyond their personal involvement in a project or initiative?

Today, visitors to Australia Zoo continue to crowd to the Animal Planet Crocoseum, the Rainforest Aviary, and the Tiger Temple. Australia Zoo and the Wildlife Warriors foundation continue to thrive. Why?

One possible explanation lies in the embedded culture associated with Steve Irwin's personal dream. Perhaps it was his recognition of the fragility of life that made the zoo the foundation of his vision for wildlife conservation. The philosophy that *zoo animals come first, the zoo team comes second, and the zoo visitors come third* has been firmly embedded in operation at the zoo. It shows in the thoughts of the following young bloggist:

> I'm Tameka and I'm currently 15. I went to Australia Zoo the other day, and it was fantastic. It really made me think about a lot of stuff. I'm really interested in working with the team. I know I'm still too young, but I'm thinking of volunteering soon and then maybe from then on I can slowly gain employment by Australia Zoo. ("My Dream," 2006)

As evidenced by this and numerous other bloggists, and indeed by our own experience of Australia Zoo, visitors are immediately struck by its special aura, partly physical, partly intangible. Certainly, care for the animals manifests itself in the almost palpable respect that zoo staff demonstrate toward the smallest creature and in the shared responsibility staff take in caring for the zoowide environment that houses the numerous fauna.

A second possible explanation lies in Steve's partnership with his wife, Terri. The 1990s must have been a whirlwind of activity for them, with little time for reflection. They must have been on a steep learning curve in relation to just about every aspect of zoo operations, with a rapidly expanding conservation enterprise that was going global. But Steve was not a loner. While his natural charisma and enthusiasm served his purpose of forefronting the wonders of the animal kingdom, his wife Terri was a hands-on insider. Steve reportedly asked Terri to promise that if anything happened to him she would make sure the zoo carried on. Additionally, Steve's children, Bindi and Robert, quite remarkable spokespersons for conservation in their own right, became integral parts of the Steve Irwin enterprise, fitting comfortably into Steve's business operations, approach, and image. His death did not create the huge obstacles that might have been expected because his ready-made "followers" were well prepared to continue on quite naturally and normally where he had left off.

Thus, four years after his death, Steve Irwin continues to be embedded in the international conservation conscience. We believe the Steve Irwin story embodies at least three essential elements of the C-B dynamic we have called *consolidating success*. First, it involves embedding an organization's distinctive values and vision in the organization's culture and ethos through the use of imagery, language, and symbolism. Second, it involves use of communications strategies, particularly modern technological communications, to enable the values and goals of an organization, cause, or movement to be brought into public consciousness. Third, it entails ensuring long-term stability in leadership through explicit strategies for succession. Fourth, it requires that attention be paid to dispersing leadership in ways that avoid undue reliance on one individual and that encourage a strong sense of shared responsibility and commitment.

These lessons from the ongoing success of the Crocodile Hunter foundation, we believe, have direct applicability in the work of school-based educational leaders in their efforts to build and sustain capacity.

CONCLUSION

In this chapter, we have acknowledged the fragility of successful school improvement and asserted that many outstanding educational achievements in the recent past have lacked sustainability, thus generating cynicism in school communities. We have proposed the sixth C-B dynamic—consolidating success—as an antidote to this situation.

We have also established that consolidating success is leadership driven, manifesting sophisticated forms of distributed leadership at both school and system levels. We have observed that teacher leaders, together with principals, play critical—and equivalent—roles at the junctures where the sustainability of success is planned.

Finally, it has become obvious as this chapter has unfolded that the relationship between consolidating success and sustaining success is complex. This thorny issue appears to be seriously undertreated in educational thinking, research, and associated literature. We offer the following tentative thoughts on this issue for the consideration of both practitioners and scholar-researchers:

Consolidating school success involves the application of a range of concerted actions, at a point in time, or points in time, to officially endorse an in-place process of school revitalization, embed its successes, orient new staff regarding the school's pedagogical priorities, and ensure the succession and sustainability of leadership.

Sustaining school success is a long-term process, beginning with the commencement of a school improvement initiative and extending beyond the formal completion of the initiative, to provide ongoing feedback about the effectiveness of school improvement processes, to contribute to maturation of teachers' expertise and professionalism, and to ensure the distribution of leadership across the school.

COSMIC C-B SIMULATION 6—EAT ALL YOUR GREENS!

CONSOLIDATING SUCCESS: BUILDING PERSONAL CAPACITY

Purpose:

To explore the meanings of consolidation and sustainability through a "greens" simulation

Rationale:

A great deal of confusion exists in education communities regarding both the short-term strategies and the long-term processes that are required for sustaining educational achievements and successes.

In this simulation, we endeavor to reduce that confusion. In so doing, we take Andy Hargreaves and Dean Fink's colorful metaphor with which we opened this chapter—*If you want to be healthy, you have to eat all your greens!*—and invite you to consider three questions:

1. Was each "green" a part of the All Hallows thumbnail and Crocodile Hunter scenario menus?
2. Was each "green" fully savored—or ignored, or merely picked at by the diners?
3. Is each of the six C-B greens a part of your school's longitudinal approach to enhancing a success that you have worked very hard to achieve in an area of school priority?

Approximate time required: 1.5 hours

Organization:

This simulation is intended primarily as a whole-school activity. Work groups of seven are recommended, with one or more school leaders in each group. If this is not possible, a degree of improvisation will be needed.

Materials for each group:

- Exhibit 7.A—The COSMIC C-B diagram
- Exhibit 7.B—Ten good health greens:
    - Asparagus
    - Bok choy
    - Celery
    - Okra
    - Spinach
    - Lettuce
    - Beans

  - o Broccoli
  - o Cabbage
  - o Sprouts

- Exhibit 7.C—Three copies of the Outside-the-Square Crocodile Hunter scenario for each table
- Exhibit 7.D—Three copies of the All Hallows snapshot for each table
- Exhibit 7.E—Two copies of the Exploring Consolidation and Sustainability worksheet for each person

Exhibit 7.E

EXPLORING CONSOLIDATION AND SUSTAINABILITY

Evidence of the *committing to revitalization* green

Evidence of the *organizational diagnosis and coherence* green

Evidence of the *seeking new heights* green

Evidence of the *micro-pedagogical deepening* green

Evidence of the *invoking reaction* green

Evidence of the *consolidating success* green

"Success" (good health today) means

"Sustainability" (good health into the future) means

Process:

Step 1—Formulate the simulation groups. Select a group facilitator, whose job it is to explain the task and process, and keep the group participants purposefully engaged and on task.

Step 2—Key instructions (to be modified to suit local circumstances):

As a school, we have spent much time and effort building the ______ pedagogical principle/curriculum/special project and testing and refining it. We can now see the results, some of which are a source of great professional satisfaction for us. In this simulation, we will explore ways to protect what we have created and ensure that our success does not disappear, fade, or get lost in the wake of new innovations. To do so, we will use an old but very simple adage for good health: *Eat all your greens.*

Step 3—The facilitator assigns the Crocodile Hunter scenario to three group members and the All Hallows case study to the three other members within each six-member group. Individual group members then each select (a) two C-B dynamics and (b) two "greens" from Exhibit 7.B, assigning a green to each of their chosen dynamics. From this point on, the "green" names replace the C-B titles.

Step 4—Participants read their assigned case study description (15 minutes) and complete their two relevant sections of the Exhibit 7.E worksheets.

Step 5—The facilitator coordinates a reflection on the Crocodile Hunter capacity-building "meal," emphasizing the adequacy, or otherwise, of each "green." That done, each member then completes the full worksheets using two data sources:

- His or her own two case study entries
- Descriptions provided by the five other group members

Step 6—This procedure is repeated for the All Hallows thumbnail, using a second copy of the Exhibit 7.E worksheet. With the two Exhibit 7.E worksheets completed, the various groups convene for a full *Eat all your greens* staff discussion. Six questions provide the framework for each case study discussion, with the green and COSMIC names being used interchangeably:

1. Were any greens ignored? If so, which?
2. Were any greens picked at, but not finished? If so, which?
3. Which greens were most nourishing?
4. Why is a healthy diet of all six greens essential to a school's good health?
5. How healthy was the overall diet in this case study?

Replicate the discussion for the Crocodile Hunter case study.

Step 7—Finally, as a group, select six greens, one for each C-B dynamic. Review your school longitudinal C-B project, using the five questions above as your guide. Prepare a gastronomical report titled "Toward Sustainable Health at __________ school." Prepare a plan to present the report to a full staff meeting.

8

Next Steps Along the Parallel Leadership C-B Pathway

Parallel leadership is a distinctive educational concept that has the potential to decisively advance the cause of schools and the teaching profession in the twenty-first century

—Crowther et al. (2009, p. 58)

INTRODUCTION

A pathway, the *Macquarie Dictionary* tells us, is a course of action in which something moves. In school improvement, several leadership pathways are well trodden. First is the *principal* pathway, where principals wave the flag, decide the direction, and point the way. Second is the *systemic* pathway, where district and system officers describe the destination and provide general directions for getting there, sometimes offering the services of a part-time guide. Third is the *experiential* pathway, where no particular end is planned, collective knowledge replaces a map, and shared responsibility does the job of the guide.

Indeed, each of these leadership approaches to school improvement sometimes works. That is not surprising, given the expertise and dedication that abound in schools and education systems. But, as our analysis in the introduction illustrated, far too often, all three pathways have led to spurious or transient end points—or to nowhere.

In this book we have asserted that a fourth pathway is available to 21st-century school leaders seeking to build and sustain the capacity of their schools. It is the *parallel leadership* pathway. As our chapter descriptions have shown, the parallel pathway places taxing demands on principals, teacher leaders, and district officers, but it also offers rich rewards for educational leaders and their schools. In this final chapter, we give the parallel leadership pathway the very close scrutiny that it demands and deserves. We also take one final look at the COSMIC C-B model, drawing attention to how parallel leaders can make practical uses of it. We conclude with suggestions for those educators who wish either to advocate for parallel leadership pathways in their school systems and workplaces or to explore it further.

COSMIC C-B IN RETROSPECT AND PROSPECT

In Retrospect . . .

Our starting premise in this book was that successful school capacity building is very much an unknown entity, even though its importance to school leaders is universally agreed on. We cited David Hopkins and David Jackson (2003, p. 87) in making this point: *Without a clear focus on "capacity," a school will be unable to sustain continuous improvement efforts or to manage change effectively. That we know.*

The capacity-building model that we commend for educational leaders' consideration is labeled COSMIC C-B, based on four features drawn from our understanding of the cosmos: ever-evolving, dynamic, harmonious, and orderly—every school leader's dream!

The school scenarios that are included in the chapter descriptions reveal our six COSMIC C-B dynamics in place in school settings and show how schools in the IDEAS Project research made use of the spirit and intent of the dynamics to achieve, consolidate, and then sustain high levels of success.

The core ingredients of the six dynamics are reflected in the questioning framework in Table 8.1. It is our clear position that, if school communities can meet the demands of the six dynamics as we have defined them in earlier chapters, and can answer the Table 8.1 principal/teacher/system leader questions affirmatively, then their chances of achieving and sustaining educational quality are very good indeed.

Table 8.1 Key Questions for Educational Stakeholders in Assessing the Integrity of a School Improvement Process

Dynamic 1—Committing to revitalization
Principal: Do I feel a deep personal attachment to the school's recent achievements (or claims of failure), and a sense of urgency to build and embed our successes? **Teacher leaders:** If a convincing values-based rationale for a school improvement process has been articulated by the principal, am I prepared to support it? **System leaders:** What must we do to ensure that the school's proposal for revitalization is linked to system priorities and expertise?
Dynamic 2—Organizational diagnosis and coherence
Principal: Am I engaging in discussion of the school's index of coherence without egotism, blame, or a thin skin? **Teacher leaders:** Does our school's report on our index of coherence (coherence) point out our achievements and needs in a "no blame" manner? **System leaders:** How can we ensure that resources and expertise are available to help correct misalignments identified in the school's self-diagnosis and subsequent index of coherence?
Dynamic 3—Seeking new heights
Principal: Do I publicly stand behind the school's vision and values, showing the courage of my convictions, and leading from the front? **Teacher leaders:** Are we pursuing elevated goals for our school through schoolwide pedagogical enhancement—with teacher leaders facilitating the process? **System leaders:** Are the school's vision and SWP consistent with the district's statement of purpose and core values?
Dynamic 4—Micro-pedagogical deepening
Principal: Do I facilitate schoolwide pedagogical deepening through support for teacher leadership? **Teacher leaders**: Are our professional learning processes assisting us to illuminate our individual gifts and talents in relation to our SWP and internationally acclaimed pedagogies? **System leaders:** How can the system deploy educational resources and expertise to contribute to pedagogical deepening initiatives in the school?

(Continued)

(Continued)

Dynamic 5—Invoking reaction
Principal: Do I ensure that the school's communications plans incorporate a balance of explanatory, promotional, networking, and advocacy strategies? **Teacher leaders:** Is the feedback that we are getting from sources both internal and external to the school being incorporated into our professional learning processes? **System leaders:** Are we encouraging double-loop feedback for the school through cluster and networking activities?
Dynamic 6—Consolidating success
Principal: How will I show my commitment to a 1 + 1 = 3 mind-set (rather than a "new broom sweeps clean" mind-set) when I move on to a new position? **Teacher leaders:** Are teacher leaders the designated custodians of our school's vision, SWP, and ongoing developmental processes, supported by a functioning ISMT? **System leaders:** Are we endorsing newly developed school knowledge and taking steps to ensure that it is enriched by key staff changes and ongoing systemic developments?

In Prospect . . .

Thus, COSMIC C-B, in our view, is a very valuable and timely tool for school leaders. We say this for five reasons that have been put forward, expanded upon at length, and defended, in the chapters of this book:

- It is grounded in values associated with social and ecological sustainability. That is, COSMIC C-B provides criteria and strategies for the incorporation of sustainability-associated values in a school's visioning and pedagogical developmental work. It also emphasizes continuous improvement, balance, and coherence over adhocracy or one-shot brilliance.
- It places concrete emphasis on the concept of knowledge generation. That is, COSMIC C-B asserts that the vision statements and pedagogical frameworks that are developed as the core means to enhanced school capacity constitute authentic and significant "new knowledge."
- It is processual in nature. That is, COSMIC C-B is not a description of a desired outcome but a guide for the ongoing decision making of school leaders as they proceed through their processes of school improvement.

- The construct of distributed leadership assumes definitive meaning in it. That is, COSMIC C-B demonstrates the workings of parallel leadership in what we believe to be the most comprehensive form yet published.
- The work of teachers is central—philosophically, conceptually, and practically. Indeed, without active and committed teacher leadership, it is very difficult for us to envision the intents of some C-B dynamics—particularly seeking new heights, micro-pedagogical deepening, and consolidating success—being achieved.

Are we, then, in a position to answer Hopkins and Jackson's challenge? We assert with confidence that we now know what a clear focus on capacity means and that we also know a great deal about how to achieve it. The answer is *yes*.

PARALLEL LEADERSHIP IN RETROSPECT AND PROSPECT

In Retrospect . . .

In proposing a parallel leadership pathway to achieve and sustain school success, we are entering a complex and somewhat contentious area of educational thinking. Is the concept of parallel leadership defensible? Is it worth developing further?

Some respected authorities are doubtful. Leithwood and Jantzi wrote recently,

> One slice of the educational literature seems mostly to be about "leadership by adjective"; a new qualifier is added to the term leadership at least annually, creating the misguided impression that something new has been discovered. (2006, p. 202)

In somewhat similar vein, Mulford (2008, p. 38) has claimed that the use of adjectives such as "democratic," "strategic," and "breakthrough" to describe school leadership implies the imposition of a "one size fits all" leadership style that is counterproductive. On the other hand, as we saw in the opening chapter, Linda Lambert (2007) is definitive that leadership in different phases of capacity development requires different functions (p. 316). Hallinger and Heck have also recently captured the importance of this assertion: "Leaders must be able to adapt their strategies to changing conditions at different stages in the journey of school improvement" (2010, p. 106).

In proposing the parallel leadership pathway as the key to sustained success through school improvement, we are optimistic that we are adding a degree of lucidness, not obfuscation, to this important debate.

We devoted a section of each of Chapters 2–7 to school-based leadership in relation to the particular C-B dynamic that was the subject of that chapter. In reflecting on the totality of the six leadership sections, we find ourselves face-to-face with two important conclusions. The first conclusion relates to the roles and functions of principals and teacher leaders respectively in the capacity-building process (see also Resource B). The second conclusion relates to particular leadership approaches that appear to characterize success with each C-B dynamic.

Figure 8.1 is drawn from the research database that is described in Resource B and that provided the basis for our discussions in the "Leadership" sections of Chapters 2–7. It contains a simplified diagrammatic representation of our statistical conclusions regarding the relative importance of principals and teacher leaders in the workings of each C-B dynamic.

Table 8.2 is also drawn from the database that is contained in Resource B, supplemented by the overview of dominant leadership approaches that was presented in Chapter 1. That is, it summarizes our research-based conclusions regarding the major leadership forms in the C-B dynamics as they relate to four broad categories of school-based leadership:

- *Transformational leadership*—emphasizing charisma, vision, inspiration, and intense energy or adrenaline
- *Strategic leadership*—emphasizing planning, accountability, objectivity, and efficiency
- *Advocacy (educative leadership)*—emphasizing social justice, consciousness raising, culture struggle, and confronting barriers to fairness
- *Organizationwide leadership*—emphasizing democracy, shared responsibility, collective thinking, and everyone a potential leader

Several key points emerge from Figure 8.1 and Table 8.2.

First, Figure 8.1 makes clear that the overall importance of principals and teacher leaders across the six-dynamic C-B process is relatively even. School revitalization cannot get underway (dynamic 1), our research reveals, without a firm commitment from the principal. It cannot penetrate classrooms (dynamic 4) without fully fledged teacher leadership. In the other four C-B dynamics, both leadership forms are essential. Successful capacity building, we conclude, is dependent on mature principal–teacher leadership capabilities and a relationship between principals and teacher leaders that is mutually respectful and grounded in trust while also recognizing each party's special needs, personal characteristics, and role-related functions.

Figure 8.1 A Diagrammatic Representation of Principal and Teacher Leader Influences in Capacity Building

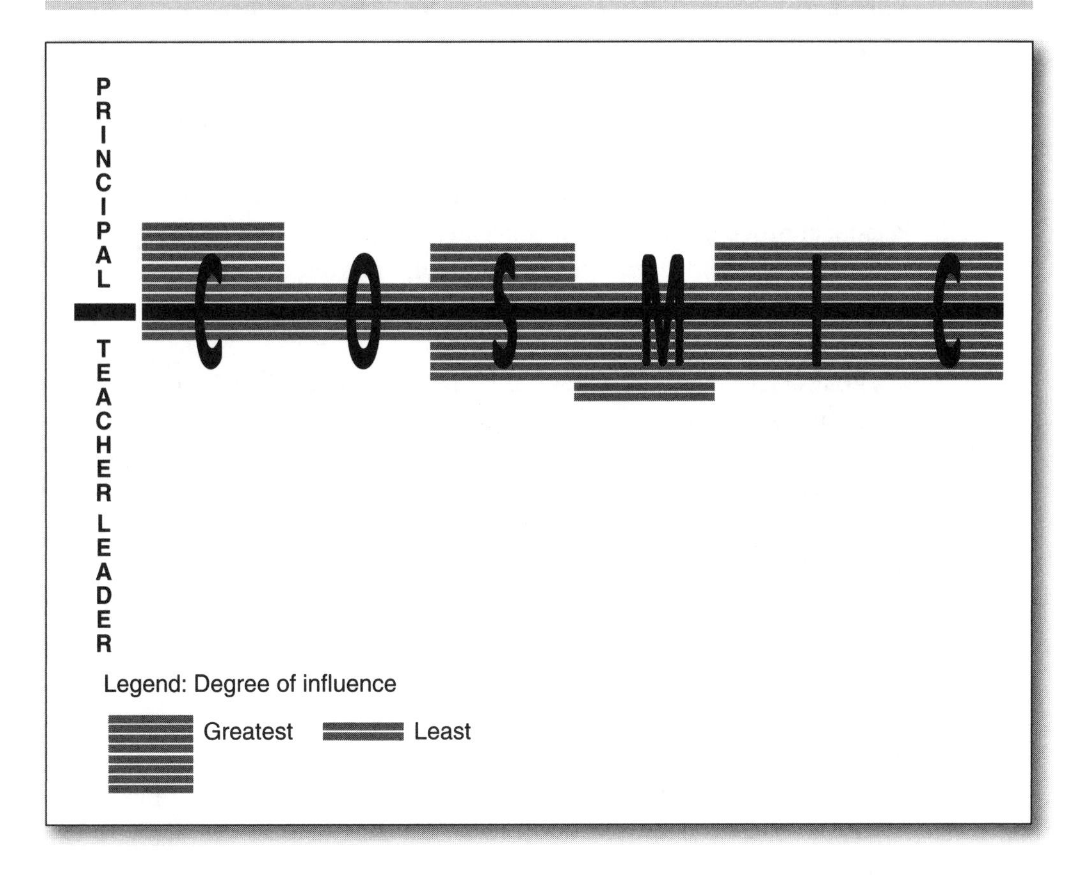

Table 8.2 Evidence of Four Leadership "Forms" in the C-B Dynamics

C-B Dynamics	*Dominant Leadership Approaches*
Committing to action	Advocacy/strategic
Organizational coherence	Organizationwide/strategic
Seeking new heights	Transformational/advocacy/strategic
Micro-pedagogical deepening	Strategic/advocacy
Invoking reaction	Strategic/advocacy/organizationwide
Consolidating success	Strategic/organizationwide

Second, teacher leadership gathers momentum as C-B processes unfold and as prospective teacher leaders engage in meaningful schoolwide activity, with the support and advice of principals and system officers. Teacher leadership assumes incontrovertible importance in the fourth (*micro-pedagogical deepening*) dynamic.

Third, teacher leadership can be undertaken by school-based professionals in a wide range of professional designations—classroom teachers, year-level and subject co-coordinators, heads of programs, and assistant principals. Positional office or designation is irrelevant. What matters is whether aspiring and prospective teacher leaders enjoy the full respect and confidence of their colleagues on the basis of evidence of the six capabilities that are contained in our Teachers as Leaders Framework (see Resource A).

Fourth, the multidisciplinary construct of "parallelism" emerges from our analyses as a highly credible framework within which to view the 21st-century teacher leader–principal leadership construct. In the IDEAS Project, parallelism in relationships was evident from start to finish but matured and acquired meaning in its own right in processes associated with the third, fourth, fifth, and sixth C-B dynamics.

We made the point in Chapter 1 that parallelism is a deeply entrenched construct in numerous manifestations of Western culture, including language, sciences, mathematics, and philosophy. Is it surprising, then, that its meanings were found to characterize principal–teacher leader relationships in school contexts where successful capacity building was achieved? Surely not.

Consider, for example, parallelism in the mathematical sense. The Mazzarino principal and teacher leaders (Chapter 4) could be said to reflect that meaning in the way they "mirrored" each other's values and goals in creating the Mazzarino *Castle to Network* vision and Janus-look schoolwide pedagogy. In the Eacham case study (Chapter 6), three "mirrors" were in evidence in the school's improvement processes—a strategic mirror (vision), a pedagogical mirror (SWP), and an accountability mirror (template), with a different leadership mosaic discernible in each mirror.

If the music construction of parallelism is employed, then the notion of parallel fifths might be seen as an appropriate metaphorical descriptor for the "tandem" leadership relationship between the Bellwood principal and teacher leaders as they negotiated a school development pathway in the context of significant within-school restraints (Chapter 3).

Epistemological definitions of parallelism seem readily applicable in the balance of affective (heart) and cognitive (head) ideals that were sought in the All Hallows' school leaders' revitalization purposes and also in their professional relationships (Chapter 7).

Finally, consider the Greenfield success story (Chapter 5). The Greenfield principal and teacher leaders employed metaphor to communicate the intents of their process of revitalization, to generate cultural consonance in the school community, and to inspire images of their school as a creative, exciting place to be each day. Their survey databases indicate that they succeeded in this endeavor and in so doing gained momentum for yet more creative metaphorical representations of their school. They could be said to capture the essence of parallelism in the form of figurative language.

Fifth, Table 8.2 indicates the diversity of leadership approaches that we observed to be associated with the six C-B dynamics as the research schools went about their improvement initiatives. We conclude from our interpretations of Table 8.2 that the leadership requirements for successful school improvement cannot be met through traditional approaches to leadership that have tended to focus on single individuals, particularly the principal. In our view, the only way that a school can meet the demands of leadership for successful school improvement is through accessing a range of leadership capabilities that go well beyond the principal's office. Taking Figure 8.1 and Table 8.2 together, we conclude also that the four approaches to leadership that are represented (i.e., strategic, transformational, educative/advocacy, and organizationwide) apply relatively evenly in the work of principals and teacher leaders across the duration of an improvement process.

Parallelism, it is apparent, is an extraordinarily rich cultural and disciplinary construct. It has the potential to become an equally rich educational construct. Parallel leadership is its most obvious educational manifestation.

In Prospect . . .

Three futuristic messages emerge from our "In retrospect" analysis. One relates to the principal, one to teacher leadership, and the third to our core concept of parallelism.

First, principals who lead "in parallel" understand and accept the close relationship between shared leadership responsibility and successful school capacity building as well as the rapidly growing maturity of the 21st-century teaching profession and of teachers in their schools. They view their due process functions in this context, ensuring that their leadership responsibilities are closely linked to key teachers' growing capabilities for schoolwide pedagogical enhancement. Their main functions we assert to be as follows:

- *Mobilizing, facilitating, and sustaining a whole-school improvement process*—making a decision to revitalize; stepping back at key junctures; ensuring that the process builds and maintains momentum; and endorsing succession planning
- *Envisioning inspiring futures*—making personal values public; encouraging creativity in school-developed imagery; and ensuring

that their school's vision meets educational, ethical, transformative, and practical criteria

- *Aligning key institutional elements*—facilitating organizational diagnosis using proven instruments; listening; encouraging purposeful group dynamics; and allowing teacher leaders to manage (or co-manage) diagnostic/analysis/reporting procedures
- *Enabling teacher leadership*—understanding the concept (especially the expert teacher/teacher leader linkage); providing opportunities and strategies for potential teacher leaders; and encouraging a school definition of parallelism
- *Building synergistic alliances*—facilitating within-school (cross-grade and -subject) networks to encourage pedagogical deepening; clarifying links to emerging systemic priorities; developing alliances with other schools, based on common interests and helping in-need schools; testing school-developed pedagogical products in public forums; and engaging in public advocacy for the school and profession
- *Culture building and identity generation*—operating across all three of Edgar Schein's levels of organizational culture (artifacts, values, assumptions), and appreciating that authentic identity generation in a school derives primarily from the dual concepts of vision and SWP

Second, teachers who lead "in parallel" facilitate principled professional action in a school in order to achieve whole-school success. They engage collaboratively with the principal, but assume major responsibility for the school's pedagogical enhancement. Their key functions we assert to be as follows:

- *Conveying convictions about a better world by*
  - transposing values-based visions into values-based pedagogical frameworks
  - contributing to an image of teaching as a profession that makes a difference
- *Facilitating communities of learning by*
  - building a shared, schoolwide approach to core pedagogical processes
  - developing and using protocols for mature professional interaction
- *Striving for pedagogical excellence by*
  - refining core teaching strategies in respect of students' needs and well-being
  - continuously developing and refining personal teaching gifts and talents
  - seeking deep understanding of authoritative pedagogical practices

- *Confronting barriers in the school's culture and structures by*
  - standing up for in-need children, especially disadvantaged and marginalized individuals and groups
  - working with administrators to find solutions to issues of equity, fairness, and justice in the school's culture and structures
  - encouraging student "voice"
- *Translating ideas into sustainable systems of action by*
  - working with the principal and other teachers to manage projects that heighten alignment between the school's vision, values, pedagogical practices, and professional learning activities
  - building alliances and nurturing external networks of support
- *Nurturing a culture of success by*
  - acting on opportunities to emphasize accomplishments and high expectations
  - facilitating continuity in school improvement processes in the face of transition in key staff

Third, parallel leadership we assert to be a process whereby teacher leaders and their principals engage in collective action to build and sustain enhanced school capacity. It embodies four distinct qualities—mutual trust, shared purpose, allowance for individual expression, and appreciation for the importance of creating school success in the context of systemic goals and priorities.

Parallel leadership, we conclude, is an educational concept of distinction and of substance.

CONCLUSION

The parallel leadership pathway is a human pathway. As such, it is marked by profound human values—deep trust, shared purpose, and explicit allowance for the expression of individual talents and values. But that is not all. It is a pathway that is grounded in a concern for social and ecological sustainability. Thus, it is a pathway for future generations, not just those treading it today. And that is not all either. It is also a pathway that is inseparable from processes of organizational regeneration, revitalization, and rejuvenation. It is part and parcel of school improvement and capacity building. When parallel leadership, school improvement, and school capacity building are intertwined, the world of the school becomes more courageous, more coherent, more creative, more focused, and, ultimately, more successful. How can they become intertwined? When school leaders ensure that the COSMIC C-B model is incorporated into their work.

If ever there was a time to feel a great sense of confidence in educational leadership, that time is now.

❖ Resources ❖

RESOURCE A

THE IDEAS PROJECT

Background

The IDEAS Project began in early 1997 as a result of dialogue between senior staff in the Queensland (Australia) Department of Education and counterparts in the University of Southern Queensland's Leadership Research Institute. The essential question that guided these discussions was deceptively simple: *Can it be ensured that school-based management is implemented so that it has positive effects in classrooms? If so, how?*

IDEAS in its present form represents the product of more than a decade of thinking, dialoguing, and critiquing of this perplexing question by educators from a wide range of schools, systems, and universities across Australia and internationally. Additionally, it has been written about widely and provided much of the material for the Corwin bestseller *Developing Teacher Leaders: How Teacher Leadership Enhances School Success* (Crowther et al., 2009).

In the period 1997 to present, the IDEAS Project has been formally implemented in more than 350 schools in several countries. It continues to be refined and expanded.

Of fundamental importance in guiding the developments that have occurred with IDEAS has been the compelling research evidence from the University of Wisconsin-Madison (Newmann & Wehlage, 1995) that when teachers engage as a professional community to shape their school's philosophy, and when they then proceed to develop shared pedagogical principles and strategies that complement their school's philosophy, the effects on student achievement, particularly for disadvantaged students, can be very significant. This insight—that the professional community of the school must be accorded key responsibility for school revitalization and pedagogical development—remains fundamental to IDEAS today, particularly through the distinctive IDEAS constructs of teacher leadership (and parallel leadership) and schoolwide pedagogy. Additionally, the Australian Research Council supported research into the IDEAS Project through two substantial research grants (1997–1999, 2000–2003), as did the Singaporean Ministry of Education. These grants engaged the services of a number of doctoral students, as well as Professor Steve Kaagan of Michigan State University as an international research partner. Then, in 2004, the Australian government lent further support to the research dimension of the IDEAS Project through a comprehensive 12-school trial in three Australian school jurisdictions. The outcomes of the trial served to confirm the transferability of IDEAS concepts and processes to a wide range of educational contexts. Finally, in 2008, the

Victorian (Australia) Department of Education facilitated the very significant R&D project that is contained in Resource B and that provided the basis for the development of this book.

IDEAS Project Protocols of Professional Engagement

Figure A.1 outlines the protocols of professional engagement used by schools engaging in the IDEAS Project.

Figure A.1 Protocols of Professional Engagement

IDEAS—Principles of Practice

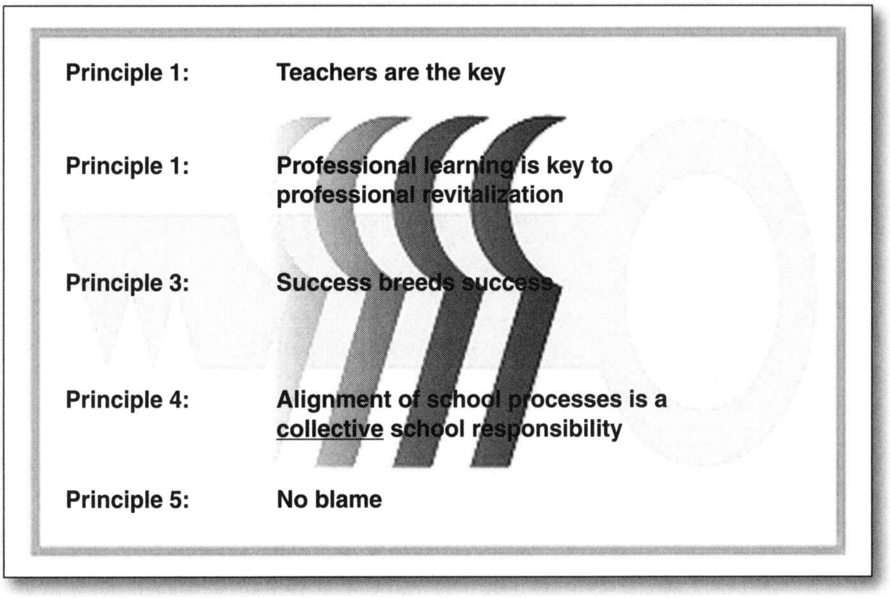

Principle 1: **Teachers are the key**

Principle 1: **Professional learning is key to professional revitalization**

Principle 3: **Success breeds success**

Principle 4: **Alignment of school processes is a collective school responsibility**

Principle 5: **No blame**

Key Components of the IDEAS Project

The vision of the IDEAS Project is uniquely focused on the dual concepts of the power of enlightened teaching and enhanced school outcomes:

> *To inspire IDEAS schools to engage in journeys of self-discovery that will ensure they achieve sustainable excellence in teaching and learning*

To this end, the IDEAS Project is distinguished by four key components. Each component is grounded in authoritative research completed under the auspices of a range of international educational agencies. The four components are as follows.

Component One: The ideas Process

The *ideas* process is a five-phase school-based revitalization approach that has drawn on sources such as metastrategy (Limerick, 1998); appreciative inquiry (Cooperrider & Whitney, 1996); action learning (Argyris & Schon, 1996; Kolb, 1984; Zuber-Skerritt, 1990); and organizational capacity building (King & Newmann, 2001). The five phases, *initiating, discovering, envisioning, actioning,* and *sustaining,* center on the pedagogical work of teachers, in terms of leadership functions and responsibilities and through the IDEAS Protocols of Professional Engagement.

A diagrammatic representation of the *ideas* process is contained in Diagram A.1.

Diagram A.1 The *ideas* Process

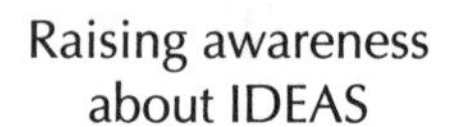

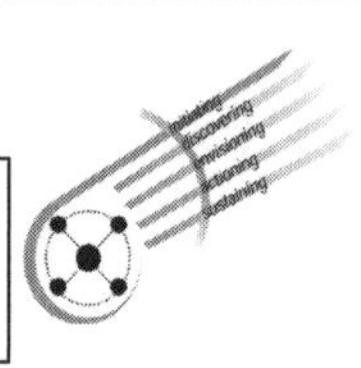

initiating	How will we manage the revitalization process? Who will facilitate the process? Who will record our history of the journey?
discovering	What are we doing that is most successful? What is not working as well as we would like it to? What is our level of alignment of key school variables?
envisioning	What do we hope our school will look like in the future? What is our conceptualization of our preferred schoolwide pedagogy?
actioning	How will we create a tripartite action plan—a pedagogical plan, a strategic plan, and a community plan? How will we work toward enhancing the alignment of key school elements and processes?
sustaining	What progress have we made in implementing our schoolwide pedagogy? How are we ensuring continuity in our development as a school?

Component Two: Organizational Alignment: The Research-Based Framework for Enhancing School Alignment (RBF)

The RBF is grounded in authoritative theory relating to organizational alignment (Drucker, 1946; Heath & Staudenmayer, 2000; Hitt & Ireland, 2002; Schneider et al., 2003) complemented by research into whole-school improvement conducted under the auspices of the University of Wisconsin-Madison's Center on Organization and Restructuring of Schools (King & Newmann, 2001). Based on the various authoritative contributions that have been considered, the IDEAS Project offers the following definition of alignment:

Alignment in educational organizations occurs when distinct and interdependent organizational elements are mutually reinforcing, thereby enhancing the opportunities for heightened school outcomes.

The five fundamental variables that contribute to alignment in educational organizations are

- the organization's leadership and strategic management capability;
- internal and external stakeholder support;
- the organization's infrastructural designs (including curricula, spatial arrangements, technologies, marketing, and quality assurance strategies);
- the organization's pedagogical practices (teaching, learning, and assessment); and
- the organization's professional learning mechanisms.

Where these five sets of variables are developed and in alignment with each other, a school's potential to enhance its outcomes are maximized.

A diagrammatic representation of the RBF is contained in Diagram A.2. Participating IDEAS Project schools use the RBF at a number of junctures during their IDEAS Project journeys, commencing with a systematic approach to organizational diagnosis using the IDEAS Diagnostic Inventory at the "discovering" phase of the process.

Component Three: 3-Dimensional Pedagogy (3-DP)

IDEAS conceptualizes the work of the 21st-century teaching professional as three-dimensional pedagogy (3-DP). The term 3-DP represents the integration of personal pedagogy (PP), schoolwide pedagogy (SWP), and authoritative pedagogy (AP) in the work of teachers. A diagrammatic representation of 3-DP is in Diagram A.3. The position is taken in IDEAS that it is the intersection of the three dimensions that generates "expert teaching" as an individual/collaborative professional construct.

Diagram A.2 The Research-Based Framework for Enhancing School Alignment

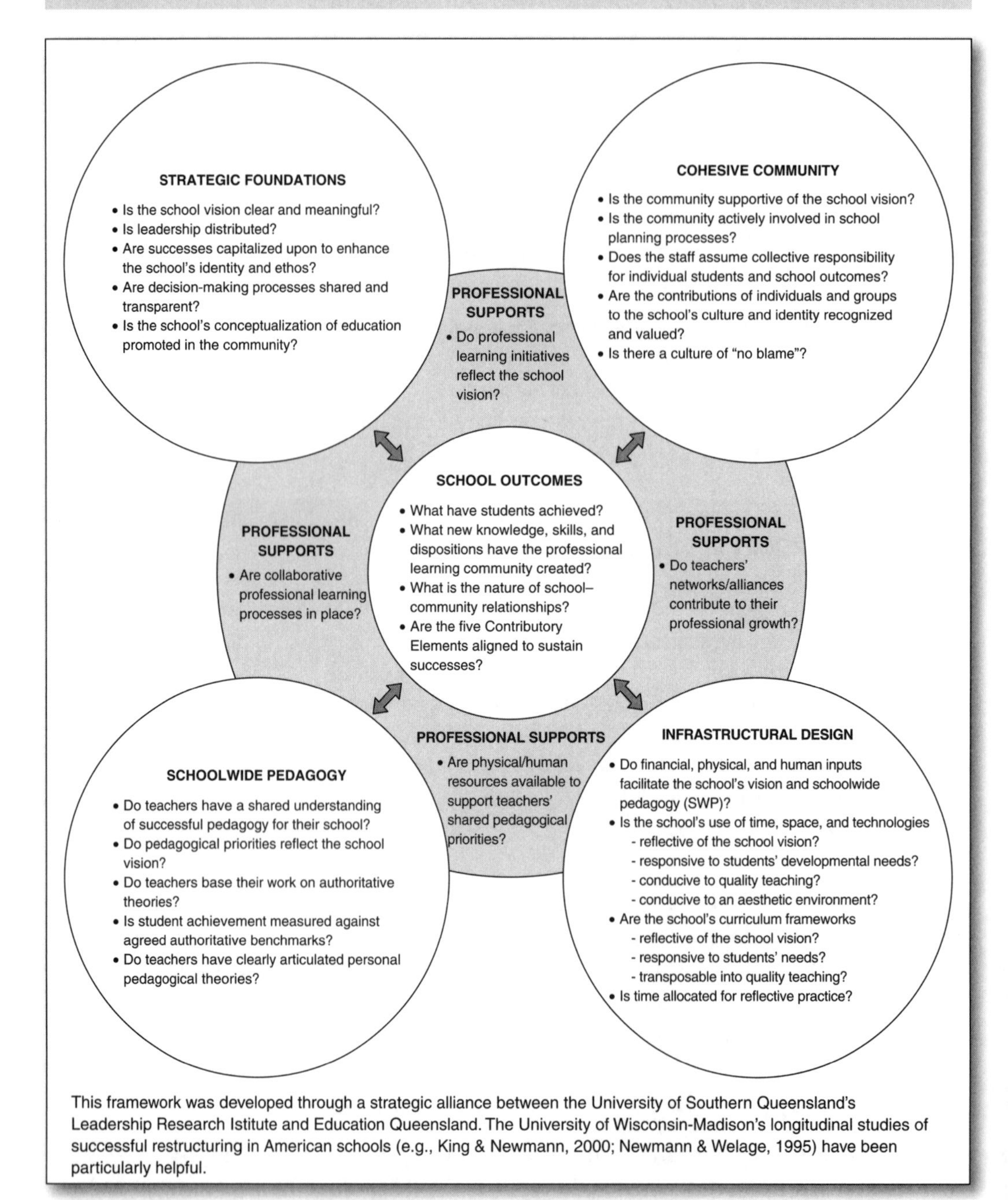

This framework was developed through a strategic alliance between the University of Southern Queensland's Leadership Research Istitute and Education Queensland. The University of Wisconsin-Madison's longitudinal studies of successful restructuring in American schools (e.g., King & Newmann, 2000; Newmann & Welage, 1995) have been particularly helpful.

Component Four: Parallel Leadership

In the IDEAS Project, parallel leadership is viewed as a process whereby teacher leaders and their principals engage in collective action for purposes of schoolwide development and revitalization to enhance the school's "capacity" (Crowther et al., 2002, 2009). The three essential characteristics

Diagram A.3 Three-Dimensional Pedagogy

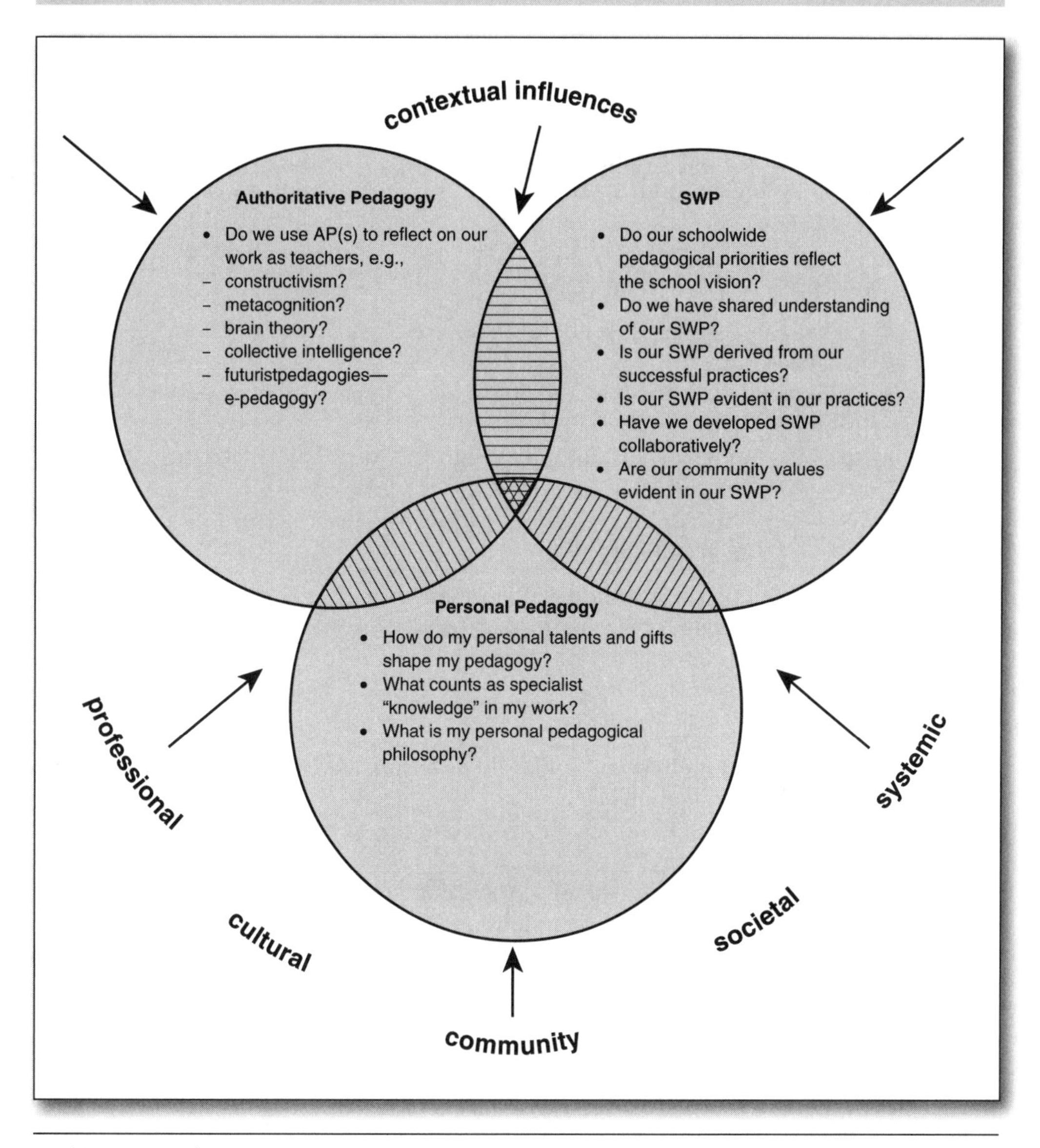

(Andrews & Crowther, 2003)

of parallel leadership are defined as mutual respect, a sense of shared purpose, and allowance for individual expression. Teacher leaders' functions in parallel leadership relationships reflect all major leadership theories but emphasize schoolwide pedagogical enhancement (Crowther et al., 2009). The Teachers as Leaders Framework that is essential to the IDEAS Project is contained in Table A.1.

Table A.1 Teachers as Leaders Framework

Teacher leaders . . .

Convey convictions about a better world by

- articulating a positive future for all students
- contributing to an image of teaching as a profession that makes a difference

Facilitate communities of learning by

- encouraging a shared, schoolwide approach to core pedagogical processes
- approaching professional learning as consciousness-raising about complex issues
- synthesizing new ideas out of colleagues' professional discourse and reflective activities

Strive for pedagogical excellence by

- showing genuine interest in students' needs and well-being
- continuously developing and refining personal teaching gifts and talents
- seeking deep understanding of significant pedagogical practices

Confront barriers in the school's culture and structures by

- standing up for children, especially disadvantaged and marginalized individuals and groups
- working with administrators to find solutions to issues of equity, fairness, and justice
- encouraging student "voice" in ways that are sensitive to students' developmental stages and circumstances

Translate ideas into sustainable systems of action by

- working with the principal, administrators, and other teachers to manage projects that heighten alignment between the school's vision, values, pedagogical practices, and professional learning activities
- building alliances and nurturing external networks of support

Nurture a culture of success by

- acting on opportunities to emphasize accomplishments and high expectations
- encouraging collective responsibility in addressing schoolwide challenges
- encouraging self-respect and confidence in students' communities

(Crowther, Ferguson, & Hann, 2009, p. 3)

Principals' leadership functions are conceptualized as "metastrategic" (Crowther et al., 2009). See Table A.2.

Table A.2 The Five Core Functions of the Principal in School Improvement

Function One	Envisioning inspiring futures
Function Two	Aligning key institutional elements
Function Three	Enabling teacher leadership
Function Four	Building synergistic alliances
Function Five	Culture building and identity generation

A diagrammatic representation of the relationship of parallel leadership to enhanced school capacity building, as it is articulated in the IDEAS Project, is contained in Diagram A.4.

Diagram A.4 Linking Parallel Leadership and Successful Capacity Building

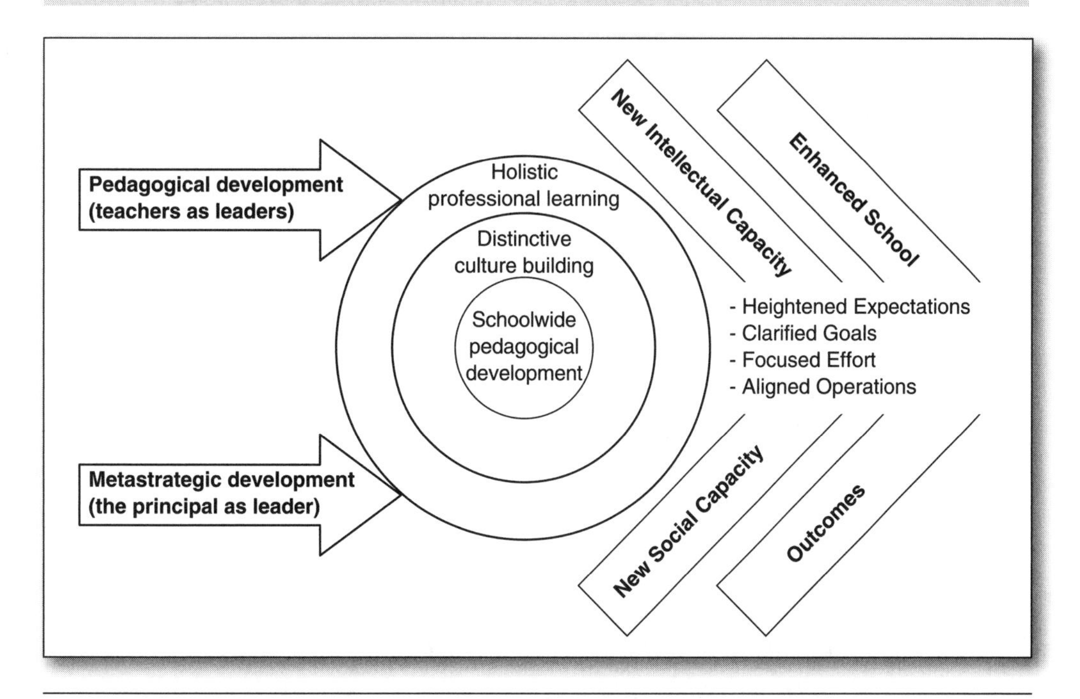

(Crowther, Ferguson, & Hann, 2009, p. 60)

RESOURCE B

THE RESEARCH DESIGN AND METHODOLOGY

Twenty-two schools undertook to complete the IDEAS Project in a metropolitan region in the Australian State of Victoria in the period 2004 to 2008. Consistent with the key principles of the IDEAS Project, they undertook to accomplish the following functions:

- Implementation of a five-phase, three- to four-year revitalization process—*ideas* (Diagram A.1 in Resource A), supported by descriptive professional learning materials and ongoing assistance and advice from the IDEAS Project consultancy team
- Establishment of parallel leadership roles and functions to manage the IDEAS process, encompassing metastrategic principal functions, teacher leadership functions, and a designated IDEAS facilitator role
- Use of an established framework for organizational alignment (the IDEAS Project Research-Based Framework for Organizational Coherence [RBF—Diagram A.2 in Resource A]) and validated diagnostic instruments to ascertain (and enhance) the school's *index of coherence*
- Development of a distinctive school vision and schoolwide pedagogical framework (SWP)
- Implementation of a range of professional learning strategies to transpose the SWP into enriched classroom pedagogical practices
- Creation of internal and external networks, encompassing project clusters, parent involvement, and student leadership teams

Preliminary analysis of Victorian Department of Education SAS (Student Attitudes to School) and SOS (Staff Opinion Survey) databases in late 2008 indicated that the 19 schools that completed the project demonstrated substantial improvements in student attitudes and engagement, as well as teacher esteem and morale, in conjunction with the project. Following discussion with senior department officials, an eight-member University of Southern Queensland research team was established and a comprehensive three-phase research design was agreed on. The research problem that guided the Phase A research was as follows:

What changes, if any, in school outcomes can be attributed to the research schools' implementation of the IDEAS Project, 2004–2008?

The improvements in teacher and student data, 2004–2008, that had been observed were found to be statistically significant (Andrews & USQ-LRI

Research Team, 2009). Given that 17 of the 22 schools had been designated as "targeted" or "underperforming" by system officials in 2004, this conclusion was deemed to be worthy of further investigation.

As an exploratory step in this regard, the SOS and SAS statistical data were grouped into three categories and the explanatory diagram that is contained in Diagram B.1 was created.

Diagram B.1 A Diagrammatic Explanation of the Achievement of "Success" in a Cluster of IDEAS Project Schools, 2004–2008

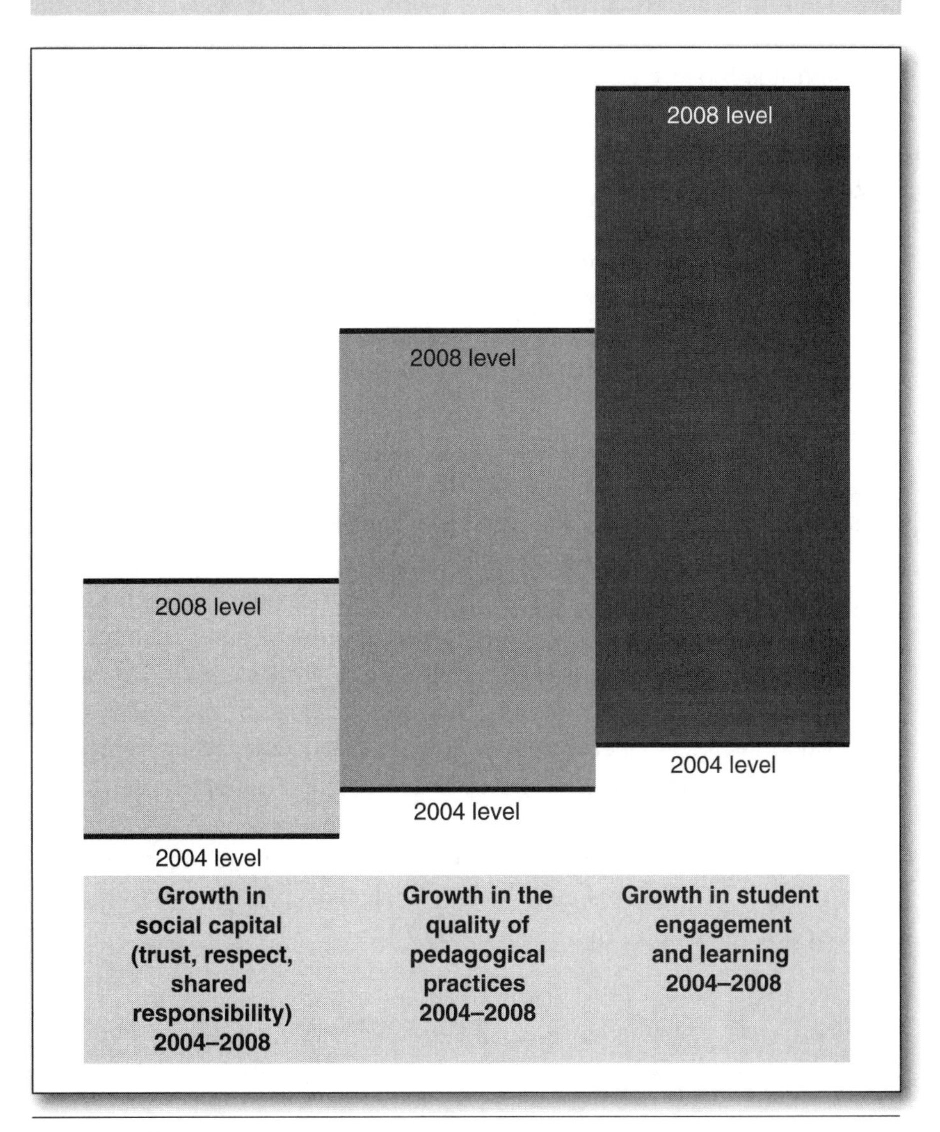

(Crowther, 2010)

In interpreting Diagram B.1, three important (and somewhat contentious) hypotheses were developed by the research team:

- *Hypothesis 1:* When a school's level of social capital increases, improvements in pedagogical practice will be at least as great.
- *Hypothesis 2:* When the perceived quality of a school's pedagogical practice increases, perceived improvements in student engagement will be at least as great.
- *Hypothesis 3:* Improvements in student outcomes that occur in conjunction with a school improvement process take a minimum of three to four years to achieve.

With this broad conceptual picture in place, a second formal phase of research was undertaken. The Phase B research problem constituted an extension of the three hypotheses that were developed out of the Phase A research. It was as follows:

> *What lessons for school improvement can be learned from the experiences of schools that have achieved enhanced outcomes in conjunction with implementation of the IDEAS Project, 2004–2008?*

The Phase B research comprised case study analyses of the documented and validated achievements of 5 of the 22 schools. It was undertaken by the university research team with the support of Professor Bill Mulford in the role of methodological and conceptual validator. In analyzing the case study data, the research team found that each of the five schools had experienced particular critical junctures—or turning points, or moments of truth—in implementing the IDEAS Project. In addressing the critical junctures successfully, each had been enabled to progress further through the five stages of the IDEAS process through concerted leadership decisions and actions. This was so even though each of the five schools had approached implementation of IDEAS in a relatively distinctive manner, reflecting its unique contextual considerations.

Samples of outcomes data for two of the schools that feature in the snapshot description in chapters in this book (Chapters 2 and 5, respectively) are contained in Tables B.1, B.2, B.3, and B.4.

Table B.1 Improvements in Student Attitude (SAS) and Staff Opinion (SOS) data at Carmichael Secondary College 2004–2007

Improvement in Student Attitudes, 2004–2008						
State (Secondary) Means			*Carmichael Secondary College Means*			
2004	2007	Improvement	2004	2007*	Improvement	
69.02	70.95	1.93	66.35	70.89	4.54	
Interpretation: Carmichael Secondary College's Student Attitudes Survey data, 2004–2007, indicated more than twice the state improvement in numerical terms, and statistical significance at the 0.05 level on all 21 items in the survey. There were particularly marked changes in student perceptions of teacher effectiveness, teacher empathy, learning environments, and student well-being.						
Improvement in Staff Opinions of School, 2004–2008						
State (Secondary) Means			*Carmichael Secondary College Means*			
2004	2007	Improvement	2004	2007*	Improvement	
55.79	57.24	1.45	54.77	62.52	7.76	
Interpretation: Carmichael Secondary College's Staff Opinion of School Survey improvement, 2004–2007, indicated more than five times the state improvement in numerical terms, and statistical significance at the 0.01 level. From 2004–2007, the staff perceived that Carmichael had improved in all 20 SOS measures, encompassing the categories of morale, professional interaction, student engagement, school ethos and environment, and teacher recognition and leadership.						
*Carmichael Secondary College closed at the end of 2007						

Table B.2 Improvements in Student Attitude (SAS) and Staff Opinion (SOS) Data at Greenfield Elementary School, 2004–2008

Improvement in Student Attitudes, 2004–2008						
State (Elementary) Means			*Greenfield Elementary Means*			
2004	2008	Improvement	2004	2008	Improvement	
79.52	82.21	1.93	78.36	87.87	9.51	

(Continued)

(Continued)

Interpretation: Greenfield Elementary School's Student Attitudes Survey data, 2004–2008, indicated about five times the state improvement in numerical terms, and statistical significance at the 0.01 level on the categories of student morale and behavior, student distress, student–teacher relations, learning environments, school connectedness, student motivation, learning confidence, and learning connectedness to peers.

Improvement in Staff Opinions of School, 2004–2008

State (Elementary) Means			*Greenfield Elementary School Means*			
2004	2008	Improvement	2004	2008	Improvement	
62.85	65.12	2.27	57.58	65.96	8.38	

Interpretation: Greenfield Elementary School's Staff Opinion of School Survey improvement, 2004–2008, indicated about four times the state improvement in numerical terms, and statistical significance at the 0.01 level. From 2004–2007, the staff perceived that Carmichael had improved in all 20 SOS measures.

Table B.3 Details of Increases in Well-Being and Climate at Greenfield Elementary School, 2004–2008

Area of major improvement, 2004–2008	*% improvement*
Classroom behavior	14.6%
Student morale	13.2%
Teacher effectiveness	11.8%
Stimulating learning environment	11.4%
School connectedness	11.2%
Teacher empathy	10.4%
Student safety	10.0%
Student motivation	9.2%
Full suspensions	
2006	10
2008	0
Afterschool suspensions	
2006	87
2008	12

SOURCE: 2008 Survey Data 2004–2008.

Table B.4 Improvements in Literacy Data at Greenfield Elementary School, 2004–2008

- Year 2 reading achievement reached the state mean in 2007 for the first time and sustained this level in 2008.
- Year 3 upward trend in all areas of literacy, 2004–2008.
- Year 5 upward trend in reading, spelling, and writing, with some 2007 and 2008 results well above state school means.

SOURCES: AIM Data 2004–2008; The 2008 Assessment of Reading DEECD Report.

As a result of the insights derived from the Phase B research, the research team, along with representatives of the five case study schools, developed the following definition of "success":

> **School success** is constituted of enhanced school outcomes in agreed high priority goal areas, based on (i) documented evidence of those outcomes and (ii) teachers' expressed confidence in their school's capacity to extend and sustain the outcomes into the future. (Andrews & USQ-LRI Research Team, 2009)

The research team then proceeded to develop the following definition of "capacity building":

> **Capacity building** is the intentional process of mobilizing a school's resources in order to enhance priority outcomes–and sustain those improvements (Andrews & USQ-LRI Research Team, 2009).

The six-dynamic capacity-building model that is contained in Figure 1.1 (this book) was then fleshed out by the research team and representatives of the five case study schools. The six dynamics that constitute the model were given precise meanings, based on developments, events, and decisions associated with the six critical junctures:

- *Committing to school revitalization*—the first capacity-building dynamic—requires that school leaders engage in intensive values interrogation, resulting in justification of a priority need for revitalization in their school. That need is then articulated with a spirit of hope, energy, and purpose.
- *Organizational diagnosis and coherence*—the second capacity-building dynamic—involves development within the school community of a sense

of shared understanding of the level of alignment of the school's key elements.

- *Seeking new heights*—the third capacity-building dynamic—involves creation of a projection of the future that is grounded in confidence and hope. This projection manifests in two interrelated forms—a vision statement and a schoolwide pedagogical framework.
- *Micro-pedagogical deepening*—the fourth capacity-building dynamic—involves teachers engaging in one or more of three forms of pedagogical practice: intensive reflection on personal gifts and talents, conceptual expansion and exploration of the school's pedagogical principles (SWP), and refinement and implementation of strategies relating to the SWP.
- *Invoking reaction*—the fifth capacity-building dynamic—involves the dissemination of significant new school-based knowledge through critique, networking, and advocacy. It provides important mechanisms for refinement of the school's creative products.
- *Consolidating school success*—the sixth capacity-building dynamic—is made possible by the embedding of core processes that have contributed to the enhancement of school outcomes. The processes involve strategic, professional learning and enculturation strategies.

To conclude Phase B of the research, the researchers labeled the model COSMIC C-B (based on the acronym for the six dynamics) and identified a series of features that they believed to be critical to it:

> *First,* it contains the core requirements (i.e., the six dynamics) that any school should ensure are in place as it proceeds through a school improvement process.
>
> *Second,* the six dynamics have an interlocking relationship, although they have individual conceptual meaning.
>
> *Third,* the centerpiece is the fourth dynamic, micro-pedagogical deepening. It is this dynamic where teaching, learning, and assessment constitute the unequivocal focus of concern.
>
> *Fourth,* it is underpinned by distributed ("parallel") forms of leadership. (The increased size of the arrows linking the six dynamics in the diagram in Figure 1.1 [this book] connotes the growth in the importance of parallel leadership as the capacity-building process unfolds.)
>
> *Fifth,* it is concerned with ensuring that success, once achieved, is sustained.

Sixth, it asserts that each school is essentially responsible for its own improvement.

The Phase C research was then undertaken by the university research team. Eight IDEAS Project schools that had achieved significant outcomes in conjunction with their engagement with IDEAS were selected for analysis in terms of their underpinning leadership processes. The research problem that guided the Phase C research was as follows:

What forms of principal and teacher leadership are associated with successful implementation of the six individual dynamics in the COSMIC C-B model?

The database for Phase C comprised four sets of data for each of the eight schools:

- Empirical and descriptive evidence of school outcomes, 2004–2008
- Descriptive evidence of the school's implementation of the five phases of the IDEAS process
- Descriptive data relating to key events and key players in facilitating IDEAS, derived from researchers' observations and post facto interviews with principals and teachers
- Focus group analyses, involving representatives of the university research team and five of the eight schools. During these sessions, all six COSMIC C-B dynamics were explored in relation to four core questions:
    - Why was this dynamic important in enabling your school to progress through the IDEAS Project?
    - How did this dynamic enable your school to progress through the IDEAS Project?
    - Who did what, and how, to facilitate achievement of this dynamic in your school?
    - What forms of leadership were explicit, and implicit, in achieving the dynamic in your school?

Broad generalizations regarding leadership principles and processes across the sample were then developed and submitted to the eight school leadership teams for validation.

The outcomes of the Phase C research are presented in Table B.5.

Table B.5 Leadership Constructs Underpinning the Capacity-Building Dynamics

The First C-B Dynamic—*Committing to School Revitalization*

Findings

- A school leader, usually the principal, either discerned a serious concern relating to student achievement or was alerted to a serious concern by systemic (regional) officers.
- A definitive decision to revitalize was made and articulated by the principal.
- The IDEAS Project was selected by the principal in part because of its *no blame, success breeds success, parallel leadership, alignment,* and *teachers are the key* principles.
- Staff were invited to endorse the process, and mostly did so at a formal meeting.
- IDEAS Project staff attended a staff meeting and outlined IDEAS principles and support mechanisms for participating schools.
- An IDEAS School Management Team (ISMT), comprising administration and teacher representatives, was created, usually with a teacher as facilitator.

Conclusions

Conclusion 1: The principal was primarily the linchpin in mobilizing the whole-school revitalization process.

Conclusion 2: Credible external support systems were essential in enabling the IDEAS process to gain momentum.

Conclusion 3: The involvement of teachers in IDEAS management roles was invited, and usually accepted by individuals and/or small teams.

The Second C-B Dynamic—*Organizational Diagnosis and Coherence*

Findings

- The IDEAS Project Principles of Practice were distributed, discussed, and posted in staff rooms.
- The RBF (Diagram A.2, Resource A) was introduced to the staff, and its integrity demonstrated, by the IDEAS Project team.
- The concepts of parallel leadership and teacher leadership were presented at school workshops and relevant materials distributed.
- IDEAS Project Diagnostic Inventories (DIs) were administered to teachers, students, and parents.
- The ISMT managed all aspects of RBF/DI activities, including the calculation of the school's index of coherence, whole-school conversation about DI data (using the IDEAS Project Rules of Skillful Discussion in Table B.6) and report card preparation.
- Principals stepped back from RBF/DI activities and encouraged facilitators to view themselves as teacher leaders.
- The school's major "alignment" needs were identified and strategies for enhancing alignment proposed.

Conclusions

Conclusion 4: Principals provided big-picture explanations to staff regarding their aspirations and support for IDEAS and the concepts of parallel leadership and teacher leadership.

Conclusion 5: Credible external agencies were important in explaining the RBF, mobilizing diagnostic processes, facilitating "no blame" relationships, and establishing the foundations for parallel leadership roles.

Conclusion 6: Preliminary teacher leadership functions were set in place through ascription to project facilitators of schoolwide diagnostic, analytical, and reporting strategies.

The Third C-B Dynamic—*Seeking New Heights*

Findings

- School and community values were explored through formal school workshops.
- Potential vision statements were generated using IDEAS resource materials.
- A school vision statement was developed, with strong principal involvement.
- The IDEAS Project Principles of Practice were reiterated.
- The IDEAS Project Rules of Skillful Discussion were reiterated.
- IDEAS Project materials were redeveloped by ISMTs for pedagogical workshops.
- A schoolwide pedagogical framework was developed, facilitated by teacher leaders.
- The IDEAS team assisted with SWP workshops.
- Leadership theories, and parallel leadership concepts, were presented to IDEAS team members, ISMT members, and project facilitators.

Conclusions

Conclusion 7: Principals were the key agents in whole-school vision development processes.

Conclusion 8: Teacher leaders led SWP developmental processes, using the school vision as the starting point.

The Fourth C-B Dynamic—*Micro-Pedagogical Deepening*

Findings

- Activities associated with the fourth C-B dynamic involved three forms: whole-school exploration of SWP principles through processes of action learning and professional conversation, exploration of personal pedagogical talents and gifts, and creation of instructional strategies to facilitate schoolwide application of SWP principles.

- Activities were led by the IDEAS Project facilitators, or by the ISMT as a team of equals (ranging from two to ten in size), or by the ISMT and one or more heads of departments, or by the ISMT and principal.
- Because of the newness to most professionals of the concept of "pedagogical deepening," the advice of IDEAS Project team members was sought on a regular basis.

Conclusions

Conclusion 9: Teacher leadership took on a life of its own in most of the schools with the fourth C-B dynamic.

Conclusion 10: Teacher leaders used principals' support and ongoing advice from the IDEAS Project team.

The Fifth C-B Dynamic—*Invoking Reaction*

Findings

- ISMTs, in conjunction with HODs, coordinated within-department reviews and refinement of SWP principles.
- Colorful IDEAS brochures and PowerPoint presentations were prepared for community awareness building, forums, and cluster meetings.
- Regional, state, national, and international forums were convened.
- Books and international journal articles were published.
- Principals promoted and advocated for IDEAS at the system level.
- IDEAS school representatives visited IDEAS schools nationally and internationally.
- Student IDEAS leader teams were formed.
- National and international educational visitors were introduced to IDEAS processes.

Conclusions

Conclusion 11: Parallel leadership became highly visible, with principals, teacher leaders, and middle managers working in cohesive teams to present newly created school knowledge (visions, SWP, and strategies for classroom implementation) in professional and public forums, and refine it, using forum feedback.

The Sixth C-B Dynamic—*Consolidating Success*

Findings

- The principal and ISMT were the key agents in the orientation of new staff (including principals) to the school's vision and pedagogical developments.
- The ISMT was endorsed as "custodian" of the school's vision and SWP.

- The fundamentals of distributed leadership, metastrategic principalship, and teacher leadership became widely understood by principals and ISMT members.
- The IDEAS process was accepted as an umbrella process for ongoing school decision making.
- Pedagogical deepening was accepted as an essential ongoing school process.
- Transitions in ISMT membership, roles, and functions were undertaken by principals and teacher leaders through formal induction activities.
- IDEAS DIs were readministered and followed up.
- Visions and SWP principles were incorporated into principals' annual and triennial strategic plans.
- A "morphing" of IDEAS products with emerging systemic priorities (particularly literacy and numeracy) began.
- Staff members were in some instances consulted in the appointment of incoming principals.

Conclusions

Conclusion 12: The consolidation of success required the embedding of processes (strategic, professional learning, and enculturation), not people. But people must still take responsibility for those processes, if they are to materialize in meaningful forms.

Conclusion 13: Principals and teacher leaders' personal understanding of parallel leadership and SWP were important in facilitating consolidation of school successes.

Table B.6 IDEAS Rules of Skillful Discussion for School Groups

- Listen for what you don't know, not what you do know.
- Speak into the middle—no eyeballing allowed.
- No "ping ponging" allowed.
- Value the silences—they may indicate a breakthrough is pending.
- If it's not positive, don't even think it.
- Build on someone else's idea, enriching it.
- Compliment a contributor you have gained a new idea from.
- Play the role of synthesizer of disparate ideas when you can do so.

❖ References ❖

Andrews, D., & Crowther, F. (2003). Three-dimensional pedagogy: The image of the 21st century teacher professionalism. In F. Crowther (Ed.), *Australian College Yearbook 2003: Teachers as leaders in a knowledge society* (pp. 95–111). Deakin West, Australian Capital Territory Australia: Australian College of Educators.

Andrews, D., & USQ-LRI Research Team. (2009). *A research report on the implementation of the IDEAS Project in Victoria, 2004–2009.* Toowoomba, Australia: Leadership Research (LRI).

Argyris, C., & Schon, D. (1974). *Theory in practice: Increasing professional effectiveness.* San Francisco: Jossey-Bass.

Argyris, C., & Schon, D. (1996). *Organisational learning II: Theory, method, and practice.* Reading, MA: Addison-Wesley.

Australian Bureau of Statistics. (2006). *2006 census statistics.* Retrieved December 2010 from http://www.abs.gov.au/websitedbs/d3310114.nsf/home/census+data

Baker, S. (2007). Followership: The theoretical foundation of a comtemporary construct. *Journal of Leadership and Organizational Studies, 14*(1), 50–59.

Barber, M., & Mourshed, M. (2007). *How the world's best-performing school systems come out on top.* London: McKinsey.

Barki, H., & Pinsonneault, A. (2005). A model of organizational integration, implementation effort, and performance. *Organization Science, 16*(2), 165–179.

Barnes, C., Camburn, E., Sanders, B., & Sebastian, J. (2010). Developing instructional leaders: Using mixed methods to explore the black box of planned change in principals' professional practice. *Educational Administration Quarterly, 46*(2), 241–279.

Baron, R. A., Byrne, D., & Branscombe, N. R. (2006). *Social psychology* (11th ed.). Boston: Allyn and Bacon.

Bartel, C., & Saavedra, R. (2000). The collective construction of group work moods. *Administrative Science Quarterly, 45*(2), 197–231.

Barth, R. (2001). Teacher leader. *Phi Delta Kappan, 82*(6), 443–449.

Bates, R. (1983). *Educational administration and the management of knowledge.* Waurn Ponds, Victoria, Australia: Deakin Press.

Bennett, N., Wise, C., Woods, P., & Harvey, J. (2003). *Distributed leadership: A review of literature.* London: National College for School Leadership.

Bennis, W. G., & Nanus, B. (1985). *Leaders: The strategies for taking charge.* New York: Harper and Row.

Blankstein, A., Houston, P., & Cole, R. (Eds.). (2008). *Sustaining professional learning communities.* Thousand Oaks, CA: Corwin.

Blasé, J., & Blasé, J. (2000). Effective instructional leadership: Teachers' perspectives on how teachers promote teaching and learning. *Journal of Educational Administration, 38*(2), 130–141.

Bolam, R., McMahon, A., Stoll, L., Wallace, M., Greenwood, A., Hawkey, K., et al. (2005). *Creating and sustaining effective professional learning communities* (DfES Research Report RR637). Bristol, UK: University of Bristol. Retrieved February 10, 2010, from http://www.education.gov.uk/research/data/uploadfiles/rr637.pdf.

Bottery, M. (2008). Educational leadership, the depletion of oil supplies and the need for an ethic of global sustainability. *School Leadership & Management, 28*(3), 281–297.

Branson, C. (2007). Improving leadership by nurturing moral consciousness through structured self-reflection. *Journal of Educational Administration, 45*(4), 471–495.

Brown, K. (2004). Leadership for social justice and equity: Weaving a transformative framework and pedagogy. *Educational Administration Quarterly, 40*(1), 79–110.

Bryk, A. (2010). Organizing schools for improvement. *Kappan, 91*(7), 23–31.

Bryk, A., Camburn, E., & Louis, K. S. (1999). Professional community in Chicago elementary schools: Facilitating factors and organizational consequences. *Educational Administration Quarterly, 35,* 751–781.

Bryk, A., Easton, J., Kerbow, D., Rollow, S., & Sebring, P. (1993). *A view from the elementary schools: The state of reform in Chicago.* Chicago: University of Chicago Center for School Improvement.

Buchanan, J. (2010, June 30). Maroons must look to within to keep the tea, alive. *Courier Mail,* p. 35.

Bucholtz, M., & Hall, K. (2004). Language and identity. In A. Duranti (Ed.), *A companion to linguistic anthropology* (pp. 369–394). Malden, MA: Blackwell.

Capra, F. (2002). *Hidden connections: Integrating the biological, cognitive and social dimensions of life into a science of sustainability.* New York: Doubleday.

Center for Courage & Renewal. (n.d.). Retrieved December 2010 at http://www.couragerenewal.org/about/

Chalofsky, N. (2003). An emerging construct for meaningful work. *Human Resource Development International, 6*(1), 69–83.

Choi, J. (2006). A motivational theory of charismatic leadership: Envisioning, empathy and empowerment. *Journal of Leadership and Organizational Studies, 13*(1), 24–37.

City, E. A., Elmore, R. F., Fiarman, S. E., & Teitel, L. (2009). *Instructional rounds in education: A network approach to improving teaching and learning.* Cambridge, MA: Harvard Education Publishing Group.

Cooperrider, D. L., & Whitney, D. (1996). *Appreciative inquiry consultation workbook.* Taos, NM: Taos Institute.

Craddock, R. (1996, February 15). Waugh meets the woman of his dreams in a Calcutta slum. *The Courier Mail,* p. 1.

Cross, R., Baker, W., & Parker, A. (2003, Summer). What creates energy in organisations. *MIT Sloan Management Review,* 52.

Crowther, F. (1994). The work we do and the search for meaning. In F. Crowther, B. Caldwell, J. Chapman, G. Lakomski, & D. Ogilvie (Eds.), *The workplace in education.* Sydney: Edward Arnold.

Crowther, F. (2010). Parallel leadership: The key to successful school capacity-building. *Leading & Managing, 16*(1), 16–39.

Crowther, F., Andrews, D., Dawson, M., & Lewis, M. (2001). *IDEAS facilitation folder.* Toowoomba, Australia: Leadership Research Institute, University of Southern Queensland.

Crowther, F., Ferguson, M., & Hann, L. (2009). *Developing teacher leaders* (2nd ed.). Thousand Oaks, CA: Corwin.

Day, C., Leithwood, K., & Sammons, P. (2008). What we have learned, what we need to know more about. *School Leadership & Management, 28*(1), 83–96.

Donnelly, K. (2010, August 2). Flaws test Gillard's proud boast. *The Australian,* p. 21.

Drucker, P. (1946). *Concept of the organization* (rev. ed. 1972). New York: John Day.

Earl, L., Torrance, N., Sutherland, S., Fullan, M., & Ali, A. S. (2003). Manitoba *School Improvement Program: Final evaluation report.* Retrieved December 2010 from http://www.msip.ca/

Ebrahami, M. (2010). [Online letter]. Retrieved December 2010 from the Médecins Sans Frontières Australia website: http://www.msf.org.au/nc/from-the-field/letters-from-the-field/letters-from-the-field/article/breathing-life-into-maternal-health-care-in-the-somali-region-ethiopia.html

Eklund, N. (2009). Sustainable workplaces, retainable teachers: The next generation of teachers. *Phi Delta Kappan, 91*(2), 25–27.

Feiler, R., Heritage, M., & Gallimore, R. (2000). Teachers leading teachers. *Educational Leadership, 57*(7), 66–69.

Ferrari, J. (2009, August 11). Call to close failing schools. *The Australian,* p. 1.

Frangenheim, E.(2006). *Reflections on classroom teaching strategies: Forty-two practical strategies to encourage thinking in your classroom.* Loganholme, Australia: Rodin Educational Publishing.

Fullan, M. (2005a). Resillency and sustainability. *The School Administrator,* (February), 16–19.

Fullan, M. (2005b). *Leadership and sustainability: System thinkers in action.* Thousand Oaks, CA: Corwin.

Gardner, H. (1995). *Leading minds.* New York: Basic Books.

Gardner, H., Csikszentmihalyi, M., & Damon, W. (2001). *Good work: Where excellence and ethics meet.* New York: Basic Books.

Garmston, R. J. (1998). Becoming expert teachers. *Journal of Staff Development, 19*(1), 1–5.

Garvin, D. A. (1998). Building a learning organization. In *Harvard Business Review on knowledge management* (pp. 47–79). Boston: Harvard Business School Press. Retrieved December 2010 from http://www.amazon.com/Harvard-Business-Knowledge-Management-Paperback/dp/0875848818#reader_0875848818

Goleman, D., Boyatzis, R., & McKee, A. (2002). *Primal leadership.* Boston: Harvard Business School.

Gore, A. (1992). *Earth in the balance.* New York: Penguin Group.

Gore, A. (Writer). (2006). *An inconvenient truth* [Documentary film]. United States: Lawrence Bender Productions.

Gore, A. (2009a). Westpac Envirodome website. Retrieved December 2010 from http://www.envirodome.org.au/information/climate-change

Gore, A. (2009b). Our Choice website. Retrieved December 2010 from http:// our choicethebook.com

Gore, A. (2010, March 2). *The Australian,* 7.

Grameen Bank. (n.d.). *What is microcredit?* Retrieved December 2010 from http:// www.grameen-info.org/index.php?option=com_content&task=view&id=28&Itemid=108

Gray, J. (2008). *Why Mars and Venus collide.* Hammersmith, London: HarperCollins.

Hadfield, M., Chapman, C., Curryer, I., & Barrett, P. (2002). *Capacity building for leadership and school improvement.* Nottingham, UK: National College for School Leadership (NCSL).

Hainsworth, F. (2008, April 2). Maths lag leaves us behind the eight ball. *The Australian,* p. 26.

Hallinger, P., & Heck, R. (2010). Collaborative leadership and school improvement: Understanding the impact on school capacity and student learning. *School Leadership & Management, 30*(2), 95–110.

Hargreaves, A. (2003). *Teaching in a knowledge society: Education in the age of insecurity.* New York: Russell Sage.

Hargreaves, A. (2008). Leading professional learning communities. In A. Blankstein, P. Houston, & R. Cole (Eds.), *Sustaining professional learning communities* (pp. 175–198). Thousand Oaks, CA: Corwin.

Hargreaves, A., & Fink, D. (2004). The seven principles of sustainable leadership. *Educational Leadership, 61*(7), 8–13.

Hargreaves, A., & Fink, D. (2006). *Sustainable leadership.* San Francisco: Jossey-Bass.

Hargreaves, D. (2001). A capital theory of school effectiveness and improvement. *British Educational Research Journal, 27*(4), 487–503.

Harris, A. (2004). Teacher leadership and distributed leadership. *Leading & Managing, 10*(2), 1–9.

Hattie, J. (2003). *Teachers make a difference: What is the research evidence?* Melbourne: Australian Council for Educational Research.

Heath, C., & Staudenmayer, N. (2000). Coordination neglect: How lay theories of organizing complicate coordination in organizations. In B. M. Shaw & R. I. Sutton (Eds.), *Research in organizational behavior* (pp. 153–191). New York: Elsevier Science.

Helland, M. R., & Winston, B. E. (2005). Towards a deeper understanding of hope and leadership. *Journal of Leadership and Organizational Studies, 12*(Winter), 42–54.

Hitt, M., & Ireland, R. (2002). The essence of strategic leadership: Managing human and social capital. *Journal of Leadership and Organizational Studies, 9*(1), 3–14.

Hopkins, D., & Jackson, D. (2003). Building the capacity for leading and learning. In A. Harris, C. Day, M. Hadfield, D. Hopkins, A. Hargreaves, & C. Chapman (Eds.), *Effective leadership for school improvement* (pp. 84–104). London: RoutledgeFalmer.

Hopkins, D., & Stern, D. (1996). Quality teachers, quality schools: International perspectives and policy implications. *Teaching and Teacher Education, 12*(5), 501–557.

Hopkins, D., West, M., & Ainscow, M. (1996). *Improving the quality of education for all (IQEA)*. London: D. Fulton.

Hord, S. (1997). *Professional learning communities: Community of continuous inquiry and improvement.* Austin, TX: Soutwest Educational Development Laboratory.

Isen, A. M. (1999). Positive affect. In T. Dalgleish & M. Power (Eds.), *Handbook of cognition and emotion* (pp. 521–539). Chichester, UK: John Wiley and Sons.

Katzenmeyer, M., & Moller, G. (2001). *Awakening the sleeping giant: Helping teachers develop as leaders.* Thousand Oaks, CA: Corwin.

King, B., & Newmann, F. (1999, April). *School capacity as a goal for professional development: Mapping the terrain in low-income schools.* Paper presented at the Annual Meeting of American Educational Research Association, Montreal.

King, B., & Newmann, F. (2000). Will teacher learning advance school goals? *Phi Delta Kappan, 81*(8), 576–580.

King, B., & Newmann, F. (2001). Building school capacity through professional development: Conceptual and empirical considerations. *International Journal of Educational Management, 15*(2), 86–94.

Klein, J. (2010, January 27). Julia's revolution should measure up. *The Australian,* p. 14.

Kolb, D. (1984). *Experiential learning: Experience as the source of learning and development.* Englewood Cliffs, NJ: Prentice Hall.

Kotter, J. (2001, December). What leaders really do. Breakthrough leadership. *Harvard Business Review,* 85–97.

Lambert, L. (2007). Lasting leadership: Toward sustainable school improvement. *Journal of Educational Change, 8*(4), 311–323.

Larance, L. (1998). *Building social capital for the center: A village-level investigation of Bangladesh's Grameen Bank.* St. Louis, MO: George Warren Brown School of Social Work, Washington University.

Larson, M., & Luthans, F. (2006). Potential added value of psychological capital in predicting work attitudes. *Journal of Leadership and Organizational Studies, 13*(1), 45–62.

LeBlanc , P. R., & Shelton, M. M. (1997). Teacher leadership: The needs of teachers, *Action in Teacher Education*, 19(3), 32–48.

Leech, J., & Moon, B. (2008). *The power of pedagogy.* London: Sage.

Leithwood, K., Day, C., Sammons, P., Harris, A., & Hopkins, D. (2008). *Seven strong claims about successful school leadership.* Nottingham, UK: National College.

Leithwood, K., & Jantzi, D. (2006). Transformational school leadership for large-scale reform: Effects on students, teachers, and their classroom practices. *School Effectiveness and School Improvement, 17*(2), 201–227.

Leithwood, K., & Riehl, C. (2003). *What we know about successful school leadership.* Philadelphia: Laboratory for Student Success, Temple University.

Leithwood, K., Seashore Louis, K., Anderson, S., & Wahlstrom, K. (2004). *How leadership influences student learning, Learning from Leadership Project.* Minneapolis: CAREI.

Levin, B. (2010). Education improvement in Alberta. *Phi Delta Kappan, 91*(7), 81–82.

Licata, J., & Harper, G. (2001). Organizational health and robust school vision. *Educational Administration Quarterly, 37*(1), 5–26.

Limerick, D., Cunnington, B., & Crowther, F. (1998). *Managing the new organisation* (2nd ed.). Warrewood, New South Wales, Australia: Business and Professional Publishing.

Limerick, D., Cunnington, B., & Crowther, F. (2002). *Managing the new organisation: Collaboration and sustainability in the post-corporate world* (2nd ed.). St. Leonards, New South Wales, Australia: Allen and Unwin.

Lindle, J. (2004). William P. Foster's promises for educational leadership: Critical idealism in an applied field. *Educational Administration Quarterly, 40*(2), 165–175.

Louis, K., Marks, H. M., & Kruse, S. (1996). Teachers' professional community and restructuring schools. *American Eduational Research Journal, 33*(4), 757–798.

MacBeath, J. (2006a). Leadership as a subversive activity (ACEL Monograph Series, *No 39*). Winmalee, New South Wales, Australia: Australian Council for Educational Leaders.

MacBeath, J. (2006b). A story of change: Growing leadership for learning. *Journal of Educational Change, 7*(1–2), 33–46.

Maden, M. (Ed.). (2001). *Success against the odds. Five years on.* London: Routledge.

Médecins Sans Frontières. (n.d.). *Charter.* Retrieved December 2010 from http://www.doctorswithoutborders.org/aboutus/charter.cfm

Mitchell, C., & Sackney, L. (2001, February 25). Building capacity for a learning community. *Canadian Journal of Educational Administration and Policy,* (19). Retrieved December 2010 from http://www.umanitoba.ca/publications/cjeap/articles/mitchellandsacney.html

Mitchell, C., & Sackney, L. (2009). *Sustainable learning communities: From managed systems to living systems.* Paper presented at the Annual Conference of the International Congress for School Effectiveness and Improvement, Vancouver, British Columbia, Canada.

Mohammed, S. (2001). Toward an understanding of cognitive consensus in a group decision-making context. *Journal of Applied Behavioral Science, 37*(4), 408–425.

Montefiore, S. (2005). *Speeches that changed the world.* Putney: Murdoch Books.

Mowat, V. (2010). [Online letter]. Retrieved December 2010 from the Médecins Sans Frontières Australia website: http://www.msf.org.au/nc/from-the-field/letters-from-the-field/letters-from-the-field/article/australian-nurse-victoria-mowat-writes-from-south-sudan.html

Muijs, D., Harris, A., Chapman, C., Stoll, L., & Russ, J. (2004). Improving schools in socioeconomically disadvantaged areas: A review of research evidence. *School Effectiveness and School Improvement, 15*(2), 149–175.

Mulford, B. (2004). Congruence between the democratic processes of schools and school principal training in Australia. *Journal of Educational Administration, 42*(6), 625–639.

Mulford, B. (2007). Overview of research on Australian educational leadership, 2001–2005, *ACEL Monograph Series.* Winmalee, New South Wales, Australia: Australian Council for Educational Leaders.

Mulford, B. (2008). *The leadership challenge: Improving learning in schools.* Camberwell, Victoria: Australian Education Review, Australian Council for Educational Research.

Munby, S. (2009). *School leadership today.* Retrieved December 2010 from http://www.nationalcollege.org.uk/docinfo?id=21843&filename=school-leadership-today.pdf

Murphy, J. (2005). *Connecting teacher leadership and school improvement.* Thousand Oaks, CA: Corwin.

Murphy, J., Elliott, S., Goldring, E., & Porter, A. (2007). Leadership for learning: A research-based model and taxonomy of behaviours. *School Leadership & Management, 27*(2), 179–201.

My dream. (2010, January 6). Australia Zoo, Home of the Crocodile Hunter Blog. Retrieved December 2010 from http://blogs.australiazoo.com.au/?author=2047

National College for Leadership of Schools and Children's Services. (2009). *School leadership today.* Nottingham, UK: National College Publishing.

Newmann, F., & Wehlage, G. (1995). *Successful school restructuring: A report to the public and educators.* Madison: University of Wisconsin, Center on Organization and Restructuring of Schools.

Norington, B. (2010). Gore concedes mistakes made on climate change. *The Australian*, p. 7.

O'Neill, J. (1995). On schools as learning organizations: A conversation with Peter Senge. *Educational Leadership, 52*(7), 20–23.

Palmer, P. (1998). *The courage to teach.* San Francisco: Jossey-Bass.

Palmer, P. (2007). A new professional: The aims of education revisited. *Change, 39*(6, Nov/Dec), 6–12.

Peters, T. J., & Waterman, R. H. (1982). *In search of excellence: Lessons from America's best-run companies.* New York: Warner Books.

Pont, B., Nusche, D., & Moorman, H. (2008). *Improving school leadership; Volume 1: Policy and practice.* Paris: Organisation of Economic Co-operation and Development.

Pounder, G., Ogawa, R., & Adams, E. (1995). Leadership as an organisationwide phenomenon: Its impacts on school performance. *Educational Administration Quarterly, 31*(4), 564–575.

Raelin, J. (2005). We the leaders: In order to form a leaderful organization. *Journal of Leadership and Organizational Studies, 12*(2), 18–30.

Reilley, B. (2010). [Online letter]. Retrieved December 2010 from the Médecins Sans Frontières website: http://www.doctorswithoutborders.org/news/article.cfm?id=4237&cat=voice-from-the-field

Richards, D. (2004). *The art of winning commitment: Ten ways leaders can engage minds, hearts and spirits.* New York: Amazon.

Robinson, V. (2001). Descriptive and normative research on organisational learning: Locating the contribution of Argyris and Schon. *International Journal of Educational Management, 15*(2), 58–67.

Robinson, V. (2007). School leadership and student outcomes: Identifying what works and why, (ACEL Monograph Series No. 41). Winmalee, New South Wales, Australia: Australian Council for Educational Leaders.

Rose, D. (2010, July 15). Women under strain. *Herald Sun,* p. 30.

Ross, J., & Gray, P. (2006). Transformational leadership and teacher commitment to organizational values: The mediating effects of collective teacher efficacy. *School Effectiveness and School Improvement, 17*(2), 179–199.

Sachs, J. (2003). *The activist teaching profession.* Buckingham, UK: Open University Press.

Schein, E. (2004). *Organizational culture and leadership* (3rd ed.). San Francisco: Jossey-Bass.

Schneider, B., Godfrey, E., Hayes, S., Huang, M., Lim, B., Nishii, L., et al. (2003). The human side of strategy: Employee experiences of strategic alignment in a service organisation. *Organisational Dynamics, 32*(2), 757–798.

Seashore Louis, K. (2008). Creating and sustaining professional communities. In A. Blankstein, P. Houston, & R. Cole (Eds.), *Sustaining professional learning communities* (pp. 41–58). Thousand Oaks, CA: Corwin.

Senge, P. (1990). *The fifth discipline: The art and practice of the learning organization.* New York: Doubleday/Currency.

Sergiovanni, T. (2005). The virtues of leadership. *The Educational Forum, 69*(2), 112–123.

Solansky, S. (2008). Leadership styles and team processes in self-managed teams. *Journal of Leadership and Organizational Studies, 14*(4), 332–341.

Spillane, H. (2010). [Online letter]. Retrieved December 2010 from the Médecins Sans Frontières Australia website: http://www.msf.org.au/nc/from-the-field/letters-from-the-field/letters-from-the-field/article/australian-doctor-heidi-spillane-writes-from-china.html

Stoll, L. (2009). Capacity building for school improvement or creating capacity for learning? A changing landscape. *Joural of Educational Change, 10*(2–3), 115–127.

Terri Irwin presents award to Attenborough. (2006, November 2). *The Australian.* Retrieved December 2010 from http://en.wikipedia.org/wiki/Steve_Irwin

Thompson, L. (2004). Moral leadership in a postmodern world. *Journal of Leadership and Organizational Studies, 11*(1), 27–37.

Timperley, H. (2005). Distributed leadership: Developing theory from practice. *Journal of Curriculum Studies, 37*(4), 395–420.

United Nations Educational, Scientific and Cultural Organization. (n.d.). *Grameen Bank.* Retrieved December 2010 from http://www.unesco.org/education/poverty/grameen.shtml

Van Manen, M. (2002). *The tact of teaching: The meaning of pedagogical thoughtfulness.* London, Ontario, Canada: Althouse Press.

Warner, D. (2006). *Schooling for the knowledge era.* Camberwell, Victoria, Australia: ACER Press.

Wessner, M., & Miller, T. (2008). Boomers and millenials have much in common. *Organizational Development Journal, 26*(2), 89–96.

Wood, J. Jr., & Winston, B. (2005). Toward a new understanding of leader accountability: Defining a critical construct. *Journal of Organizational and Leadership Studies, 11*(3), 84–94.

Wrigley, T. (2006). *Another school is possible.* London: Bookmarks Publication, Trentham Books.

Zuber-Skerritt, O. (1990). *Action learning for change and development.* Aldershot, UK: Gower-Avebury.

❖ Index ❖

The Corwin logo—a raven striding across an open book—represents the union of courage and learning. Corwin is committed to improving education for all learners by publishing books and other professional development resources for those serving the field of PreK–12 education. By providing practical, hands-on materials, Corwin continues to carry out the promise of its motto: **“Helping Educators Do Their Work Better.”**